This Is Panther Country

This Is Panther Country

A Memoir of Youth, Underdog Spirit, and Basketball Glory

Tom McKeown

BROWN BOOKS
PUBLISHING GROUP

All photographs featured on the cover and in chapter 35 are courtesy of the *Babylon Beacon*.

This Is Panther Country
A Memoir of Youth, Underdog Spirit, and Basketball Glory

Brown Books Publishing Group
Dallas, TX / New York, NY
www.BrownBooks.com
(972) 381-0009

A New Era in Publishing®

Publisher's Cataloging-In-Publication Data

Names: McKeown, Tom, 1961- author.
Title: This is Panther Country : a memoir of youth, underdog spirit, and basketball glory / Tom McKeown.
Description: Dallas, TX : Brown Books Publishing Group, [2025]
Identifiers: ISBN: 978-1-61254-730-5 | LCCN: 2024951164
Subjects: LCSH: McKeown, Tom, 1961---Childhood and youth. | Teenage boys--New York (State)-- Babylon (Town) | Basketball teams--New York (State)--Babylon (Town) | Babylon (N.Y. : Town)--History--20th century. | LCGFT: Autobiographies. | BISAC: BIOGRAPHY & AUTOBIOGRAPHY / Sports. | BIOGRAPHY & AUTOBIOGRAPHY / Memoirs. | SPORTS & RECREATION / Basketball.
Classification: LCC: GV884.M35 T45 2025 | DDC: 796.323092--dc23

ISBN 978-1-61254-730-5
LCCN 2024951164

Printed in Canada
10 9 8 7 6 5 4 3 2 1

For more information or to contact the author, please go to www.BrownBooks.com.

Patrick McKeown Sr.
(1933–1980)
Father, teacher, and leader who was always there in my youth and gave me a shining example of what a good man should be.

Margaret McKeown Donohue
(1937–2024)
Mother, grandmother, and friend who provided the love, compassion, and encouragement that could heal any disappointment and send me through life with a happy smile.

To Ernie and Brian Vickers who both meant such a great deal to me as friends and teammates in our youth and were taken from this world much too soon.

To the 1974–75 Babylon Panthers who gave a school and community this great story that I can share with the world.

"The greater the obstacle, the more glory in overcoming it."

—Molière

Table of Contents

Prologue 1

Chapter 1: Basketball Season Begins 7

Chapter 2: Hello, Crutches 17

Chapter 3: Hanging Around 23

Chapter 4: Thanksgiving Weekend in Babylon 31

Chapter 5: The Lead-Up to Game One 37

Chapter 6: Game One and the Aftermath 45

Chapter 7: One Player Down by Christmas 51

Chapter 8: Christmas and the Diagnosis 57

Chapter 9: Christmas Tournament Begins and a Rocky Start 63

Chapter 10: Tournament Championship and Goodbye to 1974 71

Chapter 11: 1975 and League Play 77

Chapter 12: The Unexpected Hole 85

Chapter 13: No Margin for Error and More Injuries 91

Chapter 14: Don't Trip Up 97

Chapter 15: Reality Steps In 103

Chapter 16: Back to Normal 109
Chapter 17: Amityville Round Two 115
Chapter 18: Out of Our Control 121
Chapter 19: Dad's Back and More 127
Chapter 20: Winter Break and Beyond 133
Chapter 21: Revenge or Flop 139
Chapter 22: No Missteps 145
Chapter 23: Back to School and the End of League V Play 153
Chapter 24: The County Playoffs 159
Chapter 25: Too Many Fouls Make It Too Close 167
Chapter 26: The Run-Up 173
Chapter 27: The Thrilla with the Villa 179
Chapter 28: What Next? 187
Chapter 29: The Big Gym 193
Chapter 30: Fatigue and Crisis 199
Chapter 31: Parties and Press 205
Chapter 32: Friday Night Showdown 211
Chapter 33: The Best of Suffolk 217
Chapter 34: The Underdog 223
Chapter 35: Two Counties Collide 231
Epilogue 239
Acknowledgments 245
Glossary of Basketball Terms 247
1975 Basketball Championship Brackets 250
About the Author 252

1974–75 Babylon Panthers Varsity Roster

Coach: Roy Koelbel

Assistant Coach: Don Bartsch

#	Class	Player	Position
42	Junior	Glenn Vickers	Forward
10	Senior	Gervais Barger	Guard
34	Senior	Stanley Davis	Guard
22	Senior	Charles (Chuck) Farley	Guard
32	Junior	Barry Davis	Center
40	Sophomore	Steven Farley	Forward
30	Freshman	Brian Vickers	Forward
52	Freshman	Chris Brust	Center
14	Senior	Mike Fischer	Guard
12	Sophomore	James Feeney	Guard
N/A	Sophomore	Greg Berger	Guard

Prologue

It had been a back-and-forth game for almost thirty-five minutes. The gymnasium was designed to seat about a thousand people. It was filled to capacity, and then some—maybe even a couple hundred more. The air was stale, still breathable, but with the odor of old gym shoes and excitement. The temperature was warm, humid from those hundreds of people exhaling, holding their breath, letting it out in relief or gasping in frustration, and then inhaling again. The temperature inside was only tolerable because outside it was a cold Long Island February night. The crowd noise rose and fell like a storm surge that came in wave after wave.

Our opponents had jumped to a halftime lead with hot shooting and a stifling defense, but we had regrouped during the intermission and had momentum swinging our way in the third and fourth periods. With less than a minute left in regulation we had the ball in our star player's hands, who held for the last shot, but he missed. Thus, the game went into overtime.

The odds looked to be in our favor going into overtime as three of our opponents' first-string players had fouled out of the game. But so far, in the extra period, we had been outplayed. The second of our starting guards had just fouled out while preventing a game-clinching layup. Now the situation was dire.

They were up by one point with seconds remaining. Their star player was about to step to the foul line (otherwise known as the free-throw line) for two free throws. There was no three-point line in 1975. If he made both, we were through. We knew this player. And not just from basketball. We dreaded him. Some of us hated him.

He had not missed a foul shot all night.

We were the proud Panthers of Babylon High School and our opponents were our longtime rivals the Crimson Tide of Amityville, otherwise known as the Warriors. Yes, *that* Amityville, although it was some years before the horror movie came out.

This was no ordinary game. It was February, and we were playing in the quarterfinals of the Suffolk County Basketball Championship on Long Island. The victor would be one win away from playing for the county title in the recently built Nassau Coliseum, what was at the time the home of Julius Erving—Dr. J—and the New York Nets. And as an additional incentive this year, the Suffolk champ would play a second game in the coliseum against the winner from Nassau County for the first-ever Long Island Championship. The loser was done.

Today's game was the twentieth of a season that had so far spanned nearly three months. At the center of it all was our school's blood rivalry with Amityville. We both played in the same League V and had split our regular season games with each team winning at home. Now this rubber match was being hosted at a neutral site. Amityville was a point up. In one moment, it could all be over.

I was crouched next to my father who had begun regularly attending home and away games shortly after the season started. I was the second-oldest of four children but was the only one who had really taken to sports. Dad and I had a special bond in that regard. Plus, he was a particular fan of my favorite sport, basketball.

The fact that he drove to the away games had given me a modicum of popularity with other students, since people were always looking to catch a ride. Four of my classmates had crowded into our Ford Granada to attend this game, for example. Dad and I were surrounded by our passengers, all of them seated near us about fifteen rows up from the Babylon bench.

The Amityville shooter moved to the line. Bounced the ball. Assumed his stance. He looked ready, at ease. This was going to be it.

Our coach called time-out to try and freeze the shooter.

The crowd simmered down, still murmuring. Despite how loud it was, because of the acoustics of this particular gymnasium, we could actually hear most of what our coach was saying to the team. Everyone on the other team would know, anyway. His advice was standard basketball wisdom and wasn't a particular secret. The first part of the message was timeless free-throw guidance: be sure to box out your closest opponent. An offensive rebound by Amityville would be as bad as a successful shot. Then the coach stressed to the team that after the second foul shot, make or miss, whoever had the ball was to call time-out. That would allow us to advance the ball to half-court with the opportunity for at least one more chance to tie or maybe win the game.

Seated right in front of me, packed tight up against my knees, was my friend Ernie Vickers, who was the younger brother to two of the players on the court about to walk back onto the floor. He was sharing a laugh with the girl seated on his left. Ernie had arrived with his family; the girl had driven with us. I couldn't comprehend what he might think was funny at this moment, but Ernie had always been social.

Babylon was one of the smaller schools on Long Island. Our graduating classes were usually barely over one hundred students. Our building, therefore, was a junior-senior high school that housed every class from seventh to twelfth grade. My classmates and I were in the eighth grade and thus felt we were part of the program, despite still being in junior high.

This loss would be a particularly bitter pill to swallow for us, for back on a muddy field in late October, we had squared up with Amityville for the conference football title. Both squads had been undefeated in what looked at the time to be an epic battle. I remember I had been sitting with Ernie then as well. And, just like tonight, despite having those same two brothers heavily involved in that game, his attention had been on a female classmate playing with the band.

Our team had run out on the field first, resplendent in their black jerseys, white pants with orange trim and numbers. Our uniforms were spotless, and we had looked very much like the confident team that had romped through the regular season by squashing nearly every opponent. However, I remember noticing and commenting when the Amityville team had taken the field that they looked much bigger than us.

Ernie had chided me with a smile, "You just see it that way because they're all black."

He would rib me like that quite often, but I could tell it wasn't entirely said in jest. His observation was correct on one point. The Amityville team was almost entirely composed of black players.

As the teams lined up for the kickoff, our band started a drumroll which lasted about thirty seconds, right up until our kicker connected with the ball. We watched it sail high into the air whereupon the Amityville player caught the ball on about the ten-yard line. A wall of four blockers formed in front of him.

The first few of our players who attempted to reach the ball carrier were swatted away by the four blockers. The ball carrier reached the thirty-yard line before being pushed out of bounds. Three plays later with the ball at the Amityville forty-five-yard line, their running back broke around the right side and went fifty-five yards for a touchdown, jigging several times en route and leaving many of our players sliding to the ground.

As the Amityville players ran celebrating off of the field, our guys walked off mostly covered in mud. The Babylon fans had still been confident when our high-octane offense had taken the field—but the Amityville defense had manhandled our guys on that first possession for a quick three-and-out. Then after our punter shanked the ensuing kick, Amityville had begun their second possession on our forty-yard line. Three plays later they were in the end zone again when a player with the name "Smith" on the back of his jersey jumped high in the air to haul in the touchdown.

From there they would go on to score the next sixteen points. Smith played both ways that day and seemed to be everywhere. When he wasn't shutting down our star receiver on defense, he was catching long passes and setting up touchdowns for his own team.

Trailing 30–0 at halftime, we scored our only touchdown and two-point conversion in the third quarter, but they answered on their next possession. When the gun sounded, we were witness to a crushing defeat. As a show of good sportsmanship, our fan bus had not left until the championship and MVP (most valuable player) trophies were presented. It was then over a crackly microphone we got to hear the full name of our nemesis, Paul Smith.

This same Paul Smith was the guy who was going back to the free-throw line in a few minutes. Would he end our basketball season as he had helped do in the football season?

The referee's whistle blew, and our team put their hands together for what could be the last "go" cheer of the season. Our remaining five players walked back out on the basketball court. Up in the stands, our seats were on the side farthest from the basket where the action was about to take place. Their team began the shorter walk to the same spot. Both coaches trailed their teams for the first few feet clapping and shouting words of encouragement before each returned to his respective bench.

Our tallest players took the bottom two spots of the rectangle that was called the foul lane. The next two spots went to their players and the final two to us. Those final two were to box out the shooter to ensure he did not recover a long rebound.

The referee blew his whistle from the middle of the lane while extending the ball at full arm's length in his right hand. He backed up to hand it to Smith. Once in his hands, Smith looked up at the basket, gave the ball a flip and spun it backwards in his hands, then took two dribbles in place. When he finished this mini-ritual he turned his eyes to the basket with laser focus.

He shot the ball. His hand made the perfect follow-through motion of a coach's dream.

As that ball hung in the air with about a thousand sets of eyes watching it, I leaned forward, not realizing or caring in the moment that I was knifing my knees into Ernie's back. Ernie didn't seem to mind. Like everyone else in the gym for the next second, he didn't make a sound.

The ball arced toward the goal.

A golden season, a near-impossible run at the first-ever Long Island Championship, all our hopes, dreams, fears, and nightmares sailing with it.

It all came down to this.

Basketball Season Begins

In our family every child was raised to hold three tenets above all others. The first was *family*, which meant we all loved each other, the home was a safe space, and if one of us had people problems it was all of our business. My mother had come from a mirror image of our household with four children composed of two boys and two girls. Her side represented the family of cousins, aunts, and uncles that gave us a large extended family. My father, on the other hand, had been an only child of two working parents. He had also been sick during his early childhood with rheumatic fever. With both parents out all day my father spent a great deal of time alone. As an adult, he perhaps overcompensated and could be extreme about putting family above everything else. He believed we were very lucky to have each other.

The second priority for everyone was *school*. My father was a high school teacher nearby, and my mother taught special education. Dad was not a physical man but on the occasion one of us came home with a disappointing report card, we knew there would be a painful talk at the kitchen table. His withering stare and silent contempt were ample incentive to get good grades.

The third priority, however, you as a family member got to choose for yourself. It had to be an out-of-the-house activity. Neither of my parents wanted to see us home from three to six in the afternoon watching television. They didn't even want us doing homework at that time. According to them, we needed to be out doing some character-building activity. My choice had always been sports.

The school day always started with a loud *click!*, followed by the voice of Elton John or some other Top 40 singer waking us up to their latest hit. Then, slowly from across the room, the hand of my brother Pat reached out from under his blanket to flip the off switch on our alarm clock. Over the next five minutes—slowly, slowly—he and I both sat up in our twin beds and walked down the stairs to our grandmother's kitchen for breakfast.

We called our grandmothers "Nana" from the time we could speak. The one who lived with us was my paternal grandmother, Nana Mary. Whenever we talked to her, she always responded to us with her trilling Irish brogue, addressing each of us as "Darlin'." Like many youths I took so much for granted growing up. For instance, Nana Mary would cook us whatever we wanted for breakfast every morning—pancakes, eggs, bacon, waffles, you name it. And that was for all four children and my two parents.

This morning, I was having bacon and eggs. I needed protein in my system. This was going to be one of the most significant days in my young life (but more on that later). I never had coffee back then because for whatever Irish reason, tea was the hot drink of the house. My brother, like me, never really considered what would be easiest for Nana to make. He'd asked for pancakes. Without fuss or comment, Nana provided.

Under the table was our trusted schnauzer, Max. He was always there to pick up any piece of food that fell and always received handouts from each of us to stay in his good graces. Max was quiet when it was just us in the house, but, befitting his German nature, he could be very noisy and unpleasant when a nonfamily member approached.

Once finished eating we both went back upstairs to the top floor to get dressed. We usually passed our sisters Peggy and Dorothy on the stairs. The girls were just waking up and heading down to eat. Pat and I both went to the high school, and the girls were still in grade school, where classes started an hour later. This made it easier to negotiate use of the children's bathroom. We had only one between the four of us at the top of our three-story house. That tranquility would change drastically in two years when we were all in the same school and vying for showers and morning bathroom time.

I usually was dressed and waiting to go before Pat. Back then it felt to me that I was always racing to something. Also, if we got ready quickly enough, we could get a ride from our father, Pat Senior, who taught at the next high school over. Riding with Dad could be a double-edged sword, although it would save us the nearly mile-long walk. He could be rather professorial, so the ride often came with a brief lecture on his disappointment with today's youth and how we should be more decent human beings. For better or worse he was already gone this morning, so we were going to have to hoof it to school today.

Pat finally met me downstairs at about seven fifty, which left us an ample forty minutes to get to school on foot. As we grabbed our lunches off the kitchen table, my mother emerged long enough to give us each a hug before she was off to work. Mom had gone back to college a year ago, so she had a lot going on and was just as busy as we were in the morning. But she was the best and made sure to check in before saying goodbye.

It was early November and the weather for Babylon, our town and village on Long Island, had already turned freezing, the mercury edging below thirty degrees. We were both bundled up in winter coats and gloves but still felt the cold. Although I was not a fan, I'd chosen a Washington Redskins red-and-gold-themed winter coat that year, which could be seen a mile away. I liked the colors. And, I have to admit, I liked to be noticed.

Pat wore a less conspicuous dark blue peacoat that I would inherit someday whenever he outgrew it. I never minded getting Pat's hand-me-down clothes as long as they supplemented and were not my main source for a wardrobe. Such was the life of the second born.

We lived on Coppertree Lane, whose street name was no mystery. Right outside our front door and across the street was a gigantic, centuries-old copper beech which dwarfed all of the nice-sized houses around it. There were six other families on the block who had children going to BHS (Babylon High School) during the days Pat and I were there. Several made the same trudge as we did in the morning, but it was early and we were all teenagers, so not a lot of extra-family communication took place. Pat and I usually had plenty to talk about, however.

On the surface my brother and I would seem to have little in common. Theater was his main school priority. Academically, he was more the literary guy compared to my strength in math. But today we had a common topic. In a few weeks the second James Bond movie with Roger Moore was coming out, and that was something we both considered to be a great event. We may not have been there opening night, but we were going to see that movie.

"What's the name of the movie again?" I asked.

"*The Man with the Golden Gun*," Pat replied.

"Sean Connery is a tough act to follow, but Roger Moore was pretty good in *Live and Let Die*."

"Yep, I agree. But this next one should be good too," Pat replied, adding, "Christopher Lee is playing the bad guy. He's great."

We arrived at the entrance to our school at eight twenty. School would start momentarily. Regardless of how late it was or how cold it might be, there were always at least thirty other kids hanging around the entrance smoking or talking without a seeming care in the world. But, as Judge Smails would say in *Caddyshack* a few years later, "The world needs ditch diggers too."

Pat and I parted and went to our respective homerooms once inside, which were arranged alphabetically and by grade. Babylon was a relatively small community compared to many of those surrounding it. Even with the junior and senior high schools combined, the building never seemed overcrowded.

My name is Tom McKeown. The correct pronunciation is *Muh-kyohn*, but most people say *Muh-kyoo-en*. Regardless, since my name began with "Mc" I was batched alphabetically with several other Irish American kids. We were all quickly seated awaiting morning announcements over the PA system. After we recited the Pledge of Allegiance and endured some banal updates on bake sales and such, the words came that I'd been anticipating hearing for months.

Tryouts for the junior high, freshman, JV (junior varsity), and varsity basketball teams would take place starting at 3 p.m. that day in the East and West Gymnasiums.

I had to get through a day of classes before basketball tryouts, but second-period art class was not so much of a burden as the rest. It was an easy load as all the teacher did was give out assignments such as "sketch a plant," and then we had a very ample number of weeks to finish while the teacher played music during class. Also, the teacher was the JV and assistant varsity basketball coach, Don Bartsch.

I would usually do my assignment at the front table in the class where Don was and he and I, along with some other athletic classmates, would talk basketball. Don had played high school and college basketball and stood about six foot six inches. With his shaggy blond hair and mustache, he was imposing but not threatening. If he didn't tower over everyone, he might be another student, based on his demeanor.

"This varsity team may be the best in the county this year," Bartsch proclaimed. "And Glenn Vickers may be the best player."

We all knew Glenn Vickers. Plus, his younger brother Ernie was our classmate and also into sports.

Glenn was a once-in-a-lifetime player for a high school coach. He was only a junior in 1975, but he'd been all-league the year before and averaged over twenty points a game as a sophomore.

"I think our junior high team is going to be pretty good this year," I chimed in to Bartsch. "We have seven players back who played on the team last year, so I'm excited."

Bartsch was quick to throw water on my excitement. "Yes, you guys have some good athletes, but the team is way small. What are you? Five foot seven? You'll probably be playing forward."

I had grown five inches over the last year to reach my new height. Bartsch's comment didn't bother me. And regardless, I was enthusiastic about the junior high team's chances that year, as well as the varsity's. Bartsch could spout all he wanted.

A few moments later, and just as the bell was about to ring, one of the senior varsity cheerleaders came in and sat down. She was quite attractive, and my male classmates and I sat frozen in her presence. When the bell rang, we all began to move toward the door, but she remained in place as the class emptied. She was joined by another female friend as the last of us exited.

The rest of the day was typical school, rushing to classes through crowded hallways, stopping off at my locker to switch books, and being yelled at by teachers who told me not to run and then lambasted me for being late to class. When the bell rang for final period, I quickly visited my locker to grab my gym bag and headed toward the West Gym. That was the older one where the junior high tryouts would be held.

As I made the last turn onto the hallway leading to the West Gym, I came across Ernie Vickers flirting with a brunette girl he had been sweet on recently. At the locker next to hers was another girl whom I'd become friends with over the past couple of years. We'd long grown out of the pulling-hair/boys-stink version of our youth.

Her name was Virginia, and she was a very pretty girl, with long blond hair and a slightly freckled face. She was only an inch or two shorter than Ernie and me.

Ernie also stood about five foot seven. However, he would grow another three or four inches later on. To my later chagrin I was at that moment unknowingly standing at my vertical peak for life.

While Ernie and his girl giggled at something, Virginia and I discussed a science project that was coming up in a class we shared. It involved tracking the moon over the course of several nights.

"Do you have a good telescope?" I asked.

"Yes," she replied. "My sister did a project like this last year before she went to college and didn't take the telescope with her."

"Same. I'm using my brother's. I'll probably have to take it out in the street since the trees in our backyard are like a dome."

She told me she was having two of her girlfriends from the class over to work with her on the project the coming weekend. I dropped several hints that I would gladly join this collaboration, but no invitation for me followed.

I glanced at a nearby clock. The time had come. Tryouts. Thoughts of moon-watching with Virginia would have to wait. I grabbed Ernie and we made our way to the locker room.

We had about three hundred students in the seventh and eighth grades. Half of these were boys, with a quarter of the boys trying out for the basketball team. Everyone crowded into the locker room and used their gym PE (physical education) lockers to change. If you made the team, you would get a separate, bigger locker, which would serve as a bragging right for the remainder of the season.

I finished getting dressed and hurried out of the aisle where my locker was, where I bumped into the junior high coach, Dave Williams. I had made the team the previous year, so I had a decent relationship with Mr. Williams, but he was a bit of a strange duck in many ways. Standing about six foot three, bald on the top, and wearing thin horn-rimmed glasses, he looked the part of a math teacher, his main teaching duty.

"Hello, Thomas. In a hurry?" Mr. Williams was one of those adults who always addressed students by their full first name.

"Hi, Mr. Williams," I replied. "Yes, I am in a hurry. The coach of the junior high team is not a big fan of players who arrive late to practice."

This got a smile. "Then you best be going."

The West Gym was the older of two athletic structures at Babylon High School. The main basketball court was in the middle, but the visiting bleachers to the far side were only about a quarter of the size of the home bleachers. At the moment, all of the bleachers were collapsed back and flush with the walls for practice. The only seats were on the floor.

In addition to the main baskets, there were two on each side that folded down from the ceiling. All of the backboards were made of wood, a major signal that this was an older facility.

As I made my way in, I could see the mass of hopefuls there to try out. In one area were the fifteen to twenty guys who had no prayer of making the team. They were easy to spot based on the type of sneakers they wore and their T-shirts. You might be a Led Zeppelin fan, but generally a band T-shirt was not the attire you'd choose to wear to basketball tryouts.

Then there were the players who had made the team the year before as seventh graders. We gravitated toward each other while sizing up who might be on the first team this year. There was one standout, Gary Farley, who would certainly be our go-to guy come game time. The other six of us were close in ability and would be battling it out for starting spots and playing time.

Finally, there was the "in-between" group of about fifteen players of decent ability who would be vying for the remaining spots. Most of them, hoping to get some tips, were trying to huddle up with one of us who had made last year's team.

There was one pointer I'd shared with friends a few weeks before who I knew wanted to make the squad. If they took my pointer to heart, it would likely at least get them on the team.

There was always one skill that was a deciding factor for a particular coach. If a potential player did not have that skill, the coach would cut them right away.

For Mr. Williams, this was being able to do a layup with your opposite hand. I knew he would cut half the players while doing layup drills in the first half hour based on that very skill.

But before we got to layups, we had a lot of running to do.

When Mr. Williams blew his whistle, everyone stopped what they were doing and gathered around. He explained his methodology and coaching philosophy. His teams would never lose, he said, by more than the margin of missed foul shots. All his players would be in top physical condition. And, although it wasn't mandatory, no one who had ever played for him had any facial hair. There were very few to whom that applied in eighth grade, but we all made note of it.

At the next whistle, we were directed through a series of stretches that lasted about twenty minutes. Then we were ordered to start running around the court, and with every whistle, we changed direction and ran the other way. Five guys were already puking and dropped out before they even touched a basketball. Led Zeppelin Shirt was among them.

In a standard layup drill, the players are divided in half at the top of the key, above the top circle of the foul line, where one player from the right would dribble the ball to the basket and shoot with his right hand. The front person from the other line would rebound the ball and pass it over to the next person on the shooting line. Since most people are right-handed this was relatively uneventful.

After ten minutes from the right, Mr. Williams switched us to taking layups from the left side. This was where the fun started. Seeing kids trying for the first time to shoot with their weak hands was like watching slapstick. Some attempted to cheat and push the ball up mostly with their right hands, but most just couldn't do it. I looked over at Mr. Williams. He was busily checking off names and culling the group.

By the time we got to the next drill—fast breaks—I estimated the coach was down to about eighteen players. In a fast break drill, three players would push the ball full court toward the basket. There they would meet only two players trying to stop them. The correct movement was for the middle player to try to draw one of the two defenders to guard him, and then pass to the player that the remaining defender left alone. An experienced defender, on the other hand, could usually fake a first-timer into giving up his dribble too far out. After that, he and his co-defender could fall back and cover a man each. These scenarios played out several times.

On what would be the last of these drills, I was on the wing with Ernie Vickers in the middle. Ernie pushed the ball up the court and was successfully able to draw the defender to him. He then head-faked a pass to the other player but delivered it to me for what would be an easy layup. As I cruised in for the shot, the back defender made an awkward lunge to try and stop me.

He stumbled, crashed into me—and took my legs from under me. I hit the floor in pain.

Ernie quickly rushed over to help me up, as did the player who knocked me down. I couldn't tell whether it was a cheap shot, but it didn't matter. The result was the same. Mr. Williams came rushing over to check on me and then recommended that I walk around for a while.

I couldn't. Each time my foot even touched the ground I writhed in pain.

I was helped into the locker room by Ernie and my assailant. There, one of the gym teachers who served as a trainer assessed that I had a fracture of some sort.

I knew what "fracture" meant immediately. I could hardly speak, I was so emotional.

Like that, my season was halted before it had begun.

I called home, and in about twenty minutes, my father was there taking me off to the hospital for a cast.

Hello, Crutches

I missed the next few days of school and arrived on a Monday morning replete with crutches and my books in a cinch sack, which contained a coat hanger that I would use to reach down inside the cast and scratch, an action I took every five minutes for the next two months. It was not hard finding a classmate when I needed help to get myself and my books from one class to another. I hated it, nonetheless. This was certainly not how I'd wanted to spend basketball season.

When I got to second-period art class, I took my usual seat up front near Bartsch. He took note of my cast and shook his head.

"Wow, looks like you just bought a few months of watching from the sidelines," he said while turning back to his drawing.

"Hopefully less than two months," I replied. "That would still get me back for the bulk of the junior high season."

"Maybe, these fractures can be tricky things."

"If I can get the cast off by Christmas I'd only miss one game."

"That only means you'll be walking," Bartsch cautioned. "It will likely be a couple of weeks after that before you're running and able to play."

"Thanks for cheering me up," I replied with more than a little sarcasm.

I went through the rest of the day still in a bit of a funk. It was surprising in hindsight that I didn't get called out for being inattentive in class or for being rude to any classmates who might have tried to strike up a conversation. I just didn't care.

My last class of the day alternated between study hall and PE, or just "gym" as we most often called it. It was normally a period that I enjoyed, but without being able to participate I could either sit in the gymnasium stands and watch, or hang in the coaches office and do some work. I chose the latter.

The office was on the second floor, which I navigated up to with the help of a classmate. Once up the stairs there was a window looking out on the East Gym court. I immediately started picturing myself playing there someday. There were banners from every championship Babylon had ever won hanging on the walls. Their background was black with orange writing, our school colors. The East Gym was brighter, bigger, and had the glass backboards.

Glass backboards were introduced into basketball as arenas were being built to allow for seating behind the baskets. The see-through glass would allow those fans to see much more play. The unintended benefit was that it made the arenas look more modern. Thus, at some point newer gyms that weren't built with behind-the-rim seating used glass as well because of this fresher look. Babylon was one of the first on Long Island to adopt them.

I continued past the window toward the coaches office, which all of the sports coaches and gym teachers could use as they saw fit. When I arrived at the doorway to what was a medium-sized room, I saw Mr. Roy Koelbel sitting there with his feet on the desk, smoking his signature pipe, and reading a magazine whose title I could not quite make out. In addition to being my gym teacher, he was also the head varsity basketball coach.

"Muh-*kyoo*-en," he said, butchering my name like the rest of them in his deep voice. "Sit down."

I did as instructed. "Hi, Mr. Koelbel."

Most players and students would generally address him as "Coach," but my father had a weird aversion to calling anyone by that title and had passed it down to me. I never understood the reason but had adopted it.

As I leaned my crutches against his desk, Koelbel shook his head.

"I think all you Irishmen are born with two left feet. But occasionally I can make an athlete out of one of you."

I knew his sense of humor, and we often went back and forth on Irish versus German greatness. Thus, I didn't bother to point out that Farley, Feeney, and McLoughlin were all names that had worked through his system.

Roy Koelbel was by no means your storybook coach or gym teacher. He was an imposing figure at close to six foot four but was large-boned and gangly. With his slightly graying hair, he resembled Fred Gwynne, the actor who played Herman Munster on *The Munsters*. You could almost picture the bolts coming out of his neck. But he had a quick wit and was very well-read, which made him a great conversationalist. And boy did he know basketball.

He had been coaching the varsity team for nearly a decade and had won the league championship a year ago. Suffolk County, which contained Babylon, had roughly fifty-six high schools stretching from the middle of Long Island all the way out to the Hamptons. Nassau was the other county on Long Island. It was more densely populated but with less geography. As Nassau was closer to New York City, they tended to look down on Suffolk's sports prowess with the occasional dig, calling us "farmers."

There were seven leagues in Suffolk County and Babylon was a member of League V. Despite winning the league crown the year prior, we had unceremoniously exited the county playoffs in the first round. That outcome was one that everyone, especially Mr. Koelbel, wanted to change this year.

After a few more ethnic jokes, we began to speak earnestly. I leaned to my good side, put my sack on the empty chair next to me, and pulled out a notebook.

"Are you going to do some work up here?"

"I'm going to try," I replied. "I have to make up for the few days of school that I missed."

I recounted to him the same prognosis that I had given Bartsch, and he added the same caution about thinking it would heal as quickly as hoped.

"Well, good luck," he said while getting up to go instruct his class. "And remember what Nietzsche said: 'That which does not kill us makes us stronger.'"

I looked at him with some astonishment. He was a man of many surprises. Of course he also had to get one more dig in before exiting.

"By the way, athletics doesn't have a very big budget, so try not to break anything else while you're in here."

My father had arranged to pick me up a few hours later on his way home, but regrettably the meeting spot I had chosen was on the other side of the school from where I had ended my day.

Fortunately, as I was trudging through the halls with crutches while hauling my books on my back, I saw my brother Pat coming out of the drama room. I corralled him into carrying the books.

As we walked to meet our father, I recounted my conversation with Mr. Koelbel. Pat liked the Nietzsche quote as well. My brother was also quite a good mime. His Koelbel impression was perfect. He would often grab a fake pipe for effect and then do a Koelbel rant from gym class for my parents and me, which would have us all laughing.

When we got to the front exit of the building my father had the car waiting for us. At that time my father drove a Dodge Monaco. All four of the children in our family could fit in the back seat, albeit uncomfortably. Pat held the door for me to get in the back where I could stretch out my leg while he climbed into the front seat next to my father.

As I had with Pat, I recounted my conversation with Mr. Koelbel. After a quick laugh my Dad immediately pivoted to when I would be caught up on my schoolwork. I noted that I had not missed much and would be current by the end of the week. Then I changed the subject to something more pleasant.

"Any chance you might come to more of the Friday-night varsity games this year, Dad? It would be easier to drive with you than with someone else in a more crowded car."

My father had made it to all my junior high games the year before but had only been to the one varsity game in the prior season when Babylon played on the road at West Islip, the school where he taught. Babylon opened the season with West Islip every year, but it was a nonconference game, as they were in League I.

"Perhaps I will. Even the coach at West Islip says Babylon may be the team to beat this year for everyone."

"Well, we start off with you guys again this year at our place. Is West Islip any good?"

"No, they graduated most of their good players last year," my father answered in his best analytical tone. "The coach's son is the best player, but he's only a sophomore."

Just as we pulled into the driveway, a light snow began to fall, but we still parked the car outside. We had a single garage that was small and always filled with bicycles and other kid stuff, so the car had to freeze. It had been that way for years.

We had moved to Babylon in the summer of 1966, just over eight years previously. In addition to being a teacher, my father was a dedicated member of every teacher's union. He had been blackballed from working across every New York City high school for trying to form a union grievance committee at Power Memorial Academy. The city school teams were renowned for basketball. My father had, for instance, taught at Power when Lew Alcindor (Kareem Abdul-Jabbar) was a student there. After my father ran afoul of school managers, we fled to Long Island where he was not known by the various administrations and was able to find employment and gain tenure. He certainly did not give up his union work, however.

He seemed to always be an officer at the West Islip local, everything from president to treasurer. Also, he often traveled to conventions for the AFT (American Federation of Teachers) and NYSUT (New York State United Teachers). But that didn't interfere much with his attending any function in which his children participated.

Babylon was a sleepy little town back then. We lived in Babylon Village, which was one of eight entities in the Town of Babylon. If you have ever ridden the Long Island Rail Road eastward, you will be familiar with the train conductor's voice announcing the train destinations: "Amityville, Copiague, Lindenhurst, aaaand . . . Babylon." Usually, the "and" would be drawn out and the *Bah-buh-lon* spoken very quickly.

You could walk to just about everywhere in Babylon. There was a decent downtown area with small retail shops, pizza, ice cream, and one of the last old-fashioned soda fountains in New York at a place called Waldman's. We called this area the Village. Every kid under sixteen had a bicycle, and we rode them everywhere.

Although we could have harsh winters on Long Island, it was definitely worth it when summertime arrived. We were a fifteen-minute drive over one bridge to Cedar Beach and a twenty-five-minute drive over two bridges to Fire Island, where all the beaches were named after that lifetime bureaucrat and builder of causeways, Robert Moses.

We had a regular sit-down dinner at our house at approximately six o'clock, and attendance was mandatory. It never occurred to us to skip it. Usually my mother cooked, but my father pitched in at times. They were a good team, my parents. My father always said we learned more at the dinner table than in school. He believed this to such an extent that he would test us on current events. Tonight was no exception.

Richard Nixon had resigned from office in the summer (to the great joy of our household), and my father was already digging into his successor, Gerald Ford. We all learned that night that when Nelson Rockefeller took over as vice president it was the first time in history that a president and vice president were both unelected to their offices.

My mood improved gradually during dinner as we all went back and forth about different things going on with each other.

We enjoyed a meal of meatloaf and mashed potatoes with Max again lurking under the table. My mother was a great cook and seemed to have no trouble getting dinner served at a normal hour while still holding a full-time job.

When I retreated to my room after dinner, I thought more about the Nietzsche quote. Maybe I would come back stronger.

We would see.

Hanging Around

I wasn't in that much of a hurry when the bell sounded to end classes the next day, as I wouldn't have to change clothes for the junior high practice. We only had two gymnasiums for four teams, so the practices had to be staggered. The junior high and freshman teams would practice from three to four thirty, and the JV and varsity teams would practice from four thirty to six thirty or seven. My father would be late picking me up tonight, so I was hoping to sit in on some of the varsity practice later on.

It was a little depressing for me as I watched the active junior high players quickly depart class, head for their school lockers, and then rush down to the West Gym to begin practice. Regardless, I slowly hobbled down the route toward the West Gym to sit and watch the junior high team practice from the sidelines.

Virginia, my science classmate, was still packing up at her locker as I hobbled around the turn toward the gym. She was alone, and the entire hallway was pretty empty.

She smiled, looking at my crutches, and said, "Sorry about your foot."

"Yes, it's not how I planned to start the season. But I'll get through it."

"Do you still get to travel with the team and all?"

"Mr. Williams said that's up to me."

We spoke for another ten minutes or so, and then we started walking toward the gym. The cinch sack with my books in it had a cord that pulled the top closed, and then the cord clipped to a bottom corner of the sack so I could carry it without using my hands. But the extra weight combined with the crutches was still awkward. Virginia offered to carry it for me up to the door. I smiled and thanked her as she handed it back to me. She returned the smile and was off.

The door to the West Gym was unlocked, but the handle mechanism and hinges made its opening very loud—especially since I was navigating it at diminished speed and physical capacity. Mr. Williams, like most of the other coaches, ran a closed practice. He would have thrown anyone else out, but when he saw it was me, he just nodded and let me plop down on the floor.

Although it was the first day, when the team ran offensive drills, I was irked to see that the guy who had taken out my knees and caused my injury was presently practicing with the first string in what I had presumed all year would be *my* spot. He was bigger than me with red hair and freckles, but I considered him more of a football player than a basketball player. I knew I was better than him, but the truth was I would not get a chance to prove it for the time being. I had a doctor's appointment over Christmas that would provide a better idea of how long I'd be out.

Toward the waning moments of the junior high practice, I made my way over to the East Gym where the varsity would be practicing. The doors there were wide open. Practice had not yet started, and as I made my way in, I saw Mr. Cosci. He was a chemistry teacher and, in his spare time, the basketball team's official scorekeeper for all games and public address announcer for home games.

I wasn't sure he knew who I was, but he eliminated that mystery when he quickly greeted me with a "Hi, Tom."

Mr. Cosci generally knew everyone in the school, even those like myself who hadn't yet taken his class. He was a very jovial and pleasant man, but from what I understood a very tough grader. Fortunately, that was a prospect I wouldn't have to face for a few years. He was several inches taller than me, with jet-black hair and a thin, rather tidy appearance.

The East Gym was even more impressive after coming directly from the West Gym. As I gazed up at the banners and glass backboards, it seemed loftier, vaster.

The capacity *was* much greater, with larger and equal-sized bleachers on both sides (which, at the moment, were all collapsed back). There were four collapsible chairs set out; Mr. Cosci was sitting in one and gestured me toward the other.

The East Gym had four additional foldable baskets on each side. Even the floor was different. It not only was polished to a richer shine, but the sound of a ball bouncing off its surface was somehow more resonant. It hit with a far more regal announcement than the lesser thud of the West Gym. If you loved the game as I did, the sound of a basketball bouncing off a hardwood floor was like no other. You could hear it from a distance, and it would pull you in like the sound of an ice cream truck to a five-year-old.

Gradually, members of the team emerged and dribbled out onto the court. Every player wore a reversible tank top jersey colored black one way and orange the other. My eyes were instantly drawn to Glenn Vickers as he emerged through the locker-room door.

Glenn was casually cross-dribbling a ball from his right to his left, looking every bit the star everyone expected him to be.

He was a handsome guy with moderately dark skin, with half or so of an inch of afro. He also sported a faint mustache. But it was the way he moved that grabbed your attention. He walked and dribbled with a perfectly fluid motion. It was as if a stream of water started at his fingertips and flowed uninterrupted to the rest of his body without chop or splash. Glenn was confident but not cocky in manner. He seemed to know that it was all there for the taking but would not be given easily. His opponents had their own dreams of glory.

Glenn was Ernie's older brother. The Vickers family was one of the two main pillars of Babylon sports greatness in the seventies. The other was a family named Farley. Over a span of seven years, they would each pass four star players through the BHS athletics and basketball programs.

Another key player was Gervais Barger. He was a serious competitor, but when the game wasn't on, he sported an infectious smile that would light up those around him. Gervais was darker complected than Glenn and had a chip on the upper right tooth that was visible when he flashed that smile. He was closer to five foot ten in height and looked more the youthful teenager than budding adult. Gervais had coached me at a camp and in the village little league at the public courts the previous summer.

Team member Stanley Davis was another story. He didn't smile often and had a definite edge about him. I rarely had a congenial conversation with Stanley. I always sensed something was burning inside him, and I did not want to be the person to uncover it.

Stanley appeared much older than his age. He was very dark as well, with long sideburns and many adult-formed outward physical features. Standing at about six foot two inches one might believe he had a job, wife, and family somewhere. He moved and played deceptively slow, but he was flawlessly effective. A defender could likely see what he was about to do but was usually incapable of stopping it.

Once Koelbel blew the whistle everyone gathered at midcourt. I couldn't quite make out what he was saying, but, in my experience later in life, the first thing the Babylon coaches would impress on us was that you, the player, were the envy of every kid in town, and nothing that disgraced the program would be tolerated. Then, there would be a few more notes on how he coached and how he expected to be received. Koelbel would emphasize conditioning, discipline, and that he was in charge. No good team was based on democracy.

While Koelbel was speaking, Mr. Cosci leaned over to me and asked, "Are you helping out here at all?"

"No," I replied. "I'm just watching until my father comes to pick me up. Do you stay for the whole practice?"

"No, I'll probably leave when they start running intervals."

At Babylon, an interval sprint had everyone start at the baseline. When the coach blew his whistle, they were to run up and touch the nearest foul-line area and back to the baseline, then similarly run to midcourt and back, then to the farthest foul line, and finally to the opposite baseline. A term more commonly used for this exercise around the country was to run a "suicide." As one might guess, it was not the most enjoyable part of practice. A team would likely do ten to twenty of these to end a session.

After warm-up stretching and the layup drill, Koelbel again blew his whistle for everyone to regroup. He then assigned who would be the first string. He did this by telling each one to turn his jersey to orange. Everyone else kept theirs black. Glenn and Stanley were first-team forwards, and Gervais was the point guard who did most of the dribbling. There was lean and graceful junior Barry Davis at center, no relation to Stanley, and Chuck Farley was the shooting guard. Chuck was the only white starter on the team. All five had played on varsity the prior year.

The second team was made up of mostly first-year varsity players, but among them were three upcoming phenoms. Brian Vickers and Chris Brust were freshmen but were obviously on the other side of their growth spurts. Brian was six three, strong, fast, left-handed, and a determined competitor. Chris was six foot eight, two hundred twenty-five pounds, and had a gifted shooting touch. Also, there was another Farley, sophomore Steven, nicknamed "Weiner." He was Chuck's younger brother but, at six foot four, was the taller of the two. Weiner was a great rebounder and was one of those guys who didn't need to warm up to be effective in a game.

Babylon ran what was called a 2-3 offense, whereby the two guards would bring the ball up court while the two forwards and center would run along the baseline setting picks. The main goal was to get the ball to a player on one of the two blocks next to the basket for either a layup or to draw a foul. A secondary option had the weak-side forward (on the side of the court opposite to where the ball is) go to the top edge of the foul line to form a triangle of offense. If nobody was open, then the corner forward would pass the ball back out and the guards would reverse the flow to the other side.

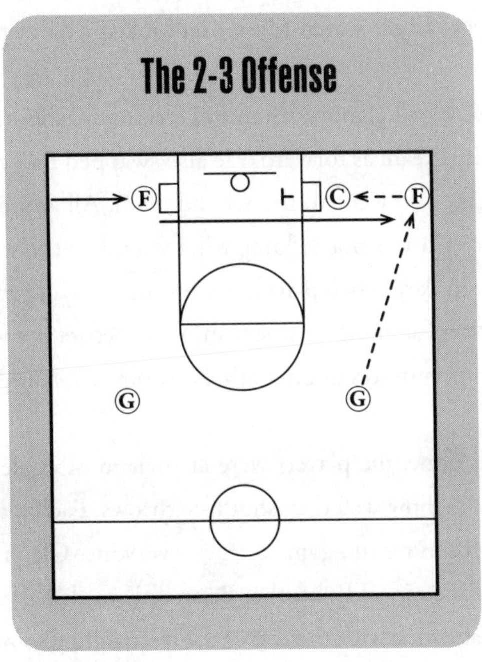

If the defense packed too many players into the lane—the shaded area between the foul line and basket—then the guards or someone else coming up might have an open jump shot. Koelbel, however, believed in making the other team play a lot of defense, so jump shots were not encouraged early in the offensive set up. As there was no time clock for high school ball back in the seventies, Babylon might run this setup for three to four minutes before taking its first shot.

In their initial trip up the court, the first team looked like they had been playing together for a decade. Gervais Barger passed the ball to Glenn, while Stanley put a hard pick on Chris Brust, freeing Barry Davis for an easy layup. The second team was less successful. Their first entry pass was intercepted by Glenn, who threw a length of the court pass to Chuck Farley for another easy layup.

On their next offensive possession, however, the second team fared better. They got the ball to Weiner in the corner. This time Chris set a hard pick (a blocking move) on Stanley, who actually fell to the ground. This freed Brian Vickers up to receive the next pass from Weiner for the layup. After this initial skirmishing and feeling one another out, both teams settled down into a more deliberate running of the offense. The next twenty minutes were an intense back-and-forth, with the first team staying ahead but the second definitely holding their own.

I was totally mesmerized by the play from both sides. When the scrimmage broke for the players to get water, Mr. Cosci looked over at me and mouthed, "Whoa."

After the break, Koelbel moved Stanley Davis out to shooting guard and put Brian in with the first team as forward. He also swapped Barry and Chris out at center. Chuck Farley also went to the second team. All appropriately inverted their jerseys. The coach was not redoing what would be the starting lineup but rather making sure his key bench players got minutes playing with the first team. The practice went on for another ninety minutes before the whole team lined up to do their twenty minutes of intervals. As promised, Mr. Cosci exited prior to the intervals

With intervals done, the players were at their most depleted. That's when Koelbel wanted to see how well they shot free throws. Each player was to shoot ten. It was tough scanning the gym to track everyone. Glenn was on the side closest to me. He made nine. His brother Brian only made half of his ten. Chuck and Stanley also made nine with the rest of the team falling somewhere between.

Toward the end of practice, Ernie emerged through the main entry and made his way over toward me and asked, "Are you going to be in town for Thanksgiving?"

"Yes, I'll be here," I replied. "We're hosting the extended family this year. Is there any action over the rest of the weekend?"

"Always," he smiled. Ernie didn't just know the location of the action; most often, he *was* the action. Where he went, crowds tended to gather.

"I'll touch base with you Friday after practice. So long as we're not walking from place to place, I can get dropped off somewhere."

Ernie agreed to this arrangement and then went up to the locker room to connect with his brothers. As he left, my father's face appeared at the outside glass door beyond the gymnasium entrance, and I made my way over. He and I would be eating leftovers for dinner.

Thanksgiving Weekend in Babylon

Holidays were big in our family, and Thanksgiving's significance was that each year, all four of the families on my mother's side would pick out one of the houses for gathering, rotating through everyone over a four-year period and starting over again. This year we were hosting at Coppertree Lane. We had added a third floor to our house a year ago, which provided an extra flight of stairs for all the kids to run up and down. In the spring or summer, we would have all been outside—we had a decent-sized backyard. Coppertree Lane was relatively quiet most of the time and void of any busy traffic. But since the pre-winter cold had settled in, we spent our time that season playing inside.

The families were evenly divided between New York and New Jersey, with my mother's parents coming from Queens. Among all the families there were ten kids between the ages of eleven and fifteen, with two much younger ones under the age of four. The ten got along very well, as there was always someone close to your own age with whom to partner up. As cousins, we saw each other seldom enough that it was a treat but often enough to form a camaraderie that allowed us to discuss the paths our lives had taken since we'd last seen one another.

Max would bark like crazy when everyone arrived. But once they were in the house and he got to sniff them he would come under control. However, with four different cars arriving we had to go through the ritual each time. When mealtime came we would lock him out in the sunroom where he would again bark for a bit but eventually calm down.

My father assumed the role of master of ceremonies, despite my mother and the other wives doing most of the work. The pressure would often get to him if whatever chore he was in charge of—such as heating the gravy—wasn't going smoothly and happened to coincide with some loud children's noise in an adjoining room. It was almost a guarantee that at least once per such event, he would yell out in frustration, "Will you people shut the heck up out there!" Often the word wasn't "heck."

Although it would scare all of us into twenty minutes of silence, the adults would always have a big chuckle, and my father would calm down and join in on the joke. He was in no way abusive, but we used to remark that when he lost his temper, teamsters would tremble. That was probably useful in running the union, but it was not great for his health.

We often had the stereotypical family seating breakdown when we ate at big gatherings. The meals occurred midafternoon this Thanksgiving, around three. There was an adult's table on the second floor where a moderate amount of booze flowed during dinner, while the kids ate downstairs in Nana Mary's apartment. She joined the adults upstairs. We were happy about the separation. It meant that our behavior was not under so much scrutiny.

It was always a fun time as we discussed everything from who was dating to schoolwork sucking. All the banter was mixed in with a lot of silliness and laughter. Once dinner was over, we faced forced conscription into cleaning the dishes upstairs while the adults continued their frivolity right outside in the dining room. Unfortunately, I did not get a pass on doing dishes that year because of my hobbled condition.

Once the dishes were done, most of the kids went back downstairs to partake in our annual tradition of watching older movie versions of *Mighty Joe Young* and *March of the Wooden Soldiers*. I opted out of the first movie and hopped over to the couch upstairs in the adjacent living room, where I was joined by my father and Uncle Steve.

"Are you out for the season, guy?" Steve asked. He always called me "guy," and since he was blessed with four daughters, he treated me like a son, as well.

"At least until January," I replied. "If it heals on time, I might be able to play some games at the end of the season."

"Their varsity has a pretty good team this year," my father chimed in. "Of course, they wouldn't win a game against Power or any city team."

His love affair with New York City would never end, regardless of where he lived. But I was thinking he might be surprised once he saw our varsity team play.

A few hours later—after the Wooden Soldiers crushed the Bogeymen—my aunts and uncles called the evening done. Within thirty minutes, four cars were filled and everybody headed back to their respective homes. We would see some of them again at Christmas. It was never *too* long between cousin visits.

My siblings and I stayed up until nearly midnight eating leftovers and watching more television. Our parents went to bed much earlier, but Nana Mary stayed up serving us tea with our pie until the last one of us retreated to bed. I had to get up early for practice the next day, but at my age, any lack of sleep could easily be recaptured with an afternoon nap.

Nothing of note happened at the two morning practices on Friday and Saturday, other than Ernie letting me know that he would be having a small party at his house Saturday night starting at eight o'clock. The Vickers family lived almost diagonally on the other side of town from us. It's a trip I had often made on my bicycle during the summer months, but with my foot in its current condition, I would need a ride.

The village of Babylon was divided into three distinct areas. It began on the shores of Great South Bay where our wealthiest citizens lived and ran north to Montauk Highway, or just Montauk, as we called it. The name comes from the Montaukett Native American tribe that populated much of eastern and central Long Island in precolonial times. The names of many of the streets and villages on Long Island have their origins with the Montauketts.

The houses got more modest and middle-class the closer you got to Montauk. Coppertree Lane was somewhere in the middle. I hadn't noticed until I reached junior high school that no black families lived south of Montauk.

Just north of Montauk, in the second area, were the commercial and public buildings. There were two long streets, Fire Island Avenue and Carll Avenue, which ran parallel up to Montauk. Across Montauk, Fire Island turned into Deer Park Avenue after a jig. Then it led through the Village area where there were shops, restaurants, and more than our fair share of saloons. North along Carll Avenue one would first pass the firehouse on the northwestern corner, then further along on the other side would be St. Joseph's Church and then Babylon High School. Across from the high school were the playing fields—football, track, field hockey, and more.

Past the high school sat the next geographic divider, the train station. And, yes, on the other side of the tracks to the western side was where many of the black families lived. It was still a nice area and by no means a ghetto. In fact, many middle-class white families lived there as well, from what I remember. But that was the only place in Babylon Village where black families dwelled.

On the east side above the tracks along Deer Park Avenue one would eventually pass two sets of streets. On the right side going north there was what we called the "Indian Streets." They were three consecutive streets that derived their names from colonial Native American tribes. The streets were Paumanake, Ketewamoke, and Cockenoe. Almost directly across from those streets were what we called the "President Streets." Those streets were Roosevelt, Lincoln, and Washington. The next street after Washington had always been named "Clinton" and would be an additional "President Street" a generation later.

My father was willing to drive me over to Ernie's but would not let me go in the standard thirteen-year-old uniform of blue jeans and a T-shirt. I had to put on corduroys, a collared shirt, and a polished shoe on my one good foot. He was this way about school as well. No McKeown kid ever showed up in school wearing blue jeans throughout our combined sixteen years of attending BHS.

I was dropped off just after eight and saw a few other of my classmates making their way inside without knocking. I had begged for an eleven o'clock curfew, which would be when my father would return. The Vickers lived in a nice house on a cul-de-sac within throwing distance of the elementary and grade schools we had all attended. Like high school, there was only one of each, so ninety percent of the people who went to kindergarten became the teenagers who graduated high school with you.

When I made my way in, I was directed to Ernie's room. Counting me, there were six of us who had arrived so far. We all sat around Ernie's room while he ran a pick through his hair. It was a comfort to me that Ernie was meticulous about his appearance. It guaranteed I would not be the only overdressed person at most events. Ernie was wearing a buttoned-up, long-sleeve shirt, black pants, and dress shoes.

Gary Farley was one of the attendees and commented, "Come on, we're not going to a fashion show."

Ernie merely smiled and continued primping. His room was not that of a typical eighth grader. For starters, he had a waterbed. Often, several of us, in a juvenile fashion, would sit on it and try and make waves to knock someone else off. The room also seemed to have been built on what had once been a porch. There was a door that led directly outside, and one of the four walls had planks of glass that could be cranked open to expose a screen. The last noticeable piece of decoration was a marijuana bong by his bed. It all conveyed a notion of independence that few of us enjoyed in junior high.

I was seated in the corner toward the front window. From there, I could see more guests arriving. Some walked up, and some pulled up in cars. Soon it became apparent this was not a party merely for Ernie and his younger friends. As I turned back Ernie had left the room and three of the others were drinking beer from Styrofoam cups. It was good my father had dropped me off early as his seeing this would have provoked a quick U-turn home for the evening.

It was fun socializing. Virginia and several of the girls from our class were there, as most of the basketball teams were from all levels. I managed to find a can of ginger ale and dump it into one of the beer cups, hoping it would foster the illusion that I was partying along. After a while, I got tired of standing and people bumping into my crutches, so I angled for the kitchen table, where I saw Brian Vickers quietly sipping on a Coke. As I took the seat next to him and leaned my crutches against the wall he welcomed me with a smile.

"How was practice today?" I asked.

"Good," he replied. Brian could actually be good company, but you had to get the conversation going. Despite his massive physical attributes and ferocious competitiveness on the court, his soul was still that of a fourteen-year-old.

"The competition will be quite a jump from what you were facing last year on the freshman team." I had seen Brian score forty-two points the year before in a freshman game when he was an eighth grader. He would be fine on varsity.

"We played a lot of the other teams in the county in summer leagues, so I know what's out there," he informed me.

Right then Glenn walked by and spewed out my name, "Muh-*kyoo*-en, what are you doing here?" When Glenn mispronounced my name, I didn't seem to mind so much. I was just happy he knew who I was.

He was holding hands with a tall, pretty blond girl, Tricia, whom I recognized as the older sister of one of my younger teammates.

"I thought it was a party for Ernie's friends, but it seems an All-Vickers, All-School event."

He laughed and then asked about my injury. I recounted the same prognosis schedule.

"Well, good luck," he said and continued to points elsewhere with his companion.

Brian had gotten up to get another Coke and asked if I wanted anything. I checked my watch and saw that it was a little after ten o'clock. It was my hope to get a ride home so as not to expose my father to the scale of this event, so I declined and set about navigating the house to find a friendly face.

In addition to seeing beer drinking, I could see outside that there were a lot of people smoking pot as well. The aroma seeped into the house. Marijuana had such a distinct smell that I did not find very pleasant. I assumed Mr. and Mrs. Vickers were still around, but they were nowhere in sight. Finally, I stumbled onto a senior friend who lived across the street from me. I knew he had a car. He wasn't enthusiastic about leaving the party, even for a short drive, but knowing my father, he was sympathetic to my plight and drove me home.

I was dropped off at ten thirty and explained to my father that I had saved him a drive. He said "goodnight" and shot me a suspicious look, but I went to bed feeling like I had gotten away with something.

It felt like—maybe even because of my injury—this would be a year where I would really move a step closer to being an adult. What I hadn't expected was that with maturity came responsibility. Was I ready for it? We were about to find out.

The Lead-Up to Game One

The emotional buildup to the first basketball game was usually noticeable at any American high school. But when there were big expectations, as we had this year, everybody seemed emotionally engaged. Banners and posters were pasted on walls and hanging from ceilings down every hallway in the building. Our tiny bookstore marketed only one cheaply made T-shirt that read BABYLON PANTHER BASKETBALL, but they were sold out by Wednesday, a full two days before the game.

I noticed that several of my teachers were mixing basketball metaphors into their lectures. "Grant's strategy at Vicksburg was like a full-court press," and "The immune system acts like a zone defense" were only some of the stories cooked up to keep our attention. It worked for me.

It had been four weeks of practice since my injury. I thought I could feel things healing up but wouldn't know until my checkup after Christmas. All accounts were that the varsity had been crystallizing and coming together, but what I heard from several people in the know was the high level at which Brian and Chris were playing. It seemed they both would be contributing greatly to the team and might have a few of the starters rattled about holding their positions.

Weiner was thought to be the best defender on the second team and continually had the difficult job of guarding Glenn during practice. But I heard Koelbel would add a sixth player to the second team to double up on Glenn. Koelbel obviously seemed certain that his star would get extra attention from whomever the opposition was.

During lunch period, my friends and I were all seated at one cafeteria table discussing plans for before and after the game. My options were limited due to my lack of mobility, so I pushed for one after-party at someone's house, but the decision was not going my way. As it was only a short walk from the East Gym to the Village area, after games most people would first head there and grab a slice of pizza or soft ice cream before heading to their ultimate destination.

There were three lunch periods between eleven thirty and one forty-five, each forty-five minutes in length. The populations were mixed, however. Seventh graders ate with seniors and everything in between during each period. There were three rows of six tables that could seat about twenty to thirty kids each. A natural hierarchy formed with seniors only sitting at the frontmost table on the west side and the grades falling in by level after that. When it got down to junior high, populations were still separated by gender. We weren't that brave yet.

As I was munching on a french fry, some of the guys discussed the junior high game, whose season had started the day before. I had a preliminary doctor's appointment and had not attended. The team had lost by eight points, with Gary Farley scoring twenty-four of the team's forty-two points.

"See, we would have won if I was there," I joked to absolutely no laughter.

"When are you due back?" Gary asked.

"I might be able to play two weeks after the cast comes off, which would mean the middle of January, but I doubt I'll be much of a force."

"Hmm." He nodded.

At that, the bell rang, and we all got up to head to our remaining classes. I had science period right after lunch and ran into Virginia and her friends heading in the same direction and tagged along. I informed them of the informal game agenda that the boys had arrived at during lunch hoping that would influence their plans and that we would all run into each other. They gave no definitive answer, but I suspected we would see them all later that night.

Pat was rehearsing with the theater group for some Christmas production they were putting on over the holiday break, so I would be picked up alone at the circle at the back of the gym today. This time it was my mother who had come to fetch me. She drove an older blue Pontiac Tempest.

"Hi, Mum," I said as I opened the backdoor and spread out across the seat.

"Hi, Bum," she replied, completing a greeting we had started using from an old Irish song.

"How was your day?" she continued.

"Good. No bad grades going into the holidays, but I'm still stuck in this cast."

It was always easier talking to my mother. She was able to separate being a teacher from being a parent much more easily than Dad. Although she did not tolerate poor performance either, she didn't always seem to be grading us, as my father did.

I always thought my parents were a handsome couple. But if I had to make a call, I would say my father married up just a bit. My mom was pretty and graceful and looked several years younger than her thirty-seven years. She also had that rare ability to know when something was wrong and could coax it out of you without prying.

My parents had been together since high school in New York City and had known each other most of their lives growing up in the same neighborhood. My father worked his way through Manhattan College, after which he and my mother married. Over the ensuing five years, my mother gave birth to four children while my father went to work. As far back as I can remember we had always lived with my father's parents. My grandfather, whom we called Poppy, had died when I was seven.

"Is that *all* that's bothering you?" she asked.

"Well, the junior high team played their first game yesterday and I really want to be playing. I'm taller, I could have started, and last year I was terrible."

"That's not going to change until you're back out there," she replied sympathetically. "Focus on enjoying Christmas and we'll get you healthy on the other side."

When I got home, I made my way up to my room and changed out of my school clothes. Then I trundled down to Nana Mary's apartment where she and my mother were enjoying a cup of tea and some Irish soda bread my grandmother had just made. I partook without an invitation, and we sat there and chatted until my father got home around five.

My father was in a good mood as he walked through the door. Fridays and holidays tended to have this effect on him as with all in the schooling community. My mother and I had moved to the upstairs kitchen so that my sisters could take over the television downstairs and get their share of Nana's spoiling love.

While he was changing, my mother heated up some leftovers from the night before so he and I could exit to catch some of the JV game, which started at six. The varsity game would follow at seven thirty to usually finish around nine.

I was impatiently tapping my fingers on my thigh out of view while my father ate and discussed some of the day's happenings with my mother. Max came and moved his head underneath my hand in an apparent gesture that if I needed to keep my hands busy then I could be petting him. My father was highlighting some aspect of the teacher's contract, but I couldn't quite grasp what. Since my father seemed calm about it, I gathered it was not a big deal. He would be much more heated if it were a large issue.

We were finally pulling out of the driveway at about six fifteen and on our way to the school. I sat in the back seat of the Monaco where I could again spread out. My father asked if I minded him sitting on the West Islip side for the game. I said I didn't and would probably join him there as those stands would be less crowded and easier for me to navigate.

We drove across Montauk onto Deer Park Avenue and through the Village. There we made a left on a side street that led to the side of the high school where the East Gym and adjacent parking lot were. We were early enough to get a decent spot. My father helped me out of the car, and we went a short distance past the circular drive through an external glass door, which brought us right to the ticket desk outside the gym.

My father had to pay fifty cents for entry, but as a student, I got in for free. We had no student identification, so it was left to whomever was in charge of entry to use his best judgment. It wasn't too much of a problem as the high schools weren't barraged with gate-crashers. At least not for this game.

Once inside the gym door, the home-side bleachers were pulled out and immediately to the right, easily accessible. One had to navigate between the baseline of the court and the opposing wall to get to the visitor side, which would require waiting for a stoppage of play. The scoreboard showed just under two minutes until the end of the second period, so we and a few others waited until halftime to cross.

In the East Gym both benches were on the visiting side. When the buzzer sounded, we made our way across and then traversed the court lengthwise to the far side where the Babylon bench was. We took two seats four rows back which enabled us to see well enough over but also enabled us to see over the heads of players seated on the bench. The sideline was, of course, currently empty as both JV teams were in their locker rooms for halftime. There was only one locker room in the East Gym, so the opposing team had to make their way to and from the West Gym locker room.

The bleachers on both sides were about half empty but would not remain so as the crowd's pace of entry had started to progressively quicken after us. The JV team was losing by five points at halftime—which was a new experience. Most had played on the freshman team the year before with Brian and Chris, where they had cruised to an undefeated season, winning by an average of twenty-plus points a game.

At the three-minute mark of halftime, the two teams returned to the courts for a couple of quick shots before the second-half tip. Mr. Bartsch was the last one out and made his way over to his coach's seat a few seconds before the buzzer went off again.

My attention to the game was soon broken when Mr. Koelbel came up and sat next to me after finishing a conversation with the athletic director. He started right in.

"Muh-*kyoo*-en, I'm glad to see you made it here without shattering any more bones."

I laughed before replying, "Just so you know, if you're going to butcher my last name, you'll have to take it up with my father here, Pat McKeown Senior. Dad, this is Mr. Roy Koelbel, the head varsity basketball coach at Babylon."

The two shook hands with a smile before Koelbel affectionately put a hand on my back and said, "I know both your boys, and other than their Irish heritage, I think they're a couple of stand-up winners."

"I appreciate that, and nobody knows a winner like a twentieth-century German," my father quipped back. The two laughed, and I sensed an instant camaraderie had been born.

Shortly after that Mr. Bartsch waved me down toward the bench and asked if I had a pen. Unfortunately, I did not, but a nearby West Islip fan selflessy offered one up. When I turned and went back to the fourth row, I saw my father had slid over as he and Koelbel continued to converse. I sat back down on the other side of my father.

At the start of the fourth quarter and with the JV trailing by ten points Koelbel departed for the locker room to prepare for the varsity game. He shook my father's hand and waved to me before crossing over to the home side and up the stairs to the home locker room.

Bartsch put the JV team into a full-court press for the remainder of the game, which pulled our guys a little closer, but when the final buzzer went off, West Islip had managed to post a four-point victory. The coaches and a few players shook hands before departing the court for the main event. By this time, about eighty percent of the bleachers were full, with a good-sized queue at the door and ticket stand.

Five minutes later, our cheerleaders ran out onto the court in their orange-and-black mini outfits with their thigh-high skirts. They tapped their white marching shoes across the court chanting, "Varsity! Victory! Varsity! Victory! . . ." This performance culminated with a human pyramid where the top girl stood up, spreading her arms high, and yelled, "Go Panthers!"

The West Islip team came out first to a smattering of boos from our side. Although they had bordered on Babylon for most of both schools' existence, West Islip had never had a black student. Hence, they had the backhanded nickname of White Islip.

After the visitors had been shooting layups for a minute, our Panthers emerged from the locker room to thundering applause. Koelbel was a great showman as well as coach and had developed a cool ritual that preceded the customary layup lines. Glenn led the team out single file, dribbling the only basketball to the far basket. Upon reaching the basket, he jumped and just touched the ball off the left side of the backboard.

Every player behind him would catch the ricochet off the backboard and do the same. After going through the line twice, Glenn switched the ball over to the right side, followed by Gervais and Stanley. They would continue twice through on the right before Glenn put the ball in the basket, and more balls were tossed out for layups. It was like watching a ballet.

When the referee blew his whistle to signify the end of warmups, both teams returned to their benches. Mr. Cosci, who was positioned behind a table near half-court, switched on his microphone and welcomed everyone to tonight's game. Then he announced the starting lineups. West Islip's five were greeted with a smattering of applause, but when the Babylon team was introduced, the gymnasium went wild. In addition to announcing the game and keeping the official score with his West Islip counterpart, Cosci was also tasked with operating the scoreboard.

Following the introductions the teams huddled up for final instructions. At that point the Babylon fans started coordinated foot stomping and we began our chant, "This is Panther Country! This is Panther Country! This is Panther Country! . . ."

Our five starters walked out to the center circle to meet the West Islip squad, with Barry Davis stepping into the middle to jump against their center, who stood an inch or two shorter. Barry's smooth features and long limbs might remind one of a gazelle, the way he moved. The chanting continued as the referee reached the ball in between the two big men and tossed it up where our chanting culminated in a giant cheer.

The season was on.

Game One and the Aftermath

Barry tapped the ball back to Gervais, who went about setting up our half-court offense. West Islip fell back into a zone defense, daring us to take an outside shot. When Gervais passed the ball to Stanley Davis in the corner, he looked inside and saw that Barry Davis was double-teamed and he was unguarded. So, Stanley accommodated the defense and calmly sank a twenty-foot jump shot.

Koelbel was not a fan of zone defenses, and as West Islip brought the ball up, we met them at half-court with a pressuring man-to-man matchup. Their guards were good ball handlers, but they were having trouble connecting passes to anyone near the basket. Finally, they found an open man near the foul line, but his shot rattled out. Barry pulled in the rebound and passed the ball out to Gervais, who pushed the ball up court.

West Islip remained in their zone defense again as Babylon attacked. This left Chuck Farley open just beyond the foul line where he drained his first shot of the season. As the first quarter was drawing to a close, their coach abandoned the zone defense for a man-to-man approach, but that only led to

Glenn and Barry easily scoring inside layups. We led by ten points as the first quarter ended.

A colleague of my father's from West Islip had arrived and sat down next to us. He shook his head and said, "This is going to be a long night."

When the second quarter began Koelbel substituted Brian Vickers in for Stanley, Chris Brust in for Barry, and moved Glenn to guard before putting Weiner in for his brother Chuck. The three who had just come out all sat next to Koelbel on the bench as the coaches conferenced with them on some matter. I wasn't sure what it could be as they had played what might be labeled a perfect first quarter. But being the good coach that he was, Koelbel was never satisfied.

The second period was no better for West Islip as Brust blocked the first two shots that came inside, and Brian scored on two gravity-defying double-pump shots. Glenn drew three fouls, which resulted in six made free throws. Drawing fouls was Glenn's superpower. He averaged in the twenties most seasons but half of his points would come from the foul line.

It looked simple as most things do from the stands. He would fake his opponent into jumping up, dip in his shoulder while the player was coming down and create contact while going up for his shot. Often, he'd make the shot as well as draw the foul, which would result in a three-point play. I would try that move for years with much less success.

When the buzzer sounded for half-time, we were up by eighteen. Gervais had played the whole half scoring only two points but dishing out five assists and making two steals. He was always the leader in those categories.

About five minutes into half-time Ernie came over and sat by me. "Hi, Mr. McKeown," he said, reaching a hand across to my father.

Ernie always made a point of pronouncing my last name correctly. That and his neat appearance elevated him as a favorite of my father who thought all high schoolers were slobs.

"How are you, Ernie?" my father replied. "Good night for the Vickers family so far."

"Yeah, sorry we have to beat up on your guys."

"Don't worry about it. Say hi to your parents."

Then Ernie turned and gave me the night's agenda. The gang was heading to get pizza at a place called Manniello's just over on Deer Park Avenue, a mere five-minute walk from the gym. I told him that I would have my father drop me off but that I would be there. He gave me a thumbs-up and headed back to the Babylon side where the mood was much cheerier.

Koelbel kept the first string in for half of the third period but with orders to not fast-break and work on the half-court offense. This would prepare them for upcoming games, and besides that, there was a collegiality amongst the veteran coaches not to embarrass one another's teams if possible. This was not merely good sportsmanship, but included the fear that the other coach might return with a stacked club a few years later when your talent happened to be depleted.

By early in the fourth quarter with Babylon leading by twenty-four, Koelbel let his whole bench rotate through. This didn't help West Islip to close the gap any. When the final buzzer went off, Babylon's margin of victory had swelled to twenty-eight. Koelbel made his way over to shake hands with the West Islip coach as my dad and I headed down the bleachers before turning toward the exit.

Before we got out of earshot, Koelbel called out to my father.

"Hey, Pat, a couple of us are heading over to the Villager for a beer. Would you like to join us?"

The Villager Tavern was also on Deer Park Avenue but about a half of a mile further north.

"I'd love to," my father responded. "I'll drop Tom off with his friends and meet you there."

I figured my father would find some way to notify my mother of our planned prolonged evening. She had probably already assumed he would be going out for a while with the West Islip crowd.

The workers at the game opened the three sets of doors at our end of the gym, and this made for easier and larger-scale exits. I was grateful not to have to navigate my way back the way we came and through the tighter main entrance. Although when they opened the doors, it threw a quick chill on everyone, at that moment it was still a relief from the stuffiness of the gym.

My father and I made our way back to the car. We sat there a bit to let the vehicle heat up and to let some other cars pull out to enable an easier exit. Then we drove over to the exit on Grove Street and made a left where, within a few hundred yards, I could see the front of the pizza parlor. I thought I saw a few of my friends entering.

Rather than drop me off to cross the street my dad drove around to the back where there was an entrance to the dining room. There, he dropped me at a narrow awning-covered entry and informed me he would be back in two hours to pick me up. Upon entering I saw Ernie and six others parked at a table. Gratefully I saw there was one seat left for me. It was a dining-style table with three chairs on each side and one chair at each end.

Ernie was at one end with his girlfriend sitting on his right. Virginia and one other girl were sitting next to her. Gary was at the other end of the table with two additional junior high teammates next to me. It was good they had gotten there when they did. The dining room was full with what looked like a wait out front.

The proprietors of the restaurant were a couple who had relocated from New York City and brought their magic with food to our fortunate town. The place boasted a full menu of pasta, meat dishes, and such, but their New York style pizza was what paid the bills. It was cooked on large silver trays that were two feet in diameter. The pizza was then cut into eight triangular slices. When prepared correctly, it was eaten by folding it in the back and starting at the tip, which should bend down a bit for the first bite.

The front entry of the place brought you to a counter where you could sit and order a slice and beverage while watching the pizza being made and put into the large steel ovens. There was a door behind the counter that led to the kitchen, which also had a door that opened to the dining room. Surrounding the counter were also a few two-person tables where a couple could order from the counter and bring their food to the table.

From the moment you walked in, the smell of cheese, sauce, and meats overwhelmed you, and your stomach would involuntarily growl as if it had been deprived of life till that point.

The waitress approached, and Ernie ordered for the table. The choices had been made before I arrived, but we all liked the same food, so it didn't matter.

"We'll have two pies, one just cheese and one with sausage. Also, a couple of pitchers of Coke."

The place served Cokes by the pitcher, like the Chianti and beer, which made it seem a little more grown up to parties of youths like us. After the two pitchers were placed on the table a few minutes later and the waitress departed, Ernie poured a glass for his date and, before putting the pitcher down again, warily maneuvered it under the table. From there he had removed a small bottle of rum from his coat pocket and emptied it into the pitcher.

Ernie then poured himself a glass. He looked at me, but I shook my head and he passed it to the fellow on my left, who did partake. Besides me, all of the guys at the table and the girl next to Virginia drank from the spiked Coke. The three of us who didn't partake drank from the other, unaltered pitcher.

Conversation flowed in every direction, but I did find myself in competition for Virginia's attention with the guy to my left. I had an advantage, I thought, in that she had sympathy for my injury. Also, we had several classes together. But he was relentless, going on about a skiing trip his family would be taking at Christmas.

Finally, our server approached, first putting two circular raised stands on our table. Then he departed and reemerged with our pizzas on the aforementioned trays with steam still coming out of them. The sight seemed to match the aroma. And the taste?

Still my definition of heaven.

Unfortunately, when the pies hit the table, all gentlemanly behavior went out the door. Each male, including Ernie, rushed to grab a slice without consideration of our female counterparts. The girls shook their heads and with more daintiness grabbed slices for themselves. Justice was swift. The pizza turned out to be very hot, and I burned the roof of my mouth on my first bite.

Ernie, always the planner, was already discussing a Saturday evening get-together. He knew if anything happened at my house, it would be dry, what with my father watching over, so he turned to the others.

"Gary," he said. "Any chance we could use your basement tomorrow to hang out?"

"Maybe," Gary replied. "Let me see what my parents and brothers have going on. I'll try and find out by practice tomorrow."

I wasn't sure a Farley party would roll out like a Vickers party—though Gary also had brothers from each grade that could open it up to their friends. I'd have to nuance my arrival and departure with my father again if this came together. Mr. Farley was a police officer, however, so things might not get quite so out of hand.

At the midpoint of our meal there were three slices of pizza left. Each guy had downed two, and each girl one. The girls said they were full, which left three slices for five guys. We played a five-way version of odds and evens to determine who would get his third slice. The fellow to my left and I put out a *one* to three *twos* from the others. Thus, we watched as the final three slices disappeared down other guys' throats.

I checked my watch and saw that my father would be arriving in fifteen minutes, so we called for the check. With each of the guys putting in two dollars and the girls adding a dollar each, the bill was covered with an ample tip.

"My dad is picking me up in a minute," I offered. "Does anyone want a ride?"

Virginia and one of the other girls popped up and quickly accepted. Although they both lived in the other direction, I knew my father would oblige. This got me some dirty looks from a couple of the other guys, but I was oblivious. Or pretended to be.

Outside the temperature had dropped another five degrees. It was teeth-chatteringly cold. Fortunately, my father was right on time. He knew both of the girls and extended a greeting, to which they replied in kind.

We headed back out to Deer Park and turned north toward an adjoining street where both girls lived two houses apart.

"Are you both planning on going to Gary's tomorrow if it comes together?" I asked.

"I'll have to see what my parents have planned—but probably yes," Virginia replied. The other girl nodded as well.

They each thanked my father as they got out of the car and we turned to head south back to Coppertree. My father was in a good mood. He had obviously enjoyed his outing with Koelbel and the others. We talked a little more basketball on the remaining ten-minute drive.

The junior high team had no games over the holidays but would continue to practice. Meanwhile, the varsity would be playing in the annual Town of Babylon Christmas tournament. With our eight-man-deep roster, I couldn't see anyone giving us trouble. But what did I know?

One Player Down by Christmas

With the exception of Christmas Day, the basketball team practiced throughout the holidays. The coaches would even tell the team to expect to practice New Year's Day, but they held making it a day off as an incentive. Only once in my years of playing basketball for Babylon was there ever a New Year's practice. After all, practice meant the coaches had to temper their New Year's libations.

On the Saturday before Christmas, my mother woke me at seven so that I would be able to have a quick breakfast before departing for eight o'clock practice. My brother had asked that I not set the alarm so he could sleep, so my mother had volunteered to wake me since she was an early riser.

Downstairs, Nana Mary had just finished making biscuits. She served Mom and me two that were still so warm the butter melted almost instantaneously when applied. With those, we also got a side of scrambled eggs. It's remarkable that I was not a much chubbier kid.

We hopped into the Tempest and were on our way.

"You seem in a much better mood today," she said. It was more of a question than a statement.

"I am," I replied. "It was a fun night last night, and I'm thinking maybe the doctor will surprise us with a good checkup next week."

"Maybe," she replied.

She dropped me off by the circular drive at about five till eight. When I arrived I found that the junior high practice had been pushed off to nine, so I went over to the East Gym to check out the varsity. I could hear the basketballs bouncing as soon as I got close. There were only five players on the floor so far, including Koelbel, who was showing Barry Davis a pivot move down by one of the baskets. I quietly took a seat without garnering any attention.

Koelbel blew the whistle a few moments after eight. Often, a Saturday practice after a victory would only be a shoot-around where everyone would grab a ball from the rack and practice his individual game at a relaxed pace. A few informal 2-on-2 games might break out at various ends of the court, but nothing too intense was expected.

Today, however, Koelbel told the team he wanted to review a few things since the Christmas tournament was coming up. If all went well, this would mean three games played in three nights starting the day after Christmas. So it was back to layup lines and a regular practice.

The drill started as usual, from the right side of the basket. Then, on his second layup attempt, Chris Brust seemed to come down awkwardly and immediately hobbled to the wall behind the basket. He was clearly in pain while he and Koelbel conversed out of my earshot. I couldn't tell what had happened as it seemed like he had just taken a normal shot.

After a few more minutes of trying to walk it off, Chris was done for the day. Weiner and the student team manager helped Chris navigate over to the stairs and up to the locker room. We didn't see him again during that practice. I recognized his limp and was afraid he had met a similar fate to mine.

Weiner came sprinting back and practice continued. The remaining bench players on the team were good athletes but none would likely be able to step up and replace Chris. The team's depth would be down to seven if Chris was out indefinitely.

During scrimmage, the first team remained the same, but the second team was much more overmatched without Chris. There were other considerations as well. Koelbel switched around a few players, obviously trying to figure out what configuration he might go with if Barry Davis were to get into foul trouble. On the first practice break, he seemed to have settled on Glenn at center, with Stanley and Brian at forward. The guards would remain unchanged.

Glenn could play anywhere, so it was no strain for him to play center. The problem was that if he was forced to play in the pivot, this might negate some of his all-around play and expose him to getting in foul trouble. This we couldn't afford. We were a solid team but not champions without Glenn on the floor.

After an hour I headed back to the West Gym to watch the junior high practice. Chris did not reemerge before I left. That did not bode well.

When my father picked me up later I recounted what had happened during practice.

"Could they tell whether it was a break or a sprain?"

"He never came back out, so I don't know for sure. But when they helped him off, he was putting zero weight on it."

By the time we pulled into the driveway, it had started snowing and there was about a quarter of an inch on our grass. It was too early to tell whether it would stick enough to get the neighborhood outside throwing snowballs and attempting sleigh riding.

Long Island was pretty flat as a land mass, and Babylon was even more so than the average. There were areas by Argyle Lake, which was directly across the street from the high school, where there were hills with enough slope for a decent downward ride. But mostly snow meant snowball fights between youths—with a few kids stupidly launching them at cars.

My priority at the moment was sleep. I had no problem making the bell for an early practice, but I would always make up sleep afterward if I could. Once inside, I immediately went up to my room, turned my television to a football or basketball game—and was out like a light within five minutes.

My usual pattern was to conk out for two hours and wake up refreshed and hungry. Fortunately, Nana Mary was downstairs always eager to feed us. Another breakfast? Why not. So she cooked a few waffles, some scrambled eggs, and bacon, and I downed them.

I spent the rest of the day idling. But then around six o'clock, I found out that a gathering had indeed come together for the evening. The meet-up time was at eight. I tried to get my mother to drop me off, but suspecting something he disapproved of might be up, my father was quick to volunteer.

The Farleys lived closer to the Vickers than to us in that northwest corner of the village. And like the Vickers they had a nice suburban house. The street was relatively quiet, but the Long Island Rail Road tracks were about a quarter mile away. You could definitely see and hear it when a train roared by.

Mr. Farley was outside putting some garbage in a steel container when we pulled up. To my horror he came over to the car. My father rolled down the window.

"How you doing, Pat," Mr. Farley asked.

"I'm good, George, how are you?"

"Good. You in a hurry to get back?"

My father shook his head in the negative.

Oh no.

Mr. Farley invited my father into the house for a beer. I was horrified that my father would now bear witness to the types of high school parties I was attending. He might never let me go out again.

We made our way up the six-step concrete stoop. As Mr. Farley walked us in, a storm door loudly slammed shut behind us. We made our way into the kitchen where Gary and Weiner were sitting at the kitchen table while Mrs. Farley was dumping chips into bowls and making other snacks in the oven.

She and my father exchanged a hug, then Mr. Farley pulled two Budweisers from the refrigerator and gave one to my father. Weiner confirmed for the group the status of Chris Brust's injury.

"I just talked to Boo," said Weiner, using the team's nickname for Chris. "He's in a cast for about two months."

He would not be playing in the Christmas tournament, or for most of the regular season.

Gary and I sidled over to an adjacent room. We were separated by a wall from the kitchen, which afforded some privacy. Mrs. Farley came in a few minutes later with a Coke for each of us. She dropped the bowl of chips on the table as well. I started to relax, thinking this might be a party that my father would approve of.

Ernie was the next to arrive and joined us in the living room. I thought it odd he didn't take off his coat. Then, after Mrs. Farley put a Coke in front of him, we saw why. He wryly smiled and pulled another unopened bottle of rum from the confines of his jacket. But Gary shook his head, and Ernie, with a sarcastic pout, placed the bottle back in his pocket.

At about eight thirty, Virginia and several of her friends arrived, as well as another five guys from the junior high team. She and one of her friends sat down on the couch next to me and we got to chatting.

"What are you doing for Christmas?' I asked.

"We're leaving on Christmas Eve to go to my aunt's. We won't be back until Friday."

"You'll miss most of the basketball tournament."

"Yeah? When are we playing?"

"The first two rounds are Thursday and Friday. If we make it to the finals that will be Saturday night."

"Do you know where that will be?"

"I think Deer Park High School, but I'm not sure. Call me when you get home if you want a ride," I said. I didn't even know for sure yet whether I could get my father to drive to the game.

Weiner eventually had several friends come by, but only as a prelude to going out elsewhere. Meanwhile, Ernie had been scheming to move the party to a place with more permissive house rules.

By ten thirty things started to break up. My father had stayed the whole time talking with Mr. Farley. So, whatever Ernie may have come up with I would not be a part of. When my father and I left, I again ruined the nights of several of the guys when three girls asked if we could give them a ride home. One of the other guys was done for the evening, as well.

My father didn't seem to mind dropping everyone off. This was Babylon, and none of them were too spread out and most other parents in the village would do the same. After we delivered the last passenger, I set about my plan to convince Dad to drive to the Christmas tournament games.

"Do you and Mom have any nighttime plans over the holidays?"

"Just Thursday night. Why?"

"I was hoping you would go to the Christmas tournament games."

"And bus along your troop, huh?"

"Yes," I answered with a pleading smile.

Dad paused and grinned back at me. He agreed to drive me and whomever to games two and three. I thought I should be able to find a ride for that first night with someone else.

It was turning into a great holiday. With any luck I would get my cast off on the twenty-sixth as well as the prognosis for my possible return to playing basketball myself. Anticipation!

Christmas and the Diagnosis

My father and grandmother were the hardcore Catholics in the family. She had emigrated from Ireland in the 1920s and was a daily churchgoer. My father attended Catholic schools and regularly adhered to the basic tenets of the church. My mother was also Catholic but much less devout. My siblings and I tended to follow her lead.

My father's devoutness often conflicted with his desire to sleep late on his days off. Any pictures we took of Christmas mornings where the kids were opening presents always showed him with a grumpy look on his face. Thus, for this year, we came up with a strategy to please everybody. We would all go to the Christmas Eve Mass, which fell on a Tuesday, come home and have a late supper, and then open presents that night. We could stay up as late as we wanted and sleep late on Christmas Day, having fulfilled our religious duties.

Others had the same idea. The mass began at six that night at red-bricked St. Joseph's next to the high school. I saw the Farley family and several of my other friends and neighbors. During communion, I saw Chris Brust making his way up. He was definitely on crutches. Chris was hard to miss as he was a head taller than anyone else.

Weiner had not been mistaken. Chris was out for a while.

Due to the cold weather, there was little socializing after the service. We retreated back to Coppertree and ate in the upstairs kitchen. Nana Mary had made biscuits, and my mother whipped up ham and cheese omelets. We also had a chocolate cake purchased from the local bakery. It was a good night for Max; we all fed him some table scraps.

Dinner ended at about nine, and we proceeded to the living room where our eight-foot tree stood, lit and shiny. All our presents were spread at the bottom. My youngest sister Dorothy had been the last to give up on Santa Claus, so no kids were disappointed. When any of us had bought presents in the last few weeks, we put them under the trees ourselves without trying to maintain the mystery as to how they got there.

The big gifts came from our parents, and at our ages then they were usually clothes. My folks were very fair; the same dollar amount was spent on each child, and everyone was even-steven at the end of the day. If you had asked for a game or toy, it was deducted from the clothes allowance.

I had asked for a Nerfoop. This was a staple of 1970s boyhood, a small basketball-shaped hoop with a net that sat on the top of a door frame, accompanied by a soft, squishable ball. I put it up in my room but would move it around the house often to wherever I was watching television. I ended up playing with that thing for years.

Our grandparents on both sides would gift us money, which we loved. Each kid bought gifts for one another and for our parents. There were two shops in the Village next to each other that we would frequent at Christmastime: a gift shop and a luggage and leather shop. They each had a hoard of things you could buy for a dollar twenty-five, and the McKeown's helped clean the places out every year.

My parents went to bed a little after ten as usual and we kids again retreated to Nana Mary's to watch television, not retiring until after midnight. None of us would wake before eleven the next morning.

Christmas Day involved another meal around three, and trying on our new clothes. In the early evening, we kids would go to the movies. My parents stayed home, preferring the peace of having us all out of the house for a few hours. *The Man with the Golden Gun* was the choice for my brother and me.

My sisters acquiesced, as the only other available movie was *The Godfather Part II*.

We would have to drive to the theater in Bay Shore, which was directly east on Montauk Highway on the other side of West Islip. The theater building itself was on the main drag so we were dropped off in front as my mother, who had driven us, sped away.

I was often surprised that our parents would let us see James Bond movies at our age, particularly with my sisters. There was no nudity or bad language, but with all of the nuanced sex scenes and outright misogyny by the lead character, it could be deemed inappropriate for youths. It had a PG rating, but that only meant if someone in the party paid the over-twelve price of four dollars, the whole group was deemed to have an adult present. For us that was Pat, and we were in. I was able to sneak by as two years younger than I was, and only paid the dollar fee. We were fair about it, however, and the three of us would square up with Pat later and ended up contributing a dollar seventy-five each.

The Bay Shore location was one of the few old-style theaters remaining. It had red velvet curtains and comfortable, fluffy matching seat cushions. The place had been built in 1926 and was part of the movie boom in the east. The entire industry eventually moved west to Hollywood and took all the production jobs with it. Several big, beautiful theaters like this one remained.

It also boasted two balcony boxes, always empty. But the fact that there *were* balcony seats provided a little mystique and tempted us to think that, at any moment, a celebrity or the president of somewhere might show up. One could still picture the theater as having a red carpet rolled out from the sidewalk into the lobby on special nights.

My sisters barely stayed awake during the movie, but my brother and I thought it was great. Christopher Lee was not quite as evil as he was in his role of Dracula, from which he'd made his reputation, but he was scary enough to provide a good foil for Roger Moore's James Bond.

The team had no practice the next day since the first game of the Christmas tournament was that night. As my father wouldn't be attending, I hitched a ride to the game with the Vickers family. But before that, the first order of business for the day was my doctor's appointment to assess progress on my injury. I was hoping for good news.

My father took me to the X-ray department at nearby Good Samaritan Hospital. The scan was done by a technician; but our family doctor, Dr. Godfrey, was in the hospital that day on other business and was also present.

Godfrey was a tall, roundish-looking man with sparkling eyes that seemed to be permanently amused. My father used to call him "Barney Google" after the song and comic strip. With twelve children, he was head of Babylon's largest household. Practically every grade at BHS had a Godfrey in it.

I sat on an examining table with my father in a nearby chair when the specialist and Dr. Godfrey entered, pinned the X-ray to a lighted panel, and mumbled together. Finally, the two broke their huddle and assumed the two other chairs in the office. The first two words from the specialist would make my day.

"Good news," he said matter-of-factly. "The break has fused together exactly as it should, and we can remove the cast."

Dr. Godfrey directed a big smile in my direction, which I returned tenfold.

The removal seemed primitive to me. I had always thought of the medical field as one of technological wonders, but a technician brought in a small electrical saw, plugged it into the wall, and cut a straight line from the top of the cast to the bottom. Then he pulled the plaster apart with his hands and snapped it off.

The skin on the leg underneath was wrinkled and pallid. I put a sock over my foot for the first time in five weeks and loosely tied my other sneaker over it (which my father had thought to bring along).

"Stand up and put some weight on it," Dr. Godfrey said.

I did as ordered. There was some pain, but not as much as I'd feared. I walked up and down the office, wincing a bit, but in no danger of falling.

"When can I start playing basketball again?" I asked.

The specialist smiled and replied, "I would spend the next week walking and no more. After that, try some slow jogging, and, if you have access to a weight room, maybe some light presses. After about two weeks, have Dr. Godfrey look at it, and he can give you the green light. You don't want to rush it."

Dr. Godfrey walked us out slowly enough for me to keep up. He spoke mostly to my father but that did not matter as my head was elsewhere. I was plotting my return to the junior high schedule.

My father often appeared stern, but on the drive home, he looked happy. You might think he was the one going back to playing basketball. In a way, I guess he was.

Once home, I carefully negotiated the half flight of stairs up to the second floor. My mother saw me without crutches and threw her arms around me in a big hug. Pat was out, but my two sisters came down with big smiles for me. It was great to finally escape everyone giving me the "poor Tom" face.

I gingerly walked up to my room and looked through the new Christmas clothes. I had not told any of my friends that the cast might be coming off today in case I got a worse diagnosis. But, in the self-regarding manner of all teenagers, I imagined people might be looking at me tonight, so I wanted to look great.

My look was always preppy. When scanning through the layer of clothes on my bed, I picked out a pair of blue corduroys, a striped collared shirt, and a tan crew neck sweater to go over it. I would still wear sneakers, which were stable and loose enough to accommodate my slightly swollen ankle.

Ernie had asked that I be dropped off at his house at 6 p.m. There were eight teams in the tournament, so there would be four games today and two tomorrow, with the championship game slotted for Saturday night. Today a game would start every two hours beginning at 2 p.m. We were playing in the last game against North Babylon, which tipped-off at eight. The Vickers wanted to get there early enough to see the result of the prior game. The winner of that game would be our opponent should we win tonight.

Ernie answered my knock and spouted out, "Hey, look at you! Two legs. I didn't know the cast was coming off today."

"I was afraid something might change, and didn't want to explain if anything went wrong. This way, the surprise is to the upside."

He accepted my logic, and we went inside, where his parents also expressed happiness at my improved condition. Gary and another friend joined us in a few minutes. The Vickers had a van, so it was easy for all of us to fit inside. I asked Ernie if his girlfriend was coming, but he said she was gone through the weekend.

From there, we were off to the tournament. In those days, a basketball tournament during the holidays was the peak of excitement for me, almost better than any Christmas present.

Christmas Tournament Begins and a Rocky Start

The tournament was in Deer Park at Robert Frost, one of their junior high schools. It was twenty minutes away. Once we arrived, we saw the impact that the multi-team tournament had on the parking situation. Mr. Vickers circled around three times, hoping to catch someone leaving, then abandoned the quest and parked in a spot at the farthest corner overlooking the street.

I didn't know Mr. Vickers—William Sr.—very well. However, I wasn't surprised to find out that he had been a standout player for Babylon basketball back in the 1940s. Standing at about six foot three inches with a lean build, Mr. Vickers looked to me like a slightly smaller version of Bill Russell. His face could go from smiling pleasantly to fixed intensity rather quickly.

When the van came to a full stop our thirteen-year-old manners escaped us once again as, eager to get inside, we rushed ahead of Ernie's parents. I tried to keep up but eventually fell behind, slowed by my limp. There were at least ten people ahead of my compatriots, so the setback wasn't permanent, and I joined them in the line.

Once inside, we found the place was electric. Most of the current crowd was there for the two teams playing, but some from earlier games had remained, no doubt to assess their future competition. With two and a half games having been played, the gym was stuffy, the crowd's exhalations and the players' sweat permeating the air.

At the moment, Deer Park was leading West Babylon by eight points, with one minute to go in the third quarter. We scanned the crowd to see if any of our classmates had taken over an area yet, but after seeing none, we muscled out some space behind the West Babylon bench.

By the middle of the fourth quarter, Deer Park had stretched their lead to fourteen, and several West Babylon fans started heading for the exits. With about one minute to go, the bleachers were half empty. Mr. and Mrs. Vickers had found a seat about three rows behind the players on the bench.

The final buzzer sounded. It was Deer Park victorious by seventeen. If we won our upcoming game, they would be our next opponent. The tip-off to our game was thirty minutes away. As a group, we moved down to the row behind Ernie's parents. The bulk of the Babylon faithful had started to arrive and, taking their cue from the Vickers family, filled up the nearby bleacher seats.

Our team charged out of the locker room first, to the strong applause of our section. Glenn Vickers led the team out single file. He dribbled the only basketball to the basket farthest from us. He tossed the ball up against the backboard, and the Babylon warm-up ritual of successive taps began.

Koelbel emerged from the locker room wearing a maroon blazer and gray slacks. He walked with a confident stride. Bartsch was a step behind him. He wore a green blazer and plaid slacks of the then-popular Johnny Miller collection.

A few minutes later our opponents emerged. For this opening game we would be playing North Babylon. They filed out looking a little cockier than West Islip had two weeks earlier. This would be a tough first-round draw due to their speed and athleticism. But North Babylon was a young team, and most thought they were a year or two away from becoming a top-flight competitor.

Mr. Cosci had been visiting with Mr. and Mrs. Vickers and was now walking over to the official scorer's table. He looked up as he walked by and gave us all a nod.

Warm-ups were whistled complete at three minutes before eight. The game would start at the top of the hour, as shown on the black-and-white clock above the basket nearest to us. I watched as the red second hand ticked down the remaining time. Our starters took off their sweats to reveal our away uniforms, black with orange trim. Koelbel made a few brief comments to the team and sent out the familiar starting five.

"Brian and Weiner should get some more time tonight," I commented to Ernie and Gary.

"Yeah, that's the bright side, I guess," Gary replied.

Once both teams were at center court, the referees went through their standard ritual of spacing out the players from both sides to ensure nobody was standing where they shouldn't. Then the ref holding the ball stepped into the circle. Barry faced his opposite number. Up the ball went, and the game was on.

Barry again won the tip and pushed the ball to Glenn, who caught a streaking Stanley Davis down the right side for the opening basket. Our side erupted at the quick hoop, as Stanley pointed his finger to Glenn in recognition of the good pass. He then raced back on defense where Chuck and Gervais awaited the North Babylon guards at half-court.

We implemented a half-court press from the start, but that didn't faze their point guard. He wasn't very tall but was stocky and used his ample body to keep a pressing Gervais at bay. The North Babylon offensive scheme involved a lot of off-ball picks that had players cutting to the basket making good use of their speed. One such player received a pass that resulted in a five-foot-lane jump shot to tie the score.

Then North Babylon went into a similar half-court press, and we didn't respond to it as well. After a forced shot by Chuck that bounded into North Babylon hands, they raced down the court for an easy layup to take the lead. The pressure from both teams kept it tight, but the first quarter ended with us down by four points.

When our team came back to the bench, Koelbel was hot. We could see his hands moving vigorously, and the constant juts of his head when he spoke left no one in doubt that he was one agitated coach. The second quarter started even worse. North Babylon upped the pressure and surprised us with a full-court press. This rattled our guards and forced several turnovers that led to easy North Babylon baskets. These soon added up, and with two minutes to go in the half, we were down by *sixteen*.

Then, following a time-out, we seemed to catch our composure. We stopped hurrying everything and started getting the ball to Barry Davis down low in the post. He scored four unanswered points. Then a North Babylon turnover led to a Glenn layup where he was also fouled with just four seconds to go in the half. Glenn made the free throw just before the buzzer sounded. We left the court trailing by nine.

Whatever Koelbel said at halftime did the trick. Although the North Babylon faithful were roaring to start the half, we went on a tear in the third quarter to tie things up at fifty-three. Barry Davis put up ten more points in the quarter, using his height to score over his defender. North Babylon was on its heels.

We continued to press our advantage in the fourth quarter on hot shooting, with Glenn and Stanley continually drawing fouls off of a tiring North Babylon defense. At one point, we went on a twelve-to-nothing run. This enabled us to pull away. It ended up a nine-point victory, and Babylon left the first round victorious.

Everyone in the stands breathed a sigh of relief when the game ended.

Along with the others, I descended from our perch toward the bottom of the bleachers. Koelbel had gone to shake the other coach's hand, but Mr. Bartsch saw me as I got down to the railing.

"Well, that was a lot closer than expected," he said. Then he looked down at my legs and smiled, saying, "All right! Back on your feet."

"Yes, I got it off this morning," I confirmed.

I then picked my foot up off of the ground and wiggled it a bit at the ankle. It was a stupid move, as I immediately felt a flash of pain and had to suppress a grunt.

"Any word on when you'll be practicing again?"

"Pretty much like you said. I won't be able to scrimmage right away, but I can jog and lift a little until then. So, a few more weeks."

He nodded and then was off to join the team, heading back to the locker room.

Just a few feet to my left Ernie's parents were conversing with Glenn and Brian over the railing as the rest of our gang waited nearby.

It was almost ten o'clock, and I decided that I would not participate if there were any postgame activities tonight. When the Vickers family dropped me off, I could see the Monaco in the driveway, which indicated my parents were home.

"Do you need a lift tomorrow?" Mrs. Vickers asked.

"No, my dad will be able to go tomorrow. But we'll see you there."

She smiled back and nodded in her motherly way.

I rushed into the house as fast as my mending legs would permit to give my dad the update. Max met and recognized me at the door so we were spared any barking. He followed me up to where I found my parents at the kitchen table having a cup of tea together, already in robes. I could hear my siblings downstairs watching television at Nana's.

"You missed a heck of a game," I shared. "We were down big in the first half but rallied back to win."

"Wow," was Dad's only reply.

"You're coming tomorrow, though, right?"

"What time?" Dad asked.

"We're the late game again, so it will start at eight."

"Good, we can get dinner in before then."

"Yes, but can we try to get there a little early to see the end of the prior game and who we might play for the title?"

"Pushy little bugger," he said to my mother, and they laughed.

"Yes, that's fine," he told me.

I relocated downstairs to join my siblings to get my own cup of tea at Nana's and, I hoped, some late-night sweet.

My father was true to his word the following evening as we finished dinner and were able to leave by a quarter to seven. We arrived in time to catch the end of the other semifinal game between Lindenhurst and Walt Whitman. Whitman was the only school not in the town of Babylon to play in the tournament. They had been substituted in to replace Wyandanch, a team that wasn't participating that year.

There were six minutes to go when we walked in the door. Lindenhurst was leading by ten. The place was packed and the man admitting people held us at the door.

A time-out was called with three minutes to go, at which point he directed us to a cluster of seats on the far bleachers. We made our way over and got seated just as play resumed.

Lindenhurst was inbounding from their own end. Whitman was the smaller of the two teams but seemed very tired, unable to make up their height deficit with speed. Lindenhurst kept pounding the ball inside to their two big men, who seemed to score at will.

With about thirty seconds to go and trailing by fourteen, a Whitman player tried to take a charging penalty on one of the Lindenhurst point guards. But the official called a blocking foul instead, and the Whitman coach exploded off of the bench and into the official's face. That resulted in an insignificant technical foul but delayed the game's finale. The Lindenhurst player hit only one of the three foul shots awarded, and the clock expired.

Apparently, that had been the most exciting part of the game. The bleachers cleared of Whitman fans, but many Lindenhurst people stayed put to see who they would be playing in the championship. I looked around to see if the Vickers family had arrived, figuring they would know the right place to sit. I spotted them in almost the same location as the night before, so we made our way over to them and exchanged pleasantries.

Shortly after we arrived, both teams for the last game had made their way onto the court to warm up. Koelbel and Bartsch were dressed similarly to the night before and were deep in discussion as the buzzer sounded to end warm-ups. Ernie and the others returned with refreshments, and we took up seats before the opening tip.

Koelbel spent more time than normal addressing the team in the opening huddle. He was likely eager to avoid another slow start such as we'd had yesterday. Finally, the referee came over and blew his whistle at the huddle. Koelbel mouthed something to the tune of, "All right, all right." And our players took the court.

Deer Park looked cocky. They had knocked us out of the tournament last year in an upset. Perhaps our performance early in yesterday's game added to their confidence that they might repeat the feat.

Barry Davis won his third tap in as many games and pushed the ball again back to Glenn, who, rather than looking for a quick basket, handed off to Gervais as we methodically went about running our offense. On the third corner pass of the sequence, Stanley saw that Barry was double-teamed on the block. He passed it to Glenn, who flashed up to the post. As Glenn's man rushed to cover him, Glenn faked him into the air and leaned in, drawing the foul and almost sinking the basket. The result was two foul shots. Glenn made both.

Our first points were on the board.

We again started with a half-court press, and this time, their guard was less successful at keeping Gervais Barger at bay. Everywhere he turned, Gervais beat the man to the spot. With Chuck Farley providing equal pressure on the opposite guard, the Deer Park center flashed up to the top of the key to make himself a target. The ball handler hit him with a high pass that he caught over his head, but Barry was instantly on him.

When he turned to make a spin move, Glenn faked collapsing with one step but then went back to his man. This was enough to trick the Deer Park center into making a pass to what he thought would be an open man. Instead, he passed right into Glenn's hands. Glenn took the ball himself up the court. The rest of the team spread out, and he went to work.

Glenn paused at the top of the key with one six-foot-two defender on him. He took a dribble right but then crossed over, shifting the ball between his legs. Then he drove down the left side. Then Glenn made his signature move. He faked up, drew the defender with him, then made contact with a minor double pump as the player was coming down, then shot. The ball banked off the backboard and into the basket. The referee blew his whistle. And there it was. Glenn was at the foul line again to complete a three-point play.

Halfway through the first quarter, we were up by ten points, and the Deer Park coach called a time-out. Koelbel stuck with the current lineup and made no substitutions. Deer Park, on the other hand, went with a smaller three-guard lineup when they returned to the court. This turned out to be a smart move.

With a third guard, they were able to get the ball up court much more easily against our press. This also confused our team as to who would cover the third ball handler. At first, it was Glenn, but this left Stanley guarding a man three inches taller than him. Deer Park sank a couple of baskets in the confusion.

On defense, Deer Park decided to leave Gervais Barger open and have the additional defender roaming close to Glenn. Gervais, though open, was not our best shooter. After a few missed attempts, Deer Park was right back in the game, trailing by only four points by the middle of the second quarter. Koelbel called a time-out.

When we returned to the court, Brian Vickers had come in for Gervais. He took a post position with Barry, and Glenn took over point duties. Stanley and Chuck were our two best outside shooters and positioned themselves not too far from Glenn. These changes proved an ample response to Deer Park's previous adjustment.

When Glenn brought the ball up court, a floating defender would leave to cover him. Stanley or Chuck were therefore open, and one of them would usually drain the open shot. It was like target practice for the two of them. Brian took to defending the second Deer Park big man, and Stanley defended one of the guards. With his long reach and jumping ability, Brian seemed to play several inches taller than his actual height.

Our lead grew to eight by halftime and swelled to sixteen by the middle of the third quarter. At this point, Gervais went back in and Glenn and Barry came out for their first breaks of the game. I wasn't sure if Koelbel planned to put them back in at all. The team on the floor with Brian and Weiner complementing the other starters was able to keep Deer Park at bay and add to the lead.

Then, with one minute left, Koelbel was able to put in his remaining players, and the starting five watched the remainder of the game from the bench. All were euphoric at advancing in the tournament and avenging the loss from last year. When the buzzer sounded, Babylon had a comfortable double-digit victory.

The team and fans departed more reassured than they had been last night with our rough start. Nevertheless, everyone knew that a good team on a bad night could go down. The next game would tell the tale and determine the tournament victor.

Tournament Championship and Goodbye to 1974

It was again almost ten o'clock as the gym cleared out and nobody was speaking about any after-gatherings, so I didn't petition my father and just drove home with him. I could tell despite his bias to New York City basketball, he was becoming impressed with Babylon and the level of competition on Long Island.

Once we pulled out of the parking lot, he was the first to speak.

"How is your ankle feeling?"

"Still a little ginger but it's nice not to have to rely on crutches."

"I'll bet."

After a little recapping of the game, we talked about other things. He was a history teacher, so we touched on what I was learning in school. I told him we were covering the post–Civil War period and Reconstruction, to which he offered up his insights. Then we turned back to my recovery workouts and when I planned to start playing again.

These were my favorite times with Dad. It seemed when he and I were alone driving in the car we never ran out of things to talk about. So long as my grades stayed up, these were very pleasant outings.

It was nearly eleven when the car pulled into Coppertree. We parted at the door. Dad went upstairs to turn in. Meanwhile, I went down to Nana's where my siblings were watching a rerun of *Hogan's Heroes*. I'd barely sat down before I had a cup of tea and a slice of cake. As long as we were up at night, Nana was there to spoil us.

Our phone was busy the next day. Virginia was back home and called to confirm her ride to the game. She asked if she could also bring her neighbor from the pizza night. I didn't think to ask my father since I believed we had plenty of room. But when the phone rang again it was Mr. Farley asking to speak with my father. The upstairs phone was on the wall next to the refrigerator.

My father was next to my mother at the table reading *Newsday*, but I was able to stretch the curly cord across to him with ample slack. After a brief conversation he handed the phone back. I hung it up. He returned to his paper, but I immediately strode over next to him.

"Well?" I said.

"Mrs. Farley's mother is not well," he replied. "So, Gary and his dad will be going with us tonight."

"What?" I asked, realizing the overbooking.

He repeated what he'd told me. I then sheepishly informed him of the added passenger Virginia had invited. Mr. Farley was a big man so there'd be nobody squeezing in front next to him. My father shook his head and said that the four of us would just have to all squeeze into the back. I was relieved, for I'd feared I might have to disinvite Virginia's friend and that they both would find other rides.

I was disappointed that it wouldn't just be me and the two girls. But Gary was always fun to have along, and he was a good basketball conversationalist.

As there would only be the championship game that night, they set a game time of seven o'clock. We picked up the girls first at a little before six. I stayed in the front while they got in. I then reluctantly told them about the Farleys coming along. They chuckled, examining the size of the back seat, and then shrugged their shoulders in assent. What else were they going to do?

Gary and his father were waiting at their front door when we arrived. I exited the front seat and left the door open for Mr. Farley, then Gary and I wedged our way into the back seats, pushing the two girls toward the middle, only to discover I had miscalculated. I'd ended up on the side with the friend and not Virginia.

The four of us joked and squirmed during the twenty-five-minute drive. Of course, none of us wore seat belts. When we pulled into the parking lot at Robert Frost there was already a short entry line stretching out from the door. We rushed our way across the parking lot but only had to spend about five minutes in the cold before we were admitted into the now very familiar gymnasium.

The Vickers family was already there seated in the same spot as the two previous nights. They were speaking with Mr. Cosci. He'd decided to come earlier than the prior nights. There was only a little extra space near them. Dad took that, and we four sought out Ernie. He was a few rows back jawing it up as usual. There we found enough space to accommodate all of us.

By about a quarter hour till game time, the stands were packed with what seemed equal parts Babylon and Lindenhurst fans. Their fans looked to be yelling, but from where we were sitting, they were drowned out by our clapping, foot stamping, and the chant, "This is Panther Country! This is Panther Country! . . ."

We kept the chant going as their team came to warm up, but then burst into a louder cheer as Glenn emerged, leading our team out into the standard ritual. After the teams broke into layup lines for ten minutes, the referee blew his whistle and it was showtime.

There were about ten of us from the eighth grade there jammed in together. Ernie's girl had returned from vacation, and they were busy chatting. Virginia was wedged in between Gary and me, with her neighbor on my right.

Koelbel had a quicker pre-tap huddle tonight and when they finished their all-in-hands cheer, they actually reached the center circle ahead of our opponents. Lindenhurst had a tall white kid jumping at center. He looked to have about two inches on Barry Davis. Once everyone was set, the referee backed in and tossed the ball.

Barry didn't win this tap as easily as the others. In fact, both centers got their hand on the ball at the same time and it fell clumsily between everyone in the circle. After it kicked around for a bit, Chuck Farley was able to gain possession and toss the ball to Gervais.

The pace was similar to the night before. Gervais and Chuck patiently moved the ball back and forth from the top waiting for someone to break free in the corner. It was almost two minutes before they found Stanley Davis in the corner. He bounced a pass to Glenn for the first basket of the game.

Lindenhurst was not by design a running team. Their offense revolved around their six-foot-seven and six-foot-five pivot men who set screens for one another aiming at a close open shot. They counted on smaller teams needing to double-team so they could pass to one of their other three players for an open jumper. But Glenn and Barry ably handled these big men one-on-one and removed this option for most of the first quarter.

Meanwhile, Stanley had the hot hand for us. He scored three mid-range jumpers that had us up by four after the first quarter. When the second quarter started, Koelbel put Brian in for Chuck and moved Stanley to guard. Stanley scored one more shot that quarter, but Brian provided an equal force down low as our post men dominated most of the second quarter. By halftime, we had doubled our lead.

Our gang all went down to the refreshment table during the break. They had a lot of baked goods and some soft pretzels for sale, so I grabbed a pretzel and a Coke, then gathered with the others.

"Party at my house after the game," Ernie said with a smile.

"Win or lose?" I asked.

Everyone looked at me like a heretic. How could I contemplate defeat? I quickly shrugged, not believing what had just emerged from my mouth.

"We'll get out at my house and then walk over," Gary said to me and the girls.

He might have been thinking the same as me—that it would be better not to have the fathers see what a fully developed Vickers party looks like. All agreed on the plan as we heard the buzzer sound to begin the second half.

We confidently assumed that our space in the bleachers would still be there when we got back, and luckily it was. I looked down and saw my father talking it up with Mr. Farley. It was also the first time I saw Chris Brust sitting all lonely at the end of the bench as the starters were heading back out onto the floor. The crutches sitting next to him jogged a familiar forlorn memory in me.

Barry had collected his third foul right before the half, so Koelbel started the third quarter with Brian joining Stanley and Glenn down low. This got Brian several looks at the basket, and halfway through the third he had added four points and two monstrous rebounds. The second one he had grabbed with his single left hand and brought it together with his right so hard I thought the air would come out of the ball.

Lindenhurst played tough but continually lost ground. When Barry came back in for Brian to start the fourth, Weiner also subbed for Glenn, who already had twenty points. The lead never got below ten points in the fourth quarter. With two minutes to go we were leading by sixteen and both sides started clearing their benches. When the final buzzer went off, we had claimed the crown with a fourteen-point championship win.

After the championship trophy was presented, the all-tournament team of six was named. Glenn, Barry, and Stanley all got the honor, in addition to three members from the other schools. We all stayed until the final minute.

My father offered to drive everyone individually back to their houses, but when I said we were all going to stay at Gary's for a bit, he was fine with that. He informed us that he and Mr. Farley would both be joining the coaches for a celebratory beer. They let us all off at the Farleys' driveway and backed out on their way to the Villager, or perhaps somewhere else.

We didn't even go inside. As soon as the car was out of sight, we trekked over to the Vickers house where the party was in full swing. Ernie met us at the door and we maneuvered to the section where the people our age were congregating. Barry White was playing on the radio or an album, I couldn't tell. We passed Glenn dancing with Tricia. He smiled and gave both Gary and me five as we walked by.

There was a keg of beer flowing and I saw the Vickers parents in the kitchen talking to some people I didn't know. Their presence might account for the fact that I did not smell any pot, inside or outside of the house. But the place was packed, and everyone was soaking in the victory.

Ernie handed us each a Styrofoam cup with an implied invitation to partake at will. Before Gary and I could offer to get the girls a drink, they all broke for the keg. I made my way to the kitchen, where there were several chilled sodas in the fridge and Brian was sitting at the kitchen table. I poured a Sprite into my cup and squeezed into a chair next to him.

"Great game," I said.

"Thanks."

"I thought for sure you were going to make the all-tournament team as well."

"No, they weren't going to let four of us on there. I'm surprised we got three."

"Yeah, I guess, but we still looked great."

"It was nice, but nothing really matters until League play starts in January."

He was right. We were four and zero but in all non-league games. League play would determine the county playoffs and all of that was still to come.

I tipped my cup against his can of Coke and said, "Well, then Happy New Year and good luck in 1975."

He nodded back. I returned to the group with my faux beverage, wondering, like everyone there, what kind of year it would be.

1975 and League Play

January always feels like the Monday of the year. There is so much holiday fun and indulgence packed into the days from Thanksgiving to Christmas and New Year's that one feels hung over for practically the whole month. When you factor in the bleak weather of the northeast it could all become very depressing.

But not if you love and play basketball.

January is the prime time of the season. League play started, and every Tuesday and Friday were game times. I had accelerated my workouts for the remainder of the holiday break and was now jogging on my bad ankle and even lifting weights with it. It was beginning to feel like I could return to normal soon.

My father insisted on one more check-up with Dr. Godfrey before letting me return to the junior high team on limited duty. I was fine with that, but the only time he could do it was the afternoon of Tuesday, January 7—the same day the varsity would be traveling to play Amityville. But I was anxious to get back to playing.

It was a short week. We cruised to a twenty-one-point win in our first league game at home against John Glenn on Friday night, January third. They hadn't been expected to be much of a challenge. However, a win was a win.

Classes came and went over the next couple of days. Our teachers, perhaps recharged from the time off, didn't seem as lethargic as the students following the holidays. They also seemed to take joy in shocking us back into reality both during class and in doling out homework. It took me about a week to get back into the academic groove.

On the day of the Amityville game, I saw several varsity players in the halls. For away games at any level in the basketball program, players were required to be dressed in suits all day during school as well as on the bus. Last year, ties had been mandatory, but as the era of the "leisure suit" had begun, the coaches became a little more flexible. As long as you were neatly attired, they were fine.

When I passed Glenn after lunch he had on a matching brown suit with a big jacket collar. Underneath he wore a floral-colored shirt with big print. The collar of the shirt was folded over the collar of the jacket to the outside. The shirt collar was also left open with no tie, to reveal a beaded necklace that he always wore on and off the court.

He also wore platform shoes but still walked quite adroitly. The rest of the team was dressed in similar fashion. But as with everything else, Glenn looked the best.

"Good luck today," I said in passing.

"Thanks, Mac," he said and continued on.

Later on, I had been planning on walking to the doctor's appointment when the time arrived, but my father offered to pick me up after school on his way home. Godfrey's office was literally a block away from Coppertree, but it was still winter so I wasn't going to pass up transportation.

My father always pressed his children to be organized and punctual, and yet he was almost always late. He agreed to pick me up at three for my three thirty at the doctor's but arrived at three twenty-five. It was going to be tight. I just shook my head when I got in the car. He went on about some stupid driver who was ahead of him on the short drive from West Islip to Babylon, but I was hardly listening. Right now, I didn't care. I did not want to miss that appointment.

Dr. Godfrey's office was a converted gray-shingled neighborhood home. It had a similar stoop to all the houses around. We passed through the door shortly after parking the car. He was talking to the woman who worked as his receptionist and nurse, and they both laughed as we walked in.

"Another traffic jam, Pat," he said to my father, well aware of his timeliness challenges.

"All right, all right," my father responded good-naturedly.

We went into his examining room, where Dr. Godfrey rolled up my trouser leg and had a look. I noticed myself how much healthier the color was, and the skin was no longer wrinkled.

He poked and prodded a bit and repeatedly asked if what he was doing hurt. I could honestly answer that none of it did. What about my exercises? I answered, and he was impressed with what I had been able to do.

"I think you're good to go in a week. Do some exercises by yourself where you're stopping and starting. If nothing hurts or feels strained, you can start practicing again."

"I will definitely do that," I said and bounded off of the table.

My father had a few more questions, but Godfrey answered to his satisfaction, and we were soon on our way home. My mother was excited to hear the news when we arrived home and gave me another big hug. At dinner that night all I could talk about was getting back to playing.

The downside of being healthy again was that Pat and I were back to walking to school. That next morning, we bundled up and were out of the door at a quarter to eight. The weather had been dipping up and down from freezing levels, and the snow we had at Christmas had melted a little to sludge and was now frozen over into a dirty gray color. Such was a Long Island January.

"Do you want to go see *The Godfather II* this weekend?" Pat asked.

There was a home game on Friday and perhaps a party or something else going on Saturday night, so I proposed Saturday afternoon.

"Let's see if there's a one o'clock show," I suggested. "It's probably a three-hour movie like the first one."

He agreed as we continued on our way.

I guess I wasn't as tuned into my surroundings as we entered the building or perhaps hadn't passed anyone in the know. But after stowing my books in my locker, I got to my homeroom class, where several other boys gathered around looking glum.

"What's going on?" I asked.

"Didn't you hear?" one replied. "The varsity lost yesterday to Amityville."

"Holy crap," I responded.

At that moment, the teacher came by and ushered us all into our seats for the morning announcements. The loss was confirmed over the loudspeaker. This was combined with a plea for everyone to come out for Friday's home game to cheer us back onto the winning track. Everyone was so stunned by the loss that the second half of the message seemed to go unheard.

It was doubtful that I or anyone would be able to sneak into the varsity practice today. I imagined the mood might be a little stern. Apparently, we had blown a seven-point lead in the fourth quarter and shot very poorly from the free-throw line. Koelbel would be working them hard today.

After the bell rang for the final class, I retrieved my bag from my school locker and started making my way toward the West Gym for junior high practice. I passed Gervais Barger and Stanley Davis on my way and gave them a smile and a wave. Gervais nodded his head with a half-smile, but Stanly kept on walking, offering no sign of recognition.

As I rounded the familiar corner where Virginia had her locker, I ran into her, packing up to head home.

"Ready for your first day back?" she asked.

"Been ready for six weeks."

"I'll bet. I can't believe the varsity lost."

"Yes, and to *Amityville* again. They seem to have our number in every sport."

"See you at the game Friday?"

"Absolutely."

I smiled and checked my watch, not wanting to be late for practice. I still had plenty of time, but I couldn't wait anymore and headed to the locker room.

It was great to be back. I had already moved my stuff from the small student locker to the larger one the athletics teams got. The extra elbow room was nice as they were only two to a column versus the three-stack configuration of the student ones. Currently, we were sharing these with the wrestlers. The tension between the two teams would occasionally erupt into a brawl, but all was quiet today.

I finished getting dressed before Gary, Ernie, and the rest of the team arrived. Mr. Williams welcomed me back as I eagerly emerged as the first player on the practice court. I told him what my doctor had said, so he allowed me to participate in everything except the scrimmages. I ran, shot foul shots, and even participated in the layup drills. In a week I should be at full speed.

It was still very difficult watching the first string scrimmage together while I had to sit on the sidelines. Ernie was a good point guard, and we had some excellent athletes on the team. But we were small everywhere except at center. This meant the whole offense was geared to getting the ball inside to Gary.

But at least I was back.

On paper, the varsity had an easy opponent that Friday night against Port Jefferson. But the faithful showed up in the East Gym as if the whole season were riding on this game. We all wondered whether there would be any signs of letdown after the Amityville loss. Would we see weakness overtake our seemingly invincible team?

I drove up with my father only because he was now going to every Friday game and hanging out with the coaches afterward. However, as he again sat over by the bench, now that I was more mobile I parted with him and sat over with my friends and classmates on the fan side.

Ernie, Gary, Virginia, and the gang were all there. We stomped our feet, chanted, "This is Panther Country!" and brought the overall noise level to a rock concert level. After we won the tip and scored the first basket everyone jumped to their feet in total rapture.

We employed a half-court press the entire game, which befuddled Port Jefferson's overmatched backcourt and forced more than twenty turnovers. The lead was thirty-one at halftime. The first string sat out most of the second half, but we were still able to increase the lead and double Port Jefferson's point total when the final buzzer went off.

This comforted us and confirmed our hope that the Amityville game had been an uncharacteristic letdown. Tonight's opponent was winless, however, and would likely finish last place in the league. They were not a real test.

I told my father that I would walk home after hanging out for a bit following the game. He was fine with that since he was likely hitting the Villager with the coaches and friends. So, we didn't connect afterward, just headed our separate ways.

I pushed for another pizza night, but one of our group, the red-haired kid who had caused my injury back in November, proposed a different idea. He had hidden some beer underneath the bleachers by the football field and wanted us to follow him there for a gathering. The temperature, he said, should have kept it nice and cold.

Being outvoted, I followed the gang, taking a right out of the gym, where we walked by St. Joseph's Church before crossing Carll Avenue, past the tennis courts and the field equipment house, and filed onto the football field. We shivered the whole way.

Once we crossed the field our organizer uncovered the two six-packs he had absconded with from his house. He peeled off the first flip-top. Then his smile quickly faded.

There was no hissing sound.

The temperature, which had dropped to twenty-five degrees during the evening, had not only kept the beer cold—it had frozen it through and through. Yet another testament to teenage brilliance. But we weren't done yet.

While most of us laughed, he and a few were convinced that if we held the cans snugly between our thighs, it would warm them up enough to drink. After ten minutes or so, and the temperature not warming in the slightest, the party collapsed beneath its own idiocy, and we all trekked home.

When I walked in the door at nine thirty, my mother and sisters were down in Nana's watching television. I wanted to recount the funny story about the beer but knew I would also be implicating myself, so I kept my comments on how the game went. My father was not yet home.

Nothing came together with my friends Saturday night, so Pat and I went to a six o'clock showing of *Godfather II* instead of the earlier one. The Babylon theater didn't have quite as grand of surroundings as the Bay Shore Theatre, but it was still comfortable and had a rather large screen.

My brother and I disagreed slightly on the movie. He thought *II* was better than the first *Godfather*. I thought it was not quite as good. That was largely due to the fact that James Caan had been my favorite character in the first movie. But *II* was definitely another classic and well-worth admission to see on the big screen.

The varsity had two home games the next week. The first was a Tuesday-afternoon game against Islip, who was undefeated in League play so far. We jumped out to an early ten-point lead thanks to some sharp shooting from Chuck

Farley, who had twelve points in the first half. Glenn would pick up the scoring in the second half as the team glided to a comfortable sixteen-point win.

Next up that Friday would be Smithtown West, who had lost to Islip earlier in the month. Most of us thought the team was rolling again and it would be a glide until the next Amityville game.

We would soon find out that was a mistake.

The Unexpected Hole

I had two agenda items ahead of me before we got to the varsity game on Friday. There was a science test on Wednesday and the junior high team had a game on Thursday. Mr. Williams had promised me that he would put me into the Thursday game if the lead or deficit were big enough by the second half. I was grateful for any time I could get.

Tuesday night I was studying for the science test and used that as an excuse to call Virginia on some matter or other for help or perhaps even collaboration. I was really trying to find out if she and her friends would be going to our game on Thursday. She was studying when I called.

"Do you have the list of what he said was going to be on the test tomorrow?" I asked.

"Sure, give me a second."

There was shuffling in the background, then she returned to the phone and read the list off to me. I pretended to be writing them down but had everything already recorded in front of me. When she finished speaking, I quickly switched the conversation.

"Are you going to the game Thursday?"

"No, the game is Friday."

"I mean the junior high game. I might get to play."

I figured she knew which one I was talking about but was teasing me.

"Probably. What time?"

"Four o'clock in the West Gym. We're only one and two, but a win there would get us back to five hundred."

"Okay, I'll try. Do you have any more science questions? I need to get back to studying."

I wanted to talk more but heard the brush-off in her voice and took the hint.

"Nope, I'll see you tomorrow."

It turned out to be a pretty easy test the next day, with half of the class scoring perfect grades—Virginia and me included. We spoke momentarily after class but then parted ways. I wouldn't see her again until Thursday.

I was able to scrimmage with the second string Wednesday afternoon. My ankle was not bothering me at all no matter how much stress I put on it. I was still consciously moving slower to protect it, however, which ironically improved my shot a little. I guess I had always relied on speed as one of my top assets and tended to hurry my release.

We ran the same 2-3 offense as the varsity, and even at my small height, I was playing forward. My red-haired replacement still played with the first string and was constantly getting picked, and I had several open shots that I made from the corner. I was careful to make sure that I didn't get toppled again.

Despite my decent practice success, I wouldn't play much on Thursday. Gary had another big game and when we were winning by twelve with three minutes to go, I finally got in as the whole starting five came out. I did make two shots during that closing run and we delivered a victory for the sparse but dedicated audience of parents and friends.

I looked around. No Virginia.

Once Friday arrived, it was all about the varsity again. The banners were up, the cheerleaders came to school in uniform, and if a student owned anything orange or black, he or she wore it. I passed several of the players in the halls that day, and although the Amityville game had brought them down a peg, for the most part, they seemed to have regained their confident strides.

In art class that morning, I sat up front as usual to discuss the game with Mr. Bartsch. The radio on in the background rattled through the current Top 40. Eric Clapton's version of "I Shot the Sheriff" was on at the time. It was one of his top-selling hits at that point, but many of the music devotees in our class didn't care for it as much. This was when Clapton was known as a pure rock 'n' roller, and they thought it was a betrayal to go that pop. I believe the aficionados just regretted sharing him with the rest of us, however.

Bartsch's talk was of the next Amityville game, almost ignoring tonight's opponent. I tried to get a critique of my play out of him, but he informed me that he had left at halftime. I asked him when the injured Chris Brust might be expected back. He said February at the earliest. That could at least be good news for the playoffs.

The rest of the school day passed uneventfully. Mr. Williams had given us the afternoon off following the win yesterday, so there was a lot of lingering around after school was out. I met up with Ernie near Virginia's locker since he was still courting her locker mate. Gary and some of the other junior high players were there as well. We all agreed to get to the gym by six tonight to cheer the JV on since their season wasn't going so well.

I didn't think my father would want to go early, so I volunteered to walk up to the game. He surprised me by being more than eager to go ahead of time. My mother ended up driving us as perhaps my father's after-game Villager runs had given her reason to play chauffeur.

When she dropped us off, she chose not to pull into the parking lot but rather stopped on the street, leaving us to walk around the outside of the gym to the ticketing entrance. The JV game had just started when we walked in. I didn't see any friends around, so I followed my father across to the far side behind the Babylon bench. Bartsch caught us from the corner of his eye and waved.

As halftime approached, Dr. Godfrey emerged and sat next to my father. At about the same moment, I saw Ernie enter the gym and so I made my departure to the fan-side bleachers. Within another ten minutes, most of my crowd had arrived.

We talked together and only half-watched the game, which our guys kept close until the fourth quarter. Two of the varsity players had stepped down to play with the JV, James Feeney and Greg Berger, who was small enough to gain the nickname "Flea." Players could play in both games according to the rules as long as their total playing time did not surpass four quarters for the night. Their presence in this game seemed to be another indication to us that tonight's game would not be a tough one.

Feeney and Flea's presence did the trick, and the JV was able to hold on for a three-point victory. After the game, both varsity players hurriedly suited up again for their upcoming appearance. Meanwhile, Ernie was, as usual, busy planning for the after-game entertainment.

"Does anyone want to be the host tonight?" he asked.

When nobody answered, he looked at me.

"I would need to have more notice," I replied. "Besides, anything at my house would be nonalcoholic and under *very* watchful eyes."

He pressed a few others as the two varsity teams burst onto the court. When the chanting and rah-rah started, he was drowned out with no resolution reached. We all joined in to psych up our team.

Smithtown shared similarities with Babylon in its evolution. With the growth of Long Island suburbs after World War II, the districts kept growing and building out into Easts, Wests, Norths, and so forth. This was the first year Smithtown West would be in our league.

I didn't say it out loud, but the reason I did not think they would be that formidable was because their team was all white and reminded me of West Islip. Ernie would surely call me out if I commented on that. So, I stayed silent and watched.

Barry Davis won the tip again, and we moved right into setting up our offense. Smithtown West went with a zone defense that seemed very effective at first. They possessed surprising quickness. Anytime we received a pass within range they had a defender immediately on us. Although Babylon thrived on making an opponent's defense work, our players seemed frustrated rather than calmly patient. But after several minutes, Glenn broke open and scored the first basket of the game.

West grabbed the ball after that, and their point guard took it up court. He had an interesting name on his jersey that I'm not sure anyone would correctly pronounce the first time: Langwost. He bounced up the court easily, evading our defenders. After a jig to his left, he drove to the middle and, before anyone could get to him, landed a six-foot jumper from the lane.

This ritual continued for much of the first half. We worked very hard for our opportunities, while on their side Langwost continued to penetrate and score—or to dish out passes to his teammates for easy buckets. This was complicated by our unusually poor shooting from the foul line. Even Glenn had missed three of his seven free-throw attempts in the first half.

Babylon was down by six when the half ended. Our fans were understandably worried. As the teams rushed off the court Koelbel was shaking his head and addressing Chuck Farley and Gervais Barger. Surely, we would figure things out and put them away in the second half.

Koelbel started Brian in the second half and moved Stanley Davis to guard as a defender against Langwost. Gervais was moved to cover the off guard. This worked in a twofold manner, as Stanley seemed finally to stymie Langwost, and Brian contributed six points in the third quarter. But Stanley's close defense came at a price. He picked up his fourth foul before the end of the quarter.

Koelbel decided to roll the dice and stuck with Stanley into the fourth quarter. Their coach must have instructed Langwost to press the initiative. With the game tied and six minutes to go, Stanley hacked Langwost and fouled out. Koelbel put Chuck back in the game and moved Gervais onto Langwost. This was not as effective.

Langwost went back to scoring and dishing from the middle to put them up by four with a minute to go. Then, after Brian missed two free throws, their center grabbed the second rebound and caught Langwost streaking down the court for an easy layup. And that pretty much put the game away. West would add two more free throws for an eight-point victory. The loss left the stands and our entire village in shock.

After shaking hands with his counterpart, Koelbel, for the first time I had seen, ran off the court with the team for what I'm sure would not be a pleasant postgame address to his players. Our group remained stunned. It took a few minutes before anyone readdressed the topic of what we might do now for fun.

I saw my father motion toward me across the way with an open palm to ask whether I wanted a ride. I pointed at the group to indicate that I would get home myself. With that, he left. I figured there might not be a Villager outing tonight.

As nobody had offered up their residence for the group, we opted for late-night food. We tried Manniello's at first, but surprisingly, there was a line out the door. So, we walked all the way down to Montauk Highway and over to a Village staple at the time, the Highway Diner.

The diner was busy as well with no booths available. So, we all sat at the counter near the corner, or the "elbow," as a friend of mine would later call it. The six of us who were there sat three to one side and three to the other. We feasted on burgers and milkshakes with no alcohol sweetening. It was too bright and exposed for us to sneak any.

"Now we're *two* games behind Amityville," Gary said.

"At least we've got them at home next time," I replied, trying to find a silver lining.

"Yeah, but now we have to go play West at West next time."

It did seem glum, particularly in regard to Amityville. Even if we won, they would have to lose an additional game for us to tie them in the standings. But Koelbel was a master at making adjustments and would find a way to gain the upper hand again. And if we could knock off Amityville at home, that might bring them down enough for someone else to pile on. Things seemed bleak but the season wasn't over yet.

No Margin for Error and More Injuries

Monday was a quiet day at school. The normal socializing, screeching noises and frivolity that went on between classes and during lunch breaks seemed almost nonexistent. It was as if the whole school was in mourning for our season. We still boasted a record of seven and two, but expectations had been set so high that a normal good record of a season was nothing to celebrate.

Our opponent Tuesday would be Comsewogue. It was one of Long Island's many towns, districts, and streets that had Native American origins. The name came from the Setalcott (Setauket) Nation, the word meaning "place where paths come together."

Comsewogue was not deemed to be a difficult opponent, but with no margin for error on our side, Koelbel would no doubt be prepping for this and every remaining game as if it were the NBA finals. We should have easily beaten Comsewogue, but they kept it close until the fourth quarter when we were able to pull away for a thirteen-point victory. There seemed to be a bit of a hangover from the Smithtown loss.

The next day Ernie, Gary, and I stuck around to watch the varsity practice after the junior high session ended. Koelbel was driving them hard as he was obviously not pleased with the prior game's performance. That really became evident when the first and second strings were scrimmaging.

The second string was playing with six guys and full-court pressing the entire time. Tempers started to flare as both sides got very physical and made some hard fouls on one another. There were several instances where I thought a punch might be thrown.

I had been discussing the physicality of play with Gary with only one eye on the court when I heard a loud thud and a bit of a shriek. It was quickly followed by Koelbel's whistle. When I turned back, I saw Chuck Farley down on the floor grasping his ankle.

One of the other players had apparently gone down with Chuck, but nobody else looked injured. We all kept quiet as Chuck was helped from the floor while getting some conciliatory pats from his teammates. It was hard to tell from where we were sitting how bad it was. But he didn't put much weight on his foot as he left the court.

Gary left us immediately and hurried over to the locker room to join Weiner and Mr. Bartsch, who were helping Chuck.

"Man, what next?" one of the other junior high players asked to no one in particular.

"Hopefully it's not a break," Ernie replied. "Otherwise, he's gone for the year."

To date Chuck was the team's third leading scorer. He was a senior and this would be his final season. What a horrible way to end it if that were the case.

Koelbel didn't end the practice but did conclude the scrimmaging. From there the team ran their intervals and proceeded to shoot foul shots. I was too distracted to mark how accurate everyone was.

After everyone left the court, I waited with Ernie and the rest of our crew for Gary to emerge with a prognosis. Eventually Gary came back with what was probably the best news we could hope to hear.

"He twisted his ankle very bad."

"How long is he out?" one of the others asked.

"Three weeks to a month."

"Damn, that means he'll definitely miss the Amityville rematch," I added.

"Yep," Gary said. "And the next one with Smithtown West."

We all broke a few minutes after those cheerful notes and headed to our respective homes. My father had attended a teacher conference at West Islip, which meant that dinner would be a little late that night. I would have to deliver the bad news then.

Nobody else was heading in my direction so I left via the streetside exit of the gym and cut between the buildings of St. Joseph's and through the back parking lots of the Village. Once I got to Montauk Highway a heavy, freezing rain started falling. Waldman's was just across the street, so I scooted over and jumped inside.

Mr. Jaffie, the owner, was wiping down the counter with only one other patron in the store. When I turned toward him and smiled, he waved me over to a seat. When entering Waldman's, you were immediately confronted with a set of shelves with every packaged candy on the market on display. Once you sat down, there were more shelves decorated with every magazine and newspaper in New York.

Mr. Jaffie had slightly tanned skin and always a friendly smile. His black hair was slicked straight back with slight graying on the sides. I can't remember ever seeing him not wearing his gray shop coat. The Jaffies lived on Coppertree Lane as well and had kids only slightly older than me. But Mr. and Mrs. Jaffie always seemed more grandparent than parent to me.

Since we moved to Babylon eight years ago my mother had always taken us to Waldman's when she thought we deserved a special treat. Without my saying a word Mr. Jaffie made me a complimentary egg cream from his fifties-era soda fountain. He knew it was my favorite. Then he leaned toward me on the counter as a prelude to a conversation.

"You look down," he said.

I put my mouth to the straw and tasted all that deliciousness but shrugged and agreed with him.

I recounted to him what happened at the varsity practice. Mr. Jaffie, like many of the merchants in town, were big supporters of the Babylon sports teams. Behind the counter there was a large mirror, and to the far left he had a big poster with the team's schedule on it where he added the scores of each game in black marker.

We spoke for a while longer until I finished my soda. At that point we both looked out and saw that the rain had lightened a bit.

"This might be your best chance," he said pointing his finger.

I thanked him for the drink, grabbed my stuff, and started out the door. The rain indeed stayed light while I ran the remaining half mile or so to our house. As I burst through the front door my parents were setting the table for dinner, so I ran up to my room and put on some dry clothes.

I was the last to the table and saw that it was chicken for dinner. As we all took our share, I recounted again what had happened at practice that afternoon.

"So, Chuck's out for a month," my dad confirmed.

"That's what Gary said."

"What do you think Koelbel will do?"

"He'll probably do what's he's done in all of the practices and move Stanley to guard and have Brian start at small forward."

"That should work."

"Yes, except Weiner is now the only forward option who can come off the bench."

My father shook his head in assent and then began his nightly current affairs quiz. I really wasn't in the mood, but I didn't call the shots.

Tonight, it had something to do with state politics and he mentioned that the governor who had succeeded Nelson Rockefeller was due to address both the New York houses, the Senate and Assembly. Then he turned to his first victim, my sister Peggy.

"You know who the current governor is, right?"

Peggy would cower like the rest of us in the face of my father's examination, but tonight she smiled broadly.

"Malcolm Wilson."

I almost fell out of my seat. She was only in sixth grade but had fielded Dad's query like a professional shortstop. We thought it would end there but then he turned to me.

"And his lieutenant governor is?"

"You're kidding me," I replied, stalling. "Who keeps track of lieutenant governors?"

"People who read newspapers," he quipped back.

When no one else answered he shared the name Warren Anderson. A name that was so significant that I would never hear it mentioned again. But that was dinner at the McKeown house.

The next day in art class I wasn't alone sitting at the front table talking to Mr. Bartsch. Word of Chuck's injury had spread. The whole school was now invested in the varsity's success and everyone wanted to know what we would do.

Bartsch confirmed my guess at what the new starting lineup would be and remarked similarly that our bench strength was now very reduced. However, he did still profess confidence, particularly in Brian's ability to step up to more minutes. I silently agreed. Brian had been playing like a third-year superstar to date.

That afternoon the junior high had an away game at Robert Frost. This was the same school where the varsity had played the Christmas tournament. As it was an away game I dressed up with the rest of the team. Leisure suits may have been in style but my father was not accepting of them yet. In accordance with his direction, I still had to dress in the standard blazer, slacks, and tie. So did most of the rest of the team, except for Ernie who followed his brother's lead and wore a similarly styled ensemble.

My amount of playing time had improved in the last two games and I was now pretty much the sixth man. That merited the first seat next to Mr. Williams once warm-ups concluded and the game started. That day we got off to a fast start.

I got plenty of playing time in the game as it was one of our few blowouts of the year. We ended up winning by eighteen points, again riding the back of Gary's twenty-point-plus performance. Ernie scored twelve and I tied him, with a few other team members scoring six. The whole team got to play, so it was a joyous bus ride home.

This trip was also unique in another way. For the first time in the two years I'd played for him, Mr. Williams decided to let some of the girls from our class come on the bus to the away games. Our junior high team had no cheerleaders, so they were just being attendees, but it was still a big deviation from normal. I wondered what had brought the change of heart, but it turned out the girls had simply asked—which hadn't happened before—and he'd agreed.

Virginia was one of the four girls. They all hung together in the front of the bus, so if you spoke to one you spoke to all. They didn't seem intimidated or uncomfortable riding with a bunch of boys. And since it was our best game of the year, I assumed Mr. Williams probably liked the result and would continue the practice.

My father had attended the game as well and decided to park out front when the bus arrived, so I had a ride home. The weather was a little milder than it had been the last few days with temperatures hovering around forty degrees. I asked if anyone wanted a ride, but neither Virginia nor any of the other girls took me up on it.

The only person who did respond to the offer was my redheaded teammate who was still holding onto what I believed was my place in the starting lineup. He hadn't had a great game today so maybe I had a chance to get the spot back for the remainder of the season. In any event he lived just around the corner from us, so we dropped him off without any incident or ill will.

Tomorrow would be the varsity's last game of the first half of their League V season. The second half would be playing the same teams, but on the opposite court from where they had played the first game. Our opponent would be a familiar one and currently tied with us for second place in the league. Other than being a tough foe, they also had a unique status that made them very well known to all Babylon students and residents. They were the all-black school.

Don't Trip Up

Wyandanch gets its name from the mid-sixteenth-century chief of the Montaukett Indians. The name means "speaks with wisdom." There is a plaque in his honor at the Wyandanch train station. As benign as that might sound, the name unfortunately conveys a much different meaning to surrounding residents.

Unlike Amityville and Copiague, which also had heavy African American populations, the perception in Babylon was that Wyandanch was entirely black and that our kids shouldn't go there without armed guards. It was a horrible and unfair stigma and one from which I'm not sure the school or community has ever been quite able to extricate itself. It was reinforced in every student's mind by several school policies.

The first was that we never played night games against Wyandanch, whether at their facility or ours. Every other team that we played on Fridays was a ramped-up, high school spirit night game. This may have been because of budgetary reasons, as Wyandanch was one of the less affluent districts. Nevertheless, the stricture sent a message.

The second policy was that our cheerleaders never went to games at Wyandanch. This conveyed the message to everyone that our girls would not be safe there, even if that was not the reason. Regardless, the compilation of this perception and these policies made it very difficult for the district to create a tax base or attract businesses, and they remained poor.

However, they had always fielded a competitive basketball team, and this year was no exception. Our league records were identical, having both lost to the same two teams. Whoever lost on this Friday would likely be locked out of the race for first place in League V. It was played in the afternoon at Wyandanch and because we still had junior high practice none of our team was able to attend.

When our practice was over that day Mr. Williams left the gym open so that we could shoot around and play a little longer. Whether he wanted to stay around and see if the varsity won, or he thought we all did, we were grateful for the extra time to have something to do while we waited.

Some practiced their foul shots or played HORSE, while others broke off into some two-on-two games. Having six baskets in the West Gym provided enough options to do whichever we pleased. It was a good low-intensity distraction.

After about an hour Mr. Williams connected with someone over the phone and got the word that we had won a relatively close game by nine points. He pressed us all to shower quickly and suggested we greet the varsity on their return and cheer them on outside when they got off the bus.

It was still cold outside so once showered we all stood peering out from the steel door to our locker room waiting for the bus to arrive. At last, it pulled up around six, and Mr. Williams lined our players up half to each side of the bus door. We cheered and gave fives to every player on the bus as they exited. We even cheered the JV team, despite not knowing how their game had turned out.

The display must have surprised the players who came out brimming with big smiles on their faces. Even the often snarling Stanley Davis seemed touched by the gesture and he cracked a half smile when he saw us. Koelbel emerged last and gave us all a big thank-you.

Finally, everything broke up and we all realized we now had a Friday night in front of us without a basketball game. We needed a plan of action.

Ernie started the dialogue. "Any ideas on what to do tonight?"

The tamer options of a movie or pizza were thrown out and rejected. Then my redheaded teammate and neighbor volunteered up.

"Hey, my parents are out at their club tonight. We could party at my house."

"That's great," Ernie answered for everyone. "What time?"

"They tend to eat late and hang around. How about nine?"

Everyone agreed. There would be no need to reach out to anyone to spread the word. A parentless high school party in suburbia was like a newly discovered gold mine. That house would be more crowded than a rock concert by five after nine.

This was good news for me. The family house being right around the corner would make for both a short walk and an easy escape. There were three high school kids in the redhead's family including a senior and a sophomore, so it was also a distinct possibility that the party would get out of hand very quickly.

I got home in time for dinner followed by tea and dessert in Nana's. My brother had control of the television, so we watched *Sanford and Son* followed by *Chico and the Man*.

"Are you going over?" I asked him, careful not to use the word "party" in case my parents were listening.

"No, it's not my crowd. I guess you are?"

"I'll make an appearance. If it gets hairy, I can always do an Irish goodbye."

"I guess," he said nonchalantly and turned back to the show.

At nine I went upstairs and got my coat and tried to quietly leave the house. I hadn't noticed that my mother had been up to something in the kitchen. When she emerged, we nearly bumped into each other.

"Where are you going this late?"

"Some friends are getting together around the block. I probably won't stay too long."

"Eleven o'clock at the latest," she said, emphasizing with her finger.

I consented and took off out the door.

It couldn't have been much past nine fifteen when I arrived, but their house was already packed. The music wasn't too loud but it could definitely be heard from the street. There were people gathered both immediately outside and inside the front door, so I had to push my way in where I found wall-to-wall people from all grades.

As I weaved through the house I came across Gervais Barger and Glenn sitting in the living room on the couch. They smiled and waved at me, which I took as somewhat of an invitation, so I went over and sat in an adjoining chair. Despite the residential lines of what seemed like a segregated village, it was not unusual for the black population to come south in force for parties.

As soon as I sat down Gervais started the conversation.

"That was pretty cool what you guys did when we got back today," he said.

"It was Mr. Williams's idea, but we were all in."

"Well, it was a tough game, and we didn't have many fans there, so we really appreciate the cheers."

"No problem."

At that moment Tricia and another girl walked up with Styrofoam cups.

"I think Ernie and your gang are out back near the keg," Glenn said with a smile.

I took that as my queue to leave—and that my seat was required—so I made my way out through the kitchen where I saw a stack of cups on the counter. I grabbed one and saw it was sitting next to a flour bowl filled up halfway with something pungent. Upon further inspection, I deduced that it was marijuana.

I was surprised someone would leave it out like that. Not for me, however. I opened the refrigerator and found the only can of ginger ale and emptied it into my cup. Continuing outside I found my friends exactly where Glenn said they were.

Everybody had a cup in their hand and thankfully nobody questioned the validity of my beverage, but I'm pretty sure they all knew. The reason everyone was outside in the cold was that someone had rolled a joint from the kitchen supply and this was being passed around the group. I wasn't the only one who did not partake but I did get a few looks when I passed up my chance.

Our group was not the only one partaking outside. The house had a quarter of an acre of yard, most of it in the back. There was a basketball hoop toward one side accompanied by a semicircle of concrete playing surface. Before the night ended there would be a few stoner two-on-two games.

I wedged my way in next to Virginia and tried to start up a conversation, but I was competing with our host for her attention. He was blathering on about his family's ski trip over Christmas and how they might go again over the upcoming February week off for winter break.

I used that opportunity to crash his monologue.

"So, you won't be here for the second Smithtown West game then."

"Oh, is that then?" He asked, seemingly caught a little off guard.

Virginia said nothing but just turned her head between the two of us.

"Yes, and if we can beat Amityville next week that game might be for the league title."

Everyone followed the games but my deeper interest gave me a little more insight forward in the season. I thought right after my remarks that I probably shouldn't have said anything, as it might be nice to have him out of town for a while. My thoughts proved prescient as he spoke again.

"I'll have to let my parents know; maybe we'll only go for half a week."

That's what I got for showing off. I think Virginia saw the look on my face and knew exactly what I was thinking. I shook my head and she smiled.

I hung mostly with my friends that evening but floated looking for Brian as he was always my fellow sober companion. He could also give me a deeper rundown as to how the game transpired. I saw Barry Davis in one room, and he waved at me. Then I saw Stanley Davis talking to someone in the living room.

When I passed the kitchen clock for the third time, it was a quarter to eleven. I decided to employ my Irish goodbye and sneak out without telling anyone. I found my way back to the front door. It was even harder pushing my way out than in. The crowd attending was at least twice the size from when I arrived.

I made my way down the gravel driveway and after walking about ten yards, I heard a siren and turned to see a police car pulling up in front of the house. I don't know why and wasn't sure what came over me, but I ran. This caught the attention of the officers, who immediately drove after me.

I made it about another fifty yards before they pulled the car in front of me and the two officers leaped out. In a near catatonic state, I just stood there unable to move or speak.

"Why were you running?" the taller of the two said.

I was shaking and took a minute or so to respond.

"I guess I've never been this close to a police car with the siren going and I freaked out."

"Were you just at that house?"

"Yes, my friend lives there and he said he was having a few people over so I went by."

"Where are you going now?"

"To my house. I live just around the corner."

The shorter one gave his partner a soft elbow and nodded to him.

"Okay, well go home. You shouldn't be out this late anyway."

Then as an afterthought he added, "And next time you see a police car, don't run. It just makes you look guilty of something."

I took his words to heart, but so far have never had cause to put them into effect. In any event, I may have given the partygoers a little extra time to clean up the house and rid it of anything that might create a problem.

When I spoke to Ernie the next day he couldn't stop laughing. I retold the story, making it sound like I reacted much cooler than I did, but he obviously imagined something closer to the truth. He told me that the police did in fact come into the house to look around, but by then all bottles and contraband had been hidden or disposed of effectively. I never did get any thanks for my unforced delaying actions.

I spent the next day worrying that the police would suddenly show up at the house and tell my parents what had happened. However, as it turned out, a much bigger and scarier occurrence dominated our weekend.

Reality Steps In

Sometime after midnight we got our second decent snowfall of the year on Long Island. It was a good snow of about two to three inches and was sticking to the ground. I would get a call if practice was canceled the next morning, but at eight o'clock the phone was silent, so I made the trudge to school.

The junior high squad combined its practice with the freshman team that morning and we mostly scrimmaged against each other. It was a relatively even match, as Gary was the best player on both teams. This made us wonder why he had not been brought up a level to play with them, but we were glad to have him with us.

When I got home Nana cooked my big post-practice breakfast. After that, I had planned to nap on the couch while watching the weekly televised college basketball game. Before I could settle in my mother interrupted my peace and pushed me out to help my brother and father shovel the driveway.

Right above mowing the lawn, shoveling the driveway was my least favorite chore. At least when mowing it was summer and could be done in short sleeves. But shoveling was done in the cold and the snow was always deeper than it looked. Often too there was ice beneath the powder which had to be chopped away with considerable effort.

After about fifteen minutes of shoveling, I saw my father leaning heavily on his shovel. My brother and I quickly made it over and heard his heavy breathing.

"Are you okay, Dad?" Pat asked.

"Yeah, but I'm think I'm going to go inside and rest for a bit."

We didn't help him as he seemed to be all right walking. But we both followed along until he got to his room. My mother was there as he sat down on the bed and put his feet up. He told us he would be fine and that we should resume the shoveling, which we reluctantly did.

It wasn't much longer before my mother came out and told us to come inside. My father was now lying in bed and looked flush. Whenever he stood up, he couldn't breathe and would nearly pass out.

"What should we do?" I asked my mother.

"His office is closed, but go over to Dr. Godfrey's house and see if he can come by."

My foot was totally healed, and I was much faster than Pat, so I bolted out of the door and around the block to the Godfrey house, which was near the southmost corner of Carll Avenue. Mrs. Godfrey was a big woman with a lovely demeanor. She met me at the door with a kind smile. After I told her what had happened, the smile quickly faded, and she pulled me inside.

"Godfrey, get your bag!" she yelled.

She always called her husband Godfrey despite it being her last name as well.

In a few minutes the doctor answered the summons and came barreling down the stairs. He had his bag in one hand while she had his coat out of the closet holding it from the back by the shoulders ready for him to slip right into it.

At that moment he noticed me and his eyes went quickly to my foot, apparently wondering if I had reinjured myself. Seeing no damage he then looked up at my face.

"What is it then?"

"My father," was all I said.

I grabbed his bag from his hands to lighten his load. It was debatable which method would be faster but he chose to drive the short distance. So, I rode with him around the block back to our house. He pulled into our half-shoveled driveway and bounded into the house without even knocking.

I yelled to my mother that we were here and directed him toward the bedroom where my father was sitting up but under the covers. I could hear Max barking from the sun deck. Someone had thought ahead and put him out there.

"What is it, Pat?" he asked.

My father went through the string of events beginning in the driveway. When he finished the explanation Dr. Godfrey took out his stethoscope and started listening to my father's heart. My mother told us to go wait outside. We did as we were told but stayed in the house.

The four kids plus my grandmother sat at the second-floor kitchen table and waited to hear Godfrey's prognosis. My youngest sister Dorothy was weeping a little, but we told her that he seemed fine. The words didn't help her much.

After about an hour my mother emerged and informed us that the doctor recommended that my father go to St. Francis Hospital in Nassau County. It housed Long Island's premier heart center. Godfrey thought my father was experiencing some sort of heart failure.

"Will he go in an ambulance?" Pat asked.

"No, we'll help him to the car and then I can drive him. He's strong enough to make that. The doctor will follow."

"Do we need to go with you to help him at the hospital?" I asked.

"The hospital staff will greet us with a wheelchair when we arrive, so I don't need both of you. Pat can come and you stay in case we need anything from back here."

My mother had gone into command mode, and I knew not to argue despite thinking I should be there as well.

After the briefing she went back into the room to help my father get dressed and Dr. Godfrey came out and sat at the table. He talked with my grandmother a bit as she clutched her rosary. Then he asked about my foot and talked to everyone a bit in an apparent attempt to lessen the tension.

When my mother called out for us, my brother and I went in and escorted my father out and down the stairs inside and down the stoop. He didn't need to be held up, but we were there in case he passed out and started to fall. He made it to the car, which had been parked on the street while we were shoveling the driveway. My mother had already started the engine, so it was warm when my father settled into the passenger seat. Pat sat in the back.

Still dazed a little, I stood there without my coat and waved as Mom departed first, then Dr. Godfrey followed. It was a few minutes before the wind hit me and I was jolted back to reality. I turned and went back inside to join my sisters and Nana in the house.

We all sat like zombies in front of the television for a while. I doubt any of the four of us could tell you what was on. After a while I needed to do something, so I went out and continued shoveling the driveway. I did this partly to keep busy, and partly out of guilt wondering why I let my father do any of it in the first place knowing his heart history.

I was nearly done when my mother pulled up, again parking in the street. When I saw my father wasn't in the car, I dropped the shovel and ran up to her.

"Is Dad . . ." I didn't want to say "dead," but that was exactly where my mind had gone.

"No," she shook her head reassuringly. "Just get inside and I'll tell everyone at once what's going on."

The three of us went in and made for downstairs where my sisters and grandmother were still in front of the television. My mother turned it off and gathered everyone around the downstairs dining room table. My sisters looked panicked, and Nana was still clutching her rosary beads.

My mother sat at the head of the table with my two younger sisters next to her. Pat and I were next to them and Nana was sitting at the other end. Mom reached across and grabbed my two sisters' hands before she spoke.

"The doctors confirmed your father suffered some kind of heart failure and they think it has something to do with one of the arteries."

"You said suffered, in the past tense?" I asked.

"Yes, he was practically back to normal when we arrived. They had him walk around and by that point his breathing and energy were quite normal."

"So, what's next?" I asked for everyone since Pat already knew.

"They are going to keep him overnight for observation and run some test where they put blue dye in the blood and see if they can trace the flow to any blockage."

This was definitely beyond my eighth grade science knowledge, but it sounded better than what I had feared when the car left.

"I'll go and get him tomorrow and we'll see what they have to say," she concluded.

We all felt a huge wave of relief. Nana got up and made my mother a cup of tea. She looked like she needed something stronger, but tea would do for now.

I didn't go out that night nor did my brother. We all dutifully stayed together most of the evening watching *Mary Tyler Moore* and *Bob Newhart*. My head hit the pillow around eleven but I didn't fall asleep for hours. My brother and I both woke up at about ten o'clock the next morning and rushed downstairs. However, my mother had let us sleep and gone to the hospital on her own.

We went to Nana's. She was in her rocker gently going back and forth, still clutching her rosary, and mumbling a prayer to herself. My grandparents had emigrated from Ireland in 1929 separately but knew each other from the old country. They met again and married in New York. My father was born in 1933 but Nana had also given birth five other times, both before and after him, and none of those babies had survived.

In a rare show of selflessness, Pat and I told Nana to stay seated and we made tea and toast to bring to her. She said, "God, bless you," to us as if we had just cured world hunger.

When my sisters woke and came down, we told them that was all the breakfast anyone was going to get this morning. They didn't protest. We waited for a few more hours until we heard the car pull up to the house.

We ran to the door and Max started barking. His barks normally sounded ferocious, but maybe because of our mood they sounded more like a welcome today. I wouldn't say my father bound out of the car, but he looked as well as I'd seen him in recent memory. I wondered what the story was.

The kids all hugged Dad at the door like he had just returned from war. Rather than make Nana come to greet him, he went down and gave her a hug and we all followed to get the hospital briefing at Nana's dining room table.

"My heart is back to normal, and they don't think surgery is necessary," he started. "I do have an irregular valve that has to be monitored. They've put me on a lean diet for the next couple of weeks. I needed to lose some weight anyway.

And they want me to take a few more days off. I can return to a normal life pretty much by the middle of the week."

Heart-valve operations, which only date back to the sixties, were still very risky at the time. My mother would recount later to us that what the doctors actually had said was that on a scale of one to four, they rated my father's need for such surgery at a two. My parents had decided to roll the dice and defer.

Back to Normal

The junior high team won its fifth game of the season on Monday and climbed above five hundred for the first time, despite a poor performance by me. I made only one basket on a fast-break layup, but otherwise missed all seven other shots, including four free throws. But outside of our team members nobody else gave attention to our games that week.

Friday was the do-or-die game for the varsity against Amityville at home. There was all the usual fanfare during the week of posters, teacher references, and morning announcements in support. But everything was tinged with a little more tension.

Every day that week when you saw one of the players in the hallway there were no smiles, just game faces. There was a Tuesday win at John Glenn, but it was barely mentioned at any of our lunch table conversations. This week was all about Friday night.

"I'm going to get there at the beginning of the JV game," Ernie said on Wednesday.

"Yeah, the Amityville people will be there in force, so seating might be tight," someone else chimed in.

"Do you think there will be a riot?" one idiot asked.

Ernie stared him down, inferring meaning to the question, and that line of conversation ceased.

Since Ernie had made the pronouncement, we all agreed to meet at the game at six. When the bell rang adjourning lunch, I went on to my next class, which was math. I was spreading the word to everyone around me to get to the game early and I continued after the bell until the math teacher shut me down with a sharp word. I remained quiet the rest of the class.

Following the junior high practice that day several of us tried to sneak over to the West Gym and see if we could sit in on the varsity practice. But Koelbel was having none of it and all doors were sealed. Every practice that week was closed.

With nothing left to do at the end of school that day I got home earlier than usual. I found my father sitting in the living room reading the newspaper. Perhaps he was preparing tonight's dinner quiz but I was still wondering how he was.

"Hi, Dad."

"Hey, buddy. How are you?"

"Good. I'm trying to shake off Monday's performance. I should play better tomorrow."

"One bad game isn't going to kill you."

I nodded and we spoke a little more about school and our games. I was curious what his plans were for Friday night—whether he would be going to the game and out with the coaches after. It would be a packed gym not conducive to any first aid requirements for the fans. How recovered *was* he?

"I'm going to skip Friday night if you don't mind," he offered.

I was relieved. He looked fine and had gone back to work that day, but I was glad he wasn't planning to push it.

"That's okay. I'll give you the blow-by-blow when I get home."

With that I got up and tried to see where he was in the newspaper but didn't get a good enough look before he snatched it up again. I went up to my room to change from my school clothes. Pat was lying on his bed reading a comic book when I came in. He would never outgrow reading or writing comics, which I guess is not a bad thing.

Pat's face grimaced in near disgust as I emptied my bag of soaked and sweat-smelling garments and tossed them into the hamper. He asked if I would put the hamper out in the hall for a while, so I did. I restocked my bag with gear for tomorrow and set it outside too. The aroma could keep me awake as well.

My mother cooked fish that night with two green vegetables to support my father's recommended diet. The fish was salmon, which was fine, but neither I nor my siblings made much of a dent in the vegetables. Both parents chastised us as a result, so we each forced down a few mouthfuls. When Dorothy almost gagged, they finally let up on us.

There was no quiz that night. This marked the third night in a row without one. I was sure once Dad got back to school and in the flow of work that the ritual would return. But tonight, he just let the conversation flow.

"My friends and I will be at the game on Friday as well," my brother said.

This surprised us all. He and his theater friends generally took little interest in sports. I guessed the import of this game must be permeating all of our school's societal groups.

"They'll be grateful for the support," I replied.

"What time are you guys heading up?"

"We're going to the JV game, so early."

"Well, we won't be there until later then."

"Don't be too late, it'll be packed."

He nodded and the rest of the evening went by without much ado.

In a reversal of Monday, I had a pretty good game on Thursday at home against Wyandanch's junior high team. It didn't help much. They trounced us by twenty points in our final home game. Next week's away game at Bayshore would be the last of the season.

Some of the varsity players had come to our game, and we got some consoling pats and fives from them after such a thorough whipping. We had played well but the other team was simply much bigger and better.

That Friday during the day the school was about as quiet as I imagined any high school in America had ever been. Everyone was aware of the situation. If the varsity lost again to Amityville, we had very little chance of repeating as League V champions. And with three losses we might not even get an at-large bid to the county championship series. The season was most definitely on the line.

I was the first of our gang to show up. I peeked inside the gym and saw that the JV was still doing its opening game layup drills, so I waited a bit for the rest of the guys. Ernie showed up next, and as we were about to go in Gary and a few others crashed through the doors. From there we entered and turned right toward the home side and pushed our way to the far bleachers so we could look across at the Babylon bench.

We climbed up about ten rows into the center of the section and set up camp. By the time we sat down, the JV was two minutes into its game. Our team looked overmatched and their opponents much bigger and faster. Mr. Bartsch was employing the slow-down 2-3 offense which allowed us to stay close. By halftime we were only down by six.

At this point the stands on both sides were nearly full. I looked around to see if Pat had followed my advice and showed up early, but I could not find him in the crowd. Virginia and several of the girls we knew showed up after halftime and made their way over to our section. Those of us sitting on the edges pushed outward to make space for them in the middle of the group.

"Tight fit," the girl sitting next to Virginia said.

"Were you expecting anything different?" I replied.

"No, I guess not."

I was sitting one row up and behind Virginia so I probably would not get much chance to talk with her during the game. Like everyone else there, though, my focus would be on the game once the contest began.

The JV had fallen behind by double digits as the third quarter ended. In the fourth they seemed unable to combat the other team's height. They continued to get inside shots against us and pull in offensive rebounds over our smaller front court. Bartsch tried a number of different player configurations and continually worked the referees to get more calls our way, but it was to no avail. When the game ended the JV had suffered an eighteen-point defeat.

As the two teams exited the court in favor of the varsities, a few of our group went to hit the refreshment stands. I stayed put. I tried shuffling around, but nothing allowed me to improve my position in relation to the girls.

The stands were now full in every section with several people standing on both sides of the bleacher sections. At that moment I saw Pat with one of his friends by his side. They stood at the entrance looking around for a seat. Nothing. Pat turned toward his friend and shook his head. Apparently, they were going to sit this one out.

The Amityville varsity was the first to enter the gym coming through the main entrance from the visiting West Gym locker room. Their cheerleaders led the fanbase in an enormous cheer that was as loud as one usually heard from the home team.

We couldn't have that!

To combat their roar, somewhere in the lower left of our stands someone started our own school chant.

"This is Panther Country! This is Panther Country! This is Panther Country! . . ."

We grew louder and louder. Many of us kept an eye to our right where our team would enter. The fans there would let us know when our varsity was on the way.

First, we heard a little cheer from that corner. When Glenn finally came into view leading the team out, our fans erupted so loud I figured it could be heard in New Jersey. He put the ball up and the opening drill layup started, even more cool and beautiful than normal. Koelbel came out at the end in his trademark maroon jacket. He was followed by Bartsch, who seemed to have shaken off the JV loss.

Once our team broke into layup lines I noted, as I had at the football game in the fall, that Amityville looked bigger. I also noted they had their game faces on. No smiles, just confident and tough-looking expressions to a man. They were the best at this point in the season, and were intent on delivering the message that nobody was going to take it from them.

A few minutes later the buzzer sounded and both sides went to their benches. Then the audio system crackled before the voice of Mr. Cosci filled the air. I would listen more intently than usual to tonight's lineup. The football teams had names on their jerseys but basketball didn't. I wanted to find Amityville's notorious Paul Smith.

"Welcome to Babylon High School and tonight's contest as the Panthers of Babylon host the Crimson Tide of Amityville."

Both sides cheered.

I watched as Cosci read off the names of their starters. Mike Voliton and Paul Smith were the guards for Amityville. Smith wore number twelve, the same as in football. Mike Sullivan and Tony Boyce were at forward, and their captain Mark Jenkins was the final name announced.

Koelbel's starters remained the same with Gervais Barger and Stanley Davis at guard and Brian, Glenn, and Barry Davis in the front court. As the teams huddled up for the pregame coaches' pep talk, we could see Chuck Farley and Chris Brust leaning in on crutches. It would be nice to have both of them able, but the situation was what it was.

As the teams approached half-court every player shook hands with every player from the other side. These guys had played multiple times in multiple sports against each other over the years and though this would likely be among the most fiercely fought games of their high school careers, there was a great deal of respect on that court. Regardless, when the ball went up it would be everyone to their battle stations.

The main referee blew his whistle. Barry Davis and Mark Jenkins faced up in the middle surrounded by the others. The secondary official moved a few of the surrounding players around so nobody was in an improper place. Then the ball was held and positioned between the two centers. Finally, up it went and the game was on.

Amityville Round Two

Jenkins controlled the tap, but when he hit the ball backward toward Smith, Stanley Davis had anticipated and swatted the ball away. After a short scramble Gervais came up with the ball and we set up our offense. The first move was ours. Smith and Voliton were right on our guards while their three big men packed the lane.

Babylon played patiently and worked the ball back and forth several times before an inside pass freed Glenn for a short bank shot and the first two points of the game. We hurried back and set up our half-court press with Gervais meeting Smith at half-court. Amityville worked patiently as well, until a forced jump shot by Voliton set up a fast break for us, resulting in a layup for Brian.

We would score the next basket as well and the home crowd was cheering loud. On their next possession Amityville got the ball down to Jenkins in the block. He pushed up a shot that went in after Barry Davis hit him on the arm. Their center then converted on the free throw.

It was six to three.

Under the basket Stanley whispered something to Gervais, who nodded in acknowledgement. As he brought the ball up court the next time, Voliton cheated over a little, anticipating a pass to the corner. Gervais faked the throw and the Amityville guard bit. He then whipped the ball in the other direction to Stanley, who hit a wide-open jump shot.

The rest of the quarter played out evenly, but on the final play during an entry pass to Jenkins, Barry was called for another foul. Koelbel erupted from the bench to yell at the official, but that did not change his mind. Amityville got the ball out of bounds. Shortly after, Smith hit a jump shot to end the quarter leaving Babylon ahead by five.

As the teams headed toward their benches Koelbel was still grumbling at the official. Then after a few seconds he hustled back over to the bench to speak to the Babylon huddle. The question was whether Koelbel would leave Barry in to start the second quarter.

"If Barry gets one more foul, Weiner's going to get some playing time," Ernie commented.

"Don't jinx it," Gary answered for everybody.

As the teams came back out Koelbel rolled the dice and left Barry in the game. And two minutes in, the jinx occurred. Barry picked up his third foul. In high school and college basketball when a player gets five fouls he is disqualified and has to leave the game. Koelbel could not leave him in now if he wanted to use him later. Barry went to the bench.

As Barry walked over shaking his head, Weiner stood up and Koelbel grasped his arm and gave him instructions. Weiner then took to the floor, and Koelbel held up a fist to signify the new configuration. Glenn moved to center while Brian Vickers and Weiner played forward and ran the baseline on offense.

Amityville capitalized on our smaller lineup and immediately started pushing the ball down low where Boyce and Jenkins both contributed multiple baskets. When Voliton hit an open jump shot with two minutes to go, Amityville took a two-point lead. Koelbel called a time-out with less than a minute to go in the half.

"Well, we didn't think it was going to be easy," I said.

I got some half-smiles, but nobody answered back. We were definitely looking vulnerable.

For the remainder of the second quarter, Koelbel put Glenn at point and moved Stanley down to the forward position. He brought the ball up with Gervais on the weak side. Because of his shooting prowess Stanley still garnered dedicated attention down low in the corner. This allowed Glenn to take his man one-on-one.

Amityville didn't react quickly enough which left a forward guarding Glenn. Their coach was yelling for a switch, but it was too late as Glenn blew by his man for an easy basket that tied the score. Immediately after the basket Babylon went into a full-court press, again catching our opponents by surprise.

Voliton picked up the ball for the inbounds but found nobody open. Smith tried to break long in a football-like play but Voliton over-threw him and the ball went sailing out of bounds on the other end. Since nobody touched it, Babylon would now inbound the ball under our own basket with about thirty seconds left in the half.

Glenn inbounded the ball out top to Gervais but then ran up and took it back from him to set up, winding down the clock for the last shot. Glenn dribbled back and forth up top for a couple of seconds with Smith now squaring up face-to-face with him. Glenn gave a quick nod to Brian in what looked to be silent communication with his sibling.

As Glenn drove for the basket, Brian darted past his defender. Glenn then tossed up a beautiful alley-oop pass to his brother, who laid the ball in for the final two points of the half as we regained the lead. Although we had lost ground in the second quarter we went into the locker room with hope—and a little momentum.

We all looked at each other and seemed to exhale for the first time since the opening tip. The teams rushed off the court for the break and the whole fan base on both sides got up to stretch. Some of our group went to get refreshments but I was among those who stayed put, still in fear of losing my seat.

Ernie headed out to get something to eat but Gary and Virginia did not, so I stood talking to them. I directed my question toward Gary.

"How do you think Weiner played?"

"Good. He didn't score much, but he got three rebounds, which helped."

"Yeah, those Amityville big men are physical."

"And fast."

He shook his head to agree while Virginia's attention had drifted to the clock and door, perhaps wondering if her friends would be back in time for the second-half start. The teams both burst back onto the court with a few minutes to go in the break to the applause of their supporters. As the buzzer sounded to start the third quarter, Ernie was stepping his way up the bleachers to us, followed by the others.

Everyone got seated and ready as the players returned to midcourt for the tip off. Barry was back in at center along with our original starting five. Amityville also began with the same starters. Jenkins again controlled the tip but pushed it to the left side into Voliton's hands this time, who passed over to Smith to set up the Amityville offense.

The Tide were more patient to start the second half, stealing a page from our book. After a couple of minutes trying to work the ball inside, Smith drove to his right where Stanley Davis collapsed to help Gervais, this leading to Smith passing the ball out to Voliton, who drained a ten-footer. Then Amityville surprised us with a full-court press that resulted in a quick turnover for Voliton to score again on a layup.

And just like that we were down two points. You could feel the tension in the stands, and the crowd grew noticeably quieter. Hopefully, this wasn't a turning point where things went rapidly downhill. We'd seen it happen before.

The next few minutes were tense. Following a three-point play by Amityville forward Tony Boyce, the Tide had built a six-point lead and Koelbel called a time-out. The Tide's bench sprung to their feet cheering along with their fans. They sensed blood in the water. Our side seemed stunned into silence.

Then our cheerleaders began the chant, "This is Panther Country! This is Panther Country! . . ."

When the referee whistled the players back to the court, Koelbel returned to the configuration that had Stanley down at forward and Glenn at point. As we brought the ball up the court Amityville adjusted by double-teaming Glenn and daring Gervais to shoot. To avoid being trapped Glenn whipped the ball over to a wide-open Gervais. When nobody rushed to cover him, Gervais stepped up and drained a twenty-footer for what would be his only points of the game. But it turned the momentum our way.

We could feel it and we could hear it.

"This is Panther Country! This is Panther Country! . . ."

After a hurried miss by Amityville on the next play Glenn brought the ball up with only one defender on him. He immediately went to work and drove to the middle where he converted a short five-footer.

We'd done it. We'd clawed our way back. It was now a two-point game.

On the next play Smith was called for an offensive foul knocking down Stanley Davis. This resulted in the Amityville coach exploding onto the floor to berate the officials. Like Koelbel's earlier dramatics, this would not change the call, and he was pulled off the court by his players and assistant coach to avoid a technical foul.

On the next Babylon sequence Barry Davis posted up high and set a screen for Glenn to take another short jumper. The ball circled the rim and fell out, but unfortunately for Amityville Brian Vickers had swooped in from the weak side to put it back in the basket for two.

The game was tied.

Amityville would have one more chance before the quarter ended, but another Voliton jumper rattled out at the buzzer. We entered the final quarter tied in a game many of us perceived to be do-or-die, and the tension was palpable in the stands. We controlled the ball to start the final period with Glenn remaining at guard and Stanley Davis down low.

Babylon worked the ball around methodically, trying to find an open shot. Then on a pass from Gervais back to Glenn, Smith knocked the ball loose, which resulted in a scramble on the floor for the ball. Glenn somehow got control of it while in a sitting position. He then proceeded to do a move that stunned everyone. He passed the ball from his right to left hand twice while putting it underneath his legs each time. It happened so quickly that I wasn't exactly sure what I had seen.

"Damn," somebody yelled out from our group or nearby.

The move seemed supernatural.

Glenn then tossed the ball to Gervais nearby who rifled it over to Brian all alone under the basket. Possibly, he'd seen these feats by his brother and was the only one unfazed. The basket gave us back the lead.

Babylon's next trip up the floor was a near repeat of the last. A scrum on the floor for a loose ball saw Glenn performing the same act with the end result again an easy layup for Brian. The Amityville coach shook his head as if not believing his eyes.

Boyce missed a short jumper for Amityville on their next play. Glenn then took the ball the length of the court and was fouled by a lunging Jenkins, halting an easy layup. Uncharacteristically, Glenn would make only one of his two free throws as we clung to a three-point lead.

Amityville seemed distraught at this point. They took two bad shots. From there on it was "Brian Time," as the younger Vickers brother would score the next four points on two foul shots and a follow-up to a missed jumper that ballooned our lead to seven with less than a minute to go. A few last-second points by Amityville would cut the final margin to two as the buzzer sounded.

Babylon had prevailed.

Our bench players erupted onto the floor toppling their teammates. Our fans jumped up and came down in the stands so hard it felt like the wooden bleachers might break. The Vickers brothers had led the way with a combined thirty-six points. But everyone in the lineup had made steady and timely contributions to put us over the top.

A few of our gang made it to the locker room entry to see if we could get a five-slap from one of the players. I wedged into a good position and caught Koelbel's gaze, as he was ten feet away. He saw me and smiled broadly. When he got close, I didn't know what to say so I stuck out my hand and said congratulations. He laughed, shook my hand with his right, and rubbed my head with his left before continuing on.

After the entire team and coaches passed by and the excitement settled a bit, I turned and saw Ernie staring at me and chuckling.

"Congratulations?" he asked sarcastically.

"I didn't know what else to say. I guess I choked."

He shook his head as we headed back to rejoin the rest of the group. We now had to figure out how and where to celebrate the biggest win of the season to date. It would be a day or two after the euphoria died down when I, like many in Babylon, realized that we were still in second place.

Unless someone else knocked off Amityville, we would remain there. But where could that help possibly come from?

Out of Our Control

As an adult in the Northeast, the most tolerable thing about February and its biting weather was that the month was short. For a kid in school in the 1970s there was also the freedom of winter break added in. This was an entire week when the state combined Lincoln and Washington's birthdays to provide five glorious days without class. I imagine it was as much for the teachers' sanity as the students' enjoyment, but no students complained.

On Monday after the game when I was heading to lunch during school, I saw Glenn coming down the hallway toward me. When he got close, I stopped to chat.

"Great game on Friday."

"Really," he replied, leaning against the wall. "I thought I played terribly."

This was among the many things to like about Glenn. He was practically a celebrity at Babylon but he would always talk to people in a very sincere way. That and he was still humble about himself, although realistic enough to understand his contribution.

"Well, when you weren't scoring you were setting Brian up with some great passes."

"Now *he* played great."

"Amityville plays Smithtown West tomorrow, don't they?"

"Yep. If West can win we're back in business."

After that he patted my shoulder and continued on. I went along to lunch a few minutes late. There I bought whatever they served on a tray at the cafeteria and joined my buddies at the eighth grade table.

Almost as big as the two varsity games that week was our junior high season finale on Thursday. From a team standpoint we could finish the year with a winning record if we beat Bay Shore. This would also be my last chance to start until next year. I would need a couple of good days at practice to show I had the stuff to get that chance.

We had a full practice on Monday and a short one before the home varsity game against Port Jefferson the next day. Mr. Williams didn't put me with the first team, but I played well both days, particularly against the redhead, who was still starting. The better I played the more physical he got, and I continued to make sure I didn't get toppled again. There would be no coming back from another injury.

The whole junior high team sat together to watch the Tuesday-afternoon game. We soon put our opponents away early by jumping out to a seventeen-point lead in the first quarter. By the end of the game the whole first team and Weiner were watching their hardworking teammates getting some well-earned game time. As we got deep into the second half, everyone's attention was elsewhere. We were hoping somebody would get word of the Amityville vs. Smithtown West game.

Our fates were not in our own hands.

We had heard nothing when the final buzzer went off and surmised we'd have to wait until tomorrow to find anything out. Then, as we were all getting up to exit, someone spied our AD (athletic director) by the entry door. He was signaling something over to Mr. Cosci, who was still sitting at the announcer's table.

As he walked briskly over, Koelbel and Bartsch saw him as well and headed to meet up at the table. We all watched to see if there would be an announcement. When the AD made it over and relayed his news, Koelbel pounded his fist against the table with a gritty smile. Then Cosci turned on his microphone.

"For all you Babylon fans, we have some additional good news to take home tonight. Word is in that Smithtown West has defeated Amityville today 61–55. Babylon is now in a three-way tie for first place in League V."

He shouted the last two words, since the entire gym had already erupted in cheers. The place wasn't as full due to it being an afternoon game, but what we lacked in numbers we made up for in volume. It was now game on for the rest of the League season to see who of the big three would break down the stretch.

Babylon still had a tough road ahead with an away game against Smithtown West, and we were still down two key players. The important thing was that our destiny was now in our own hands for a shot at co-champion. Talk among our group immediately went to the near-future games.

"Who do we play next?"

"At Islip on Friday."

"When do we play Smithtown West?"

"Next Tuesday at their place."

Normally that would be a problem. But with the junior high season ending Thursday, and next week being winter break, we all planned to be at those games. It was only a question of getting rides. I would need to find out my father's availability to travel over dinner tonight to determine if he would be up for driving. We hadn't told anyone what had happened to him, and his recovery seemed to be complete, but our worry lingered.

That night at dinner I gave the update of both the Babylon win and the Amityville loss. I jokingly asked if that could be the current events answer for the evening. My mother laughed at that one and I proceeded to my main line of inquiry.

"How are you feeling, Dad? Would you be able to drive to the next two games?"

I felt a little selfish as the words came out of my mouth. I should be more worried about him than my social standing via providing rides to the games. But neither parent seemed taken aback.

"Yes, I was planning on going," my father replied. "Where are they?"

"This Friday night at Islip and next Tuesday afternoon at Smithtown West."

"I can't do Tuesday. I'll be upstate for a NYSUT conference, but Friday is good."

Darn, that meant I'd have to find a ride for Tuesday—although I had heard the school might be putting together a fan bus. I'd rather drive with somebody. Maybe I could find a trade with someone to whom I'd offer a lift on Friday. In my mind, I had two seats for Virginia and her friend and one to bargain with.

Virginia and her friend jumped all over the drive invitation on Friday, but I was having trouble finding a trade for the final spot. The only person I could find in a complimentary situation was my redheaded adversary. This presented a number of concerns, but unless I wanted to take the bus, he had to be my man.

I guess at this point it makes sense to put a name to my "redheaded adversary." He was Jonathan Shiebler. We had known each other since kindergarten.

Jon wasn't a bad guy, and I'd say if it wasn't for the fact that the two of us both aspired to play basketball, we might have become closer friends.

The year before when we both tried out as seventh graders, I made the team at what might have been considered the twelfth and last spot. He believed that spot should have gone to him. We had a few confrontations during that time but nothing became physical. Seeing that he had about twenty pounds on me, I tried to avoid this more than he did.

Wednesday was the last practice before our final game. I was hoping that Mr. Williams had been impressed with my play in the last game and might consider me to start in the finale. Thus, on that day I hurried to be the first one in the locker room when he arrived. I even skipped the usual flirting session with the other guys over by Virginia's locker.

Before my injury I was one of the faster players on the team and was now feeling one hundred percent. So I made sure I finished first in all of the early running drills. However, after layups concluded and we moved into scrimmaging, I was once again put in to play with the second team. This time I made certain that I was covering Jon. He seemed to welcome the challenge too, perhaps worrying that his spot was on the line.

After about fifteen minutes we had played about even. Then on a set play he got the ball in the corner with only me between him and the basket. I overplayed his right side, but he didn't go to his left as I intended for him to do. Instead, he tried to dribble right at me. I managed to swat the ball away to a teammate and then took off toward the other basket. There I was hit with a long pass for an easy layup. At that point Mr. Williams called a break. As we queued up at the water fountain outside, I could feel Jon's wrath and the heat of his stare on my back, but I did not turn to acknowledge it.

When we came back out, I heard the words I had been waiting for all season.

"Thomas, put your shirt on," Mr. Williams said in his formal dialect. "Jonathan, you go skins in this round."

Scrimmaging with the first team always provided an advantage. With the better players alongside, you got sharper passes and were rarely double-teamed. My game improved immensely, and I felt like I had put some distance between myself and Jon by the end of the scrimmage. I would not know until game time the next day whether I would start. Mr. Williams never revealed that fact until the very last moment before the game began.

The next day during science class I confirmed with Virginia that she and the other girls would be coming along to the game. If I was going to start, I wanted her there. We didn't see each other again until everyone boarded the team bus that afternoon.

Despite the girls' presence, I sat toward the back, drawn away from them. I stared out the window lost in my own head thinking about the game. It took a teammate shaking me to realize we had arrived at Bay Shore, and everyone was getting off the bus.

There were no playoffs or official standings for junior high basketball. Due to Bay Shore's close proximity to Babylon, however, a few of our players had friends on their team. Through those connections we learned that they also had a five-and-five record. The winner of this game would not only claim a winning record but could brag that they'd finished ahead of the other.

It felt to me like our warm-up drills went by in a flash. The referee blew his whistle, and we all retreated back to our benches.

Then I got my wish.

Mr. Williams rattled off our starting lineup and I heard my name instead of Jon Shiebler. I didn't look his way because I knew the disappointment I would witness.

During the first quarter the two teams played about as even as our records. We clung to a two-point lead but they had the ball. After a short jumper by their oversized guard, Ernie brought the ball up court. We ran our version of the 2-3 and worked the ball down to Gary. During a sequence where he missed his first shot, but then followed it with a rebound and put back, our other forward hit the ground in pain. I hadn't seen what happened, but I recognized the look on his face. He held his ankle and moaned.

As he was helped back to the locker room Mr. Williams called Jon to come in. With the other forward out, Jon and I would both play the remainder of the game together. And the game would come down to the last play.

Ernie brought the ball up court with thirty seconds left and the score tied. We patiently worked the 2-3 trying to spring Gary open. He was having his typical outstanding outing with twenty-four of our forty-six points so far. But Bay Shore kept doubling down on him every time we passed the ball into the corner.

With about ten seconds left, Ernie was about to pass it down to me out wide, but instead shot a no-look pass to Gary at block. There wasn't enough time for their other big man to make it over to double-team and Gary scored with three seconds left to put us up by two.

Their coach tried to call a time-out, but the referee did not see him and the buzzer went off.

And so, the 1975 Babylon junior high team went out winners.

We all mobbed Gary as much for that basket as for carrying us all season. Ernie finished with eight points while Jon and I both had six. From what I could tell we both left the court happy and perhaps left our unwelcome bitterness behind.

The ride home was a great one for all except our injured teammate. But he'd only sustained a sprain, and the season was over anyway.

As he did every season, Mr. Williams treated the entire team and guests to McDonald's on the way home. He wouldn't ask what we wanted, but just ordered hamburgers, french fries, and Cokes for everyone. Our appetites soared as high as our spirits at that point. We all talked, laughed, and ate. By the time we left the restaurant not a morsel remained.

With our season over, the next day we could all turn our total attention to the varsity. The question was how far they could ride their current win streak. Success was in sight, but for each game, the chance for failure also peeked around the corner.

Dad's Back and More

In high school there are fewer times happier than a Friday night before a week off. That's only compounded when you're a sports fan and your team is on a roll. Even though that night's game was on the road, it was still a big event during the school day. Our players paraded through the hallways dressed to the nines. They sported a confident gait that had been almost nonexistent two weeks ago.

My father and I hadn't planned to attend the whole JV game that night considering it was an away game. Our opponent was Islip which is only a short twenty-minute drive east. Islip shared a kinship with Babylon in that both were villages located within towns of the same name. The town of Islip was slightly larger than Babylon and boasted eleven villages, or entities, to our eight.

We did have time for a quick bite of dinner before exiting at about six thirty. Our caravan first stopped to pick up Jon, around the corner, then we went on to collect the girls about five minutes later. I unfortunately had to sit in the front seat while Jon got to be in back with the girls.

By the time we made our way into the Islip gym it was the fourth quarter of the JV game and Babylon was holding a ten-point lead. We were only inside a few minutes when we saw Ernie, Gary, and a few of the others on the far-side bleachers behind the bench. Jon and the girls hustled over to join them, but I sat alone with my father for a bit as he elected to stay on the near side. We chatted some about the game and he reassured me that he was feeling fine. A few minutes later Koelbel entered the gym standing tall and surveying the surroundings. He had his usual game-time maroon jacket on. He soon spotted us and with a nod up with his head made his way over.

"Hey, Pat, haven't seen you for a bit. How are things?"

"Yeah, sorry I couldn't make the Amityville game," my dad said without revealing the reason. "Heard it was a real battle."

"No kidding. We'll probably see them again. Tough team."

At that moment he looked down at the current game going and saw an Islip player trying to get a shot off from inside the lane. After three pump fakes that didn't work, he passed the ball out to a teammate and the referee called three seconds. Koelbel then looked sideways at me with his right finger extended.

"If you're ever in the lane for that long you have to shoot," he instructed. "If you're trying to get the ball up, the ref won't blow the whistle. But if you pass it out, he'll nail you every time."

Koelbel was always coaching, and I appreciated the tip. A few minutes later Dr. Godfrey arrived and took a seat with us. Now that my father had regular company, I felt better about leaving to join my crowd on the other side. By the time I got there the final buzzer went off and the JV had notched a victory.

When I sat down with the group everyone was discussing their plans for the break. Most families were staying in town. Mr. Williams had informed us that he would be holding additional voluntary basketball sessions during the week off for the junior high players. Most of us planned on attending those. Jon told the group that his family had pushed their ski trip back until Wednesday so they could indeed attend the Smithtown West game.

The gym was still only half full when Glenn led our team out first in the warm-up drill. At that point it looked like we had twice as many fans as they did. Islip currently had a record of five and five. They had started the season strong with a win against Smithtown West but were now riding a three-game losing streak. I noticed Koelbel came out alone without Bartsch by his side.

When the Islip team emerged for their layup drills, more of their fans started to arrive. They didn't seem to show much enthusiasm despite the Islip cheerleaders trying their best to whoop them up. When the Babylon cheerleaders began their routine, our side experienced a similar hush, but for a different reason. There seemed to be some sort of distraction arising at the lower corner of the bleachers. This evolved into a game of telephone as a message was passed from ear to ear through the stands.

At that moment I saw Bartsch darting out of the locker room to join Koelbel at nearly a run. The word got to us almost as soon as the two coaches came head-to-head on the court.

"Wyandanch beat Amityville," somebody yelled nearby.

"Holy crap!" three of us voiced at the same time.

I forgot that all of Wyandanch's games were played in the afternoon so they would be concluded by the time Babylon's game started. Also, it had not occurred to me, or likely anyone at our school, that Wyandanch could beat Amityville. But the impossible had happened.

This meant that if Smithtown West and Babylon both won tonight, the game on Tuesday would be for sole possession of first place. The buzzer to start the game seemed to jar everyone back to the present. The two teams adjourned to their respective benches to start the game, which now took on a greatly heightened importance. We were all pretty sure what Koelbel's motivation speech in the team huddle would be tonight.

Also, something that was overlooked by most of us was that Chuck Farley was suited up. Gary had said nothing to this point.

"Hey, look at that. Is Chuck ready to play?" I asked him.

"Yeah, it was a game-time call. That's why I waited."

Wow, things *were* really looking up, I thought. Also, we noticed that although he wasn't suited up, Chris Brust was no longer on crutches. Maybe he was in the final phase of recovery as well. What a night so far and the game had not even started.

Following the team's all-hands-in *cheer* from the bench, our starters walked out onto the floor with a confident, hungry stride. Gone was the do-or-die look, which seemed to be replaced by a step-on-the-gas one. This could be bad news for Islip. The teams gathered around the midcourt circle again and the referee tossed the ball. Despite Chuck Farley's return Koelbel stuck with the starting five of the last several games.

Barry Davis again easily won the tap and flipped the ball back to Gervais, who after a few quick dribbles passed the ball to Brian in the corner. Barry then set a screen for Glenn who received the entry pass from Brian for a quick basket. This scenario would repeat itself several times in the first quarter, which saw a Babylon lead grow to ten points.

After a quick huddle the teams returned to the floor for the second quarter. The Babylon fans rose in applause when they saw Chuck substituted in, replacing Brian. The shift had Stanley going down to forward. Chuck looked a little embarrassed but gave a half-wave in acknowledgment.

Babylon continued its hot hand, stretching the lead to fourteen after a few more minutes of play. The game was a forgone conclusion in our minds; we were all just waiting for Chuck to get an open shot. He was moving well but the opportunity had not yet presented itself.

Then with four minutes to go until halftime, Stanley Davis had the ball in the corner but could not make the pass down to Barry, who was covered in the post. Normally he would have thrown the ball back up court to Gervais Barger, who was the nearest guard out top. But instead, he spied Chuck wide open at the far top spot. Stanley gripped the ball with both hands over his head and whipped it cross-court to his wide-open teammate.

This gave Chuck a few seconds to take his time while squaring up to the basket. He let the shot fly long before the defender was anywhere close to him. The flight of the ball had a beautiful arc and rotation as it soared toward the basket. I could swear we all heard the sound of it swishing through the net without touching any iron of the rim. Our bleacher erupted in cheers.

Gervais Barger was the first to congratulate Chuck with a slap on the back, but eventually the whole squad would show their appreciation and congratulations for their teammate. Shooting guard Chuck Farley was back. Chuck would score five more baskets in his triumphant return, but as usual Glenn would lead everybody with twenty-five points while going seven for eight from the foul line.

Glenn scored his twenty-fifth point on a three-point play midway through the third quarter and Koelbel decided to rest him for the remainder of the game. It was another night during which Koelbel had the luxury of playing the whole team in the eventual victory. Even Mike Fischer got in the game and scored two baskets. He was a moderately tall, curly-haired senior with a big smile. Mike had enthusiastically embraced the role of being the team-spirit leader from the bench. He was always the first guy up to greet the players coming off the floor or standing and clapping to motivate play on the court. Mike was very popular with his teammates.

Babylon would complete what was a big night for all the many reasons with a twenty-four-point victory. As we all rose to start putting on our coats, I looked over to see that my father was still in the same place. Dr. Godfrey had remained there as well with a few of the other village elders who must have trickled in during the night.

Neither my group nor those around my father seemed in a big hurry to leave. But as it was Friday night, our conversation took its normal route.

"All right, where do we go from here?" Ernie started.

After a few hems and haws, Virginia's neighbor spoke up.

"I have a basement we could use. My parents will be upstairs, but if we can smuggle anything in, they don't check on us much."

Everyone jumped at the idea. We all were wearing big winter coats with multiple inside and outside pockets. Plus, the bulky nature of the garments made it easy for even a single person to smuggle in a six-pack. After all, there were eight of us. I told them that my father would only drop us off at one place, which got Jon and me out of the job of retrieving and transporting the beverages.

The plan evolved that Ernie, Gary, and a few of the other boys would raid their respective houses for any refrigerated beer. Then the group would have to walk over to where we were while carrying the loot. I liked the plan particularly because it didn't involve me having to do any heavy lifting.

Once everything was agreed, Jon, the girls, and I walked over to my father. The older gents' postgame chatter was winding down as well. After I told my father the part of the plan that he wouldn't object to, he agreed to drop us at Virginia's friend's house. Later, Jon and I would have to walk back. I didn't ask whether Dad was heading home or joining the coaches afterward, but because he was still under orders to take it easy, I was relatively sure he would end up just heading home.

The beer heist worked like a charm as the mules easily made their way back and past the parents upstairs without giving away their cargo. There was even a refrigerator in the basement which, to that point, had only been stocked with sodas. Among these was a ginger ale that would cover me for the evening.

Between the four guys who arrived they filled the shelves with almost twenty beers. When a few more friends from the neighborhood joined us, we had swelled to a party of ten. This lessened the chance of me taking any abuse for not imbibing because that shrunk the beer-to-person ratio enough to keep me inconspicuous.

It was a fun and memorable night. We all sat around in a circle and talked about all sorts of things. No fights broke out and everyone was generally nice. We all just seemed to revel in our youth with no responsibility on the horizon until returning to school a week from Monday. Plus, we had just witnessed a strategic victory for our school on the court.

Both Jon and I were granted additional curfew hours due to the vacation. We left the gathering around eleven thirty with most of the others. Our route home was straight down Deer Park Avenue through downtown Babylon. There hadn't been any snow in the last few weeks, but it was still biting cold outside with temperatures in the high twenties. This was Long Island in February, after all. We kept our hoods up and gloves on.

The first commercial building we passed was the Villager, where all of the coaches hung out with the interested dads after games. In hopes of a possible ride home, we peeked in to see if there was anyone left that we knew. The only person we spied was Mr. Bartsch, who seemed engaged with a couple of people I didn't know. We didn't bother him.

Jon and I continued the rest of the journey on foot through town and past Waldman's. We didn't talk that much but there was an implied sense of camaraderie we hadn't shared through much of the season. We came to Coppertree Lane first and parted ways until extended practice the next day.

However well things seemed then, it would be Jon who would bring me the next bit of bad news in the coming weeks.

Winter Break and Beyond

The varsity and JV wanted to practice early Saturday morning so the junior high session would not get underway until two. This allowed me a Saturday sleep-in for the first time in three months. Nevertheless, I was the first one upstairs to wake and immediately went down to the bottom floor where Nana Mary was waiting to serve me whatever I wanted for breakfast.

I asked for waffles and bacon and she immediately went to work while I lazily curled under a blanket on the couch to mindlessly watch some cartoon show. Outside the sliding glass door that led to our backyard I could see the red on our outside thermometer was just under thirty degrees. It gave me an anticipatory shiver just thinking of being outside.

My brother was the next to meander down the stairs. After he got comfortable and put in his order, we started talking about movies that were out.

"Do you want to see *Towering Inferno* this week?" he asked.

"Sure, any day but Tuesday."

"Yeah, I figured," he answered with a smile.

My father came down next. His attire threw us off a bit. He had on a coat and tie as if he were heading to school. Then we recalled that he was flying to Albany for the union meeting. He had just enough time for a cup of tea and an English muffin before his shuttle arrived. My mom emerged as he was heading to the door. He gave her a kiss and told us to be good before heading out.

My mother then sat at the kitchen table where Nana brought her a cup of tea before making one for herself. She sat down beside her. If they were talking about anything important Pat and I could not hear it since we were zoned out watching the television. By the time my sisters woke, I was already upstairs getting dressed to head to practice.

I hung out in my room, lying on my bed for an hour or so staring at my schoolbooks stacked on the desk. Most of the teachers were pretty good about not doling out meaty assignments during a vacation. But I had one sadistic math teacher, Mr. Kalfus, who believed all school-aged kids were pampered, lazy, and entitled loafers. Yesterday, the last Friday before we left school, he gave us four hours of work to do over the break. And you could be sure he'd be quizzing us on it the day we got back. In my head, I'd planned to start on Wednesday. It was only the first Saturday of break, and I hadn't so much as opened the book.

I walked downstairs dressed and ready to go. My mother was still in her robe and slippers, which meant I was walking to school. So, I put on my gloves, pulled my wool hat over my ears, grabbed my bag, and off I went.

The locker room was a little more crowded than I thought it should be when I arrived. Apparently, a few members of the freshman team had asked to participate in our post-season sessions. This was good in that it would enable us to have more teams for drills and scrimmage.

I counted an even twenty players when we got out to the court in the West Gym. I also spied that Glenn, Gervais, and Stanley Davis had joined us. They were still in their practice attire. I didn't think they were going to play with us, and the bleachers were folded up so there was no place for them to sit.

Mr. Williams then blew the whistle, and we all met at center court. He appointed four captains who selected their players in a round-robin fashion. We were going to have a mini tournament. I was disappointed to be one of the captains because Gary was also one. It was a defeatist attitude but that meant I wouldn't be on the winning team.

Once the teams were picked, the varsity players were introduced as additional referees. We would play the first two games simultaneously on the courts running width-wise across the gym. Then we would move to the central court where the two teams who lost the earlier rounds would play each other, followed by the two winning teams meeting in the finale.

Ernie was also a captain and my team played his in the first round. In order to avoid the pretense of favoritism, Glenn refereed the other game with Stanley while Gervais and Mr. Williams called ours. It was a close but fun contest, as Ernie's squad won a three-point victory over mine to advance. Predictably, Gary's team won the other game.

We had a quick water break after the first round and then commenced with the two losing teams playing first on the main court. During the break a janitor had come in and pulled out one section of the bleachers so the non-contestants could sit more comfortably while watching. This time, again to avoid conflict, Glenn and Stanley refereed our game.

My team's second game was a pretty close one like the first. It wasn't as enjoyable, though, since Stanley kept calling controversial fouls on me. Of course, whenever I complained he would just stare me down. Out of the corner of my eye, I could see Glenn chuckling. Despite the officiating, my team managed to prevail and win the unofficial third place. We then migrated over to the bleacher seats as the other two teams got up and took the court.

While they got into position Glenn came and sat next to me and put an arm around my neck.

"I know you don't have much of one," he started, "but you need to stick your butt out more when you make your power move from the block. It makes it harder for someone to block your shot from behind and you'll create a lot more fouls."

"Thanks," I said, looking down at my rump with a smile. "I'll make as much use of what little I have."

He laughed and turned back toward the game.

Gary's team got up early and prevailed in the championship game as expected. Despite Ernie having two forwards from the freshman team on his squad, no one could stop Gary either on the block or off the dribble. When it was all over, everyone had really enjoyed the event and were grateful to Mr. Williams for scheduling more such contests for the rest of the week.

True to form, Ernie went to work in the locker room attempting to plan some sort of nocturnal event. But upon exiting the building we could all see that a heavy snow had started. It looked as if three inches had accumulated while we were playing. Thus, we all agreed to see how the weather turned out before scheduling anything.

It wasn't a snowfall of upstate or Midwest proportions, but it was enough to keep us all in on a Saturday night. My family, sans Dad, would watch much of it from our bay window on the second floor with Max on guard barking at the few cars that drove by. My mother made hot chocolate as we stared out at the accumulation, which would eventually hit seven inches. It was the largest snowfall of that winter.

We were still up at eleven o'clock that evening, but rather than go down and watch television we stayed by the window and turned on the radio. One of the local stations was running old-time radio programs on weekend nights. Tonight's episode was *The Shadow*. My parents had always spoken of these shows when growing up and so my mother stayed with us to listen. It was really a great time.

My father called the next morning to let us know he arrived in Albany without incident. But they had gotten close to twelve inches of snow, nearly double ours. Hopefully there would be no more storms before or during his trip home on Wednesday.

Pat and I got out early that morning to shovel the driveway before my father returned home and had the notion to do it himself. While out, we received requests from two of our neighbors to shovel theirs as well for ten dollars each. It wasn't necessarily our preferred use of a day off, but when an elderly woman or mother of infants asks and agrees to pay, it's hard to say no.

Over the course of the day, Coppertree turned into a winter playground as kids collected from all around to throw snowballs, build snowmen, and sled down the few front yards that had declinations from the house to the street. Our block had very little traffic and lots of school-aged children. Also, since this was the weekend before a week off, everyone's spirits were already elevated.

On Monday my focus—and many others' in the village, no doubt—was back on the basketball showdown with Smithtown West. The local and state governments had gotten the plows out in plenty of time, and most of the highways and side streets were navigable, so no school travel bans were in place. All our faithful would be easily transported to the game.

The game on Tuesday was at two o'clock, so I confirmed with Jon that his family would be by to pick me up at one. Both games would be played on the same court, but, in a reversal from normal, the varsity game would be played first. Thus, there was no reason to arrive too early, but we would likely be staying later for the JV game. I assumed the fan bus was still available, so Babylon would have a good crowd to back them up.

Jon's family station wagon pulled up to get me the next day and I saw it was a very packed car. Two families' worth. There were no dads, as they had to work. In addition to the two moms sitting up front, there were six other kids. The back seat was full, so I had to go in through the rear entry of the wagon and cram myself in over Jon and his brother on the folded-down back. It was a thirty-minute drive to Smithtown under normal circumstances, but the snowy roads added more time to the voyage.

"Are any of the girls going to the game?" I asked Jon.

"I don't know about all of them," he responded, "but Virginia is going with the Farleys."

I wondered what that meant. I could feel Jon staring at me waiting for a reaction. I kept my head turned away from him and looked out the window. A few minutes of silence went by before he continued.

"Do you think something is going on with her and Gary?"

"I wouldn't know. You couldn't have fit her in here anyway."

He kept probing while I deflected and eventually, we returned to talk of the game. When we arrived at our destination, it felt like I was in a wrestling match as we climbed out over each other to exit the car. Just as we got out and felt the first sting of cold air, the fan bus pulled into the parking lot. Despite the weather, the passengers had slid down the windows and were chanting at the top of their voices, "This is Panther Country! This is Panther Country!"

We hurried to the entry so we wouldn't have to wait in line behind the bus people. Once inside, I could see that their gym was as nice as our East one back at Babylon, with glass backboards, big bleachers, and an overall newly constructed feel to it. Jon and I saw our group on the far side in the visitor bleachers, which faced the player benches across the court. We headed over quickly as the rest of the Shiebler family followed after.

There was nobody on the court yet. And when we got closer, I could see Gary and Virginia were sitting next to each other. They weren't holding hands or anything but were laughing and engaged enough to insinuate something might be going on between them. I decided to steel myself and pretend not to notice anything. After all, it was the game that mattered today.

I did end up grabbing a seat behind them. Ernie was sitting to Gary's right but had a different girl on his arm than the one he'd been courting all year. I wondered what had happened there. Once I was seated, Virginia turned around to face me.

"Hi, Tom."

"Hey, Virginia. I'm glad you found a ride."

"Umm, ah, yeah," she responded, looking toward Gary as she spoke.

I couldn't tell if she inferred anything from my statement, but I was glad she was there.

The gym was at capacity when game time arrived. The home and visitor stands were both packed with apparently equal emotion. The Smithtown West team was entirely white, and their fan base was representative of that demography as well. But they had an outstanding game support system. In addition to a very acrobatic cheerleading crew, they had an indoor kick line that marched out onto the court twirling batons and whipping the crowd into a frenzy. Even as visiting fans, it was phenomenal to watch their antics.

After warm-ups and the ensuing huddle, the teams headed to center court. I was interested to see who would draw the defensive assignment of covering Langwost. He was the guy who killed us last time. As our players matched up around the circle, Stanley Davis took up the spot next to the Smithtown West star. I guess he would be the man.

It could be a risky strategy in that Stanley was one of our top scorers. If he were chasing Langwost around all game, he might tire enough to limit his shooting effect. Apparently Koelbel thought that was worth the risk. We would know soon enough.

The ball went up, and the game was on.

Revenge or Flop

Barry Davis again controlled the tap over to Gervais, and Babylon got the first possession. He passed the ball to Brian in the corner, who bounced it to Glenn on the post. Glenn was immediately double-teamed. But rather than pass it back out to Brian, he spotted Stanley wide open on the opposite guard spot up high. He shot a crisp pass to Stanley, who squared up and drained the first basket of the game.

West inbounded the ball quickly afterward to Langwost, who pushed the ball up the court. Babylon was slow to set up its defense so the guard shot to the middle with Stanley in his face the whole way. Still, Langwost pulled up in the lane and answered with a five-footer to tie the game.

The teams played pretty evenly in the first quarter, with all five starters from both teams contributing points. West's big men were causing trouble underneath for Babylon, with both Glenn and Barry incurring two fouls. Koelbel opted not to juggle the lineup for the second quarter and left the same starting five on the floor. Brian provided height and strength that Chuck Farley could not.

In the second quarter, Langwost remained hot from outside and continued to score. Yet Stanley seemed to keep pace with him, preventing further damage.

Then, halfway through the second quarter, Glenn picked up his third foul. That meant our superstar was going to have to sit out for a while.

"Does coach go with Chuck?" someone in the group asked.

But the question was answered in the next few seconds as Koelbel waved Steven "Weiner" Farley over next to him.

"Yeah, we need help inside," Gary offered.

Glenn stayed on the floor for another few seconds as Koelbel gave instructions to the sophomore. Weiner then jumped up toward the scorer's table, with the coach patting him on the rump for encouragement. When the game stopped for an out-of-bounds play, Weiner came in, and a dejected Glenn headed for the bench for the rest of the half.

We were leading by one when Weiner came into the game, and he proved his mettle right away. On a play where Brian got the ball down low to Barry, our center banked his shot a little too hard off of the backboard. Weiner was right there from the weak side to clean up the miss and put the ball in for his first basket.

In West's next offensive possession, they continually tried to push the ball down low to take advantage of Glenn's absence, but time and again, Barry, Brian, and Weiner rebuffed them. With only a few seconds left in the half, Langwost put up a hurried twenty-five-footer, again with Stanley right in his face. Amazingly, the shot rattled in as the buzzer sounded. This cut Babylon's lead to one at halftime.

As the teams rushed off, it became clear that we were in another close fight. Everybody got up and stretched, and a few of us headed over to the concession stand. However, we hurried back to our seats to watch as West's kick line came out again and put on a college-level halftime show.

As I was approaching my seat, I could see Virginia whispering to Gary while clutching his upper arm. It confirmed what I already knew, but still it was a bit of a gut punch. I sat back in my seat with a fake smile, watching the lead twirler launch her baton twenty feet in the air and catch it behind her back. Everyone applauded.

The kickers left the court just in time for the teams to reenter. After a few rounds of layups both sides were back in the huddle getting final instructions. Glenn was standing ready to get back in the game and did. Weiner stayed close by Koelbel on the bench.

The second half started similarly to the first, with Barry Davis tapping it back to Gervais, but rather than move slowly, he threw a half-court pass to Stanley

Davis, who had caught his defender napping for an easy layup. When West inbounded the ball, Babylon went into a full-court press. Langwost managed to negotiate through the obstruction to get the ball up the court but was nearly called for a ten-second backcourt violation.

A pass inside to one of their big men resulted in a partial block by Barry. Brian grabbed the rebound, which he proceeded to push out to Glenn. Glenn took the ball coast to coast and scored a basket, plus drawing a foul. He sank the free throw. As a result, Babylon took a six-point lead.

We kept up the pressure and Stanley's relentless defense started having its intended effect. Langwost continued to shoot well but couldn't find any outlet passes due to Stanley's pressure. Stanley was also matching him basket for basket. Nevertheless, the lead was only four as we headed into the final quarter.

Glenn picked up his fourth foul only a minute into the quarter, but Koelbel rolled the dice and kept him in the game. At this point, Brian got hot and scored Babylon's next five points, but West wouldn't shake. The lead never got past six, and West knew they couldn't afford at that point to just trade baskets. They moved into a full-court press.

Soon, they cut the lead to four with a minute to go. At this point, Glenn took the ball up court and slowly played keep-away from Langwost and the other West guard. With about ten seconds left, Glenn threw a backdoor bounce pass to Stanley, who fittingly scored the final points of the game. The Babylon side erupted, and the players rushed the floor in celebration.

Koelbel took a longer amount of time to congratulate the opposing coach. In fact, the two walked off the court together, speaking continuously. The respect was clearly visible. Bartsch went off with the team, putting an arm over Stanley's shoulders as our fans clamored around the rest of the team in a congratulatory fashion.

The Shieblers were staying for the JV game, which of course suited me fine. Much of our fan base stayed as well because the varsity players would be out to watch the next game. That would allow for some face time with them and Koelbel himself. A smaller portion of the West fans stuck around.

As we waited between the games for the Babylon squad to reemerge, I went out in the hallway with Jon, Ernie, and Ernie's new girlfriend. Gary and Virginia stayed in the gym. The school was constructed similarly to ours. Beyond the door leading to the gym, one could either go left down a hallway or straight outside through a heavy glass door.

The hallway wound past the student-run concession stand, where there was also a trophy case. We kept walking down the hall until the rest of the building was cut off by an expandable steel gate that would be removed during school hours. When we stopped, I had Ernie's sole attention for a second.

"So, it looks like Gary and Virginia are a thing."

"Yeah, that kind of happened over the last week."

He knew why I was asking but was kind enough to let me be nonchalant about it. I wasn't quite sure how I missed the whole thing developing.

"How long have you two been together?" I said changing the subject to him and his new girl.

"About the same amount of time."

"Anything going on at your house tonight?"

"Not tonight, tomorrow. I'll give you the details again during practice tomorrow."

"Thanks."

With that we all started walking back into the gym to see if the players were out, which they were. Glenn, Stanley, Gervais, and Barry were all sitting together in the middle of the home bleachers closest to the locker room. There, they allowed the faithful to pay homage. Brian was a little off to the side, befitting his shy demeanor.

I saw Koelbel on the opposite side talking to our cheerleading coach and made a beeline for him while the others made their way toward the players. He saw me when I got a few feet away and stuck out his hand to shake. This was, I took it, a reciprocal funny response to our last game encounter.

"Congratulations again, Mr. Koelbel," I said.

"Thanks again, Muh-kyoo-en," he said, looking around. "Where's your papa?"

"He's upstate until tomorrow."

"Ahh, NYSUT, huh?"

"Yep."

Most teachers knew the workings of the various union groups and when the meetings were. Although schools might have their own delegations representing their own interests, when one got a raise, they all got raises.

"He'll be at the game Friday," I continued. "Stanley had a great game."

"Yeah, at both ends. That Langwost kid is tough. Got some good minutes from Weiner, too."

"I saw Chris Brust walking around on the sidelines. How close is he to full recovery?"

"Soon. I might try giving him some minutes next week."

I always liked the way he would speak to me as if I were an adult. No condescension, just an occasional ribbing. Some of the other parents were coming over, and I did not wish to hog his time, so I excused myself and joined my friends over by the players. I went and sat with Brian off to the side. It felt like we hadn't spoken in a while.

"Way to go, Bri."

"Thanks, I still suck at the foul line."

"It didn't matter."

"Yeah, but it might next time."

He had made only one of his four foul shots but still scored fifteen points. Like Glenn, he was always focused on improving. We both then turned to watch the JV game, which was tied heading into the fourth quarter. Both Greg Berger (Flea) and James Feeney were again playing with the JV as they had accumulated no minutes in the varsity game. Their play was helping the game stay competitive.

Babylon notched its second win of the day when, down by one with only a few seconds left, a West guard overshot his teammate on a pass, and the ball sailed out of bounds to end the game. At that point, everyone was ready to go home. The stands emptied quickly. I didn't get a chance to speak with any of the other players, but I did get a quick look from Glenn. He gave me a thumbs-up. That was all I needed.

We all piled back into the Shiebler car in the same cramped manner as we arrived. Once on the road, I half expected Jon to rub the Gary and Virginia thing in my face, but he was uncharacteristically quiet himself. It made me suspect that he might have been a little sweet on her as well.

It took a lot longer to get home from the game as there was an accident on the Sagtikos Parkway, which ran north to south across Long Island and was the main road of our journey. (This name also has Native American origins and means "head of the hissing snake.") The accident had slowed traffic to a crawl behind the wreck.

As our car slowly passed, we could see a totaled Ford Mustang and pickup truck with its right side smashed in. There were also two police cars, an ambulance, and a fire truck. Someone was being loaded into the ambulance. We all checked but did not recognize anyone from Babylon, but it was still a gruesome sight.

After moving past the wreck, we picked up speed, and I was home a little before seven. I said goodbye and thanked Jon's mother before running inside. I wished them all a fun time on their ski trip the next day as well.

My family was still at the dinner table, but it looked like my mother had kept a plate hot for me. My sisters and brother left when I began to eat and talk about the game. I know my mother would have listened, but I decided to save it all for my father when he returned the next day.

I didn't feel like going out that night but rather decided to stay inside and brood. I couldn't tell you what we watched on television either, as I stared like a zombie at the screen. I was hoping a good night's sleep and fun practice tomorrow would cure everything, but that would only come with time.

No Missteps

When I returned from the gym in the early afternoon, I found that my father was back from his trip. He was sitting in the upstairs kitchen speaking with my mother. It didn't occur to me that they might be speaking about anything important. All I wanted to do was recount to him the play-by-play of the game with Smithtown West. My mother ceded the floor with a smile as I launched into my monologue on how great the game had been.

When I finished the game update, I mentioned that Mr. Koelbel had asked after him.

"When I said upstate, he knew you were with NYSUT. He asked if you would be at the next game."

I fibbed a bit not telling that I had volunteered that he *would* be at the game. I figured two days' rest from his trip would be enough time and that his curiosity and social desire to get out would have peaked by then. He responded as I'd hoped.

"Yes, that will be fine. Where is it?"

"Comsewogue. Do you know how to get there?

"It's a good forty-five minutes. We'll be back a little later than usual. You bringing anybody?"

"I don't know yet. I wanted to check with you first."

I would find out at Ernie's party that night if anyone needed a ride. After a few more minutes of banter over basketball and stuff, I went downstairs for my afternoon feeding and nap. I fell asleep watching a North Carolina–Duke basketball game. By the time I woke up, it was almost five, and Carolina had won by eight.

It was another cold night in Babylon, so most of the action at the Vickers house was inside. The majority of the players were there but the crowd was a little lighter than on previous occasions as some families had taken vacation for all or part of the remaining off days ahead. Spirits were high due to our current winning streak and now having sole possession of first place.

My mood was taken down a notch when I saw how cozy Gary and Virginia were, so I tried to balance that out by moving about the party a little more than usual. Ernie was also there with his new girl. I didn't want to seem as if I were avoiding them but did want to find some more convivial entertainment elsewhere in the crowd. So, I hung out with the gang a bit and talked about the next game.

"Does anyone need a ride?" I asked.

Nobody responded, there were just a few shaking heads. This was largely due to the game not being very important and some of the group being out of town. I also figured that Virginia and her girlfriend were going with the Farleys.

When Ernie and his girl excused themselves, I took the opportunity to stroll around in hopes of finding Brian to talk some game. I saw him at his usual spot at the kitchen table, but he was not alone. Brian had never been unpopular, but he was starting to gain a nearly equivalent star status to his brother and more people wanted to get in on that.

He smiled when he saw me, and I wedged my way into a seat. We couldn't really establish a dialogue then, as several older kids were firing questions at him. "How good are you?" "Have you ever dunked a ball in a game?" "Do you think you'll ever play in the NBA?"

I could tell he was not overly comfortable with the rapid-fire questions, but with his gentle demeanor, he answered as best as he could. After a few minutes,

I shrugged and got up to circle around some more. Brian would have to handle fame without my contribution.

Glenn was sitting in the living room with Tricia on his lap. I knew he didn't want me lingering around too much but I felt compelled to walk over and put in a quick word.

"Great game yesterday," I said. "By the way, I stuck out my butt in practice a little more today and did draw a lot more fouls. Nice tip."

Tricia laughed at my wording.

"See, I told you," he replied smiling.

Not wishing to overstay my welcome, I moved on from there.

After an hour I realized there was not much more for me to hang around for, so I made another Irish Goodbye. I thought I would have to hoof it home in the cold, but I encountered my neighbor Joey Jaffie, the son of the Waldman's owners, who was home from college on a visit. He kindly gave me a lift home. I arrived well ahead of curfew.

The next night Pat and I returned to the Bay Shore Theatre to see *The Towering Inferno*. *The Godfather II* was having a good run and was still showing at Babylon, but the Bond movie was a little less popular and had moved out a week ago to make room for the next release. We were fine with the change since we'd already seen the Bond flick.

Inferno had been an extremely hyped-up movie prior to its release. There were more than a dozen top Hollywood names in the film as well as a few NFL players. The theater was packed for a weeknight. Also, since it was a school vacation week, it's likely many parents were happy to get their kids out of the house, regardless of the cost.

The film was a little over the top and almost three hours long, but we enjoyed all of the action. I read sometime after that Steve McQueen demanded equal billing with Paul Newman on the posters and marquee and that the two would have exactly the same number of words in the dialogue. I found that amusing but was not inclined to count and validate the rumor.

When it was over Pat and I waited outside for our mother to come get us. While we stood there, Pat made a surprising request.

"Do you mind if I come to the game with you and Dad?"

"Sure, but you don't have to ask me."

"Yeah, I wanted to make sure you weren't bringing a large gang."

"Nope, this time it will be just me."

"Oh, I thought . . ."

At that moment Mom pulled up, and I used the excuse to shut down the next query, which I imagined might involve Virginia. Mom was the only one in the car, so Pat took the front seat and I the back. This put some distance between us and made it easier to change the subject, which my mother did by asking about the movie.

We talked the film up on the drive home. Mom liked many of the actors in the movie, particularly Newman. However, when she heard how long it was, she said she'd wait to see it on television. When we got home, Nana was ready as usual downstairs, making tea and cakes. We always drank tea at night back then regardless of the caffeine.

Pat ended up developing other plans and didn't join us for the game Friday. It was the last night game of the regular season and Valentine's Day. I may not have had a girlfriend, but I contented myself knowing that I would spend Valentine's doing the things that I currently loved, which were going to a basketball game with my father and watching my Babylon Panthers. It was dark when we left. Sunset on Long Island was very early this time of year. I figured plenty of people would still be going to the game but it seemed on the way that we were the only ones on the road.

This made the journey feel even more solitary. Dad and I never had problems making conversation. I always had questions, and he always seemed to have answers. But tonight, he started.

"Where's the rest of your gang?"

"Some got other rides, some on trips, and . . . whatever."

"Anything else going on?"

"No, just school and this. How was your trip to Albany?"

Our whole family had been to Albany once but I didn't remember much about it. My parents took us on a lot of trips by car when we were young. Long Island is less than six hours' drive to Boston, Philadelphia, Washington, D.C., Baltimore, and many touristy rural areas in upstate New York and New England. At times it felt like I spent half of my life in the back of a car on long family drives with my siblings.

No matter how much we complained, we were scolded and told to enjoy the sights and count ourselves fortunate that we got to view such great things. It was true, I knew, but that didn't make it more palatable. Somebody always got carsick, or we started arguing with each other. Family sightseeing trips were one of those things you grow more grateful for in hindsight.

Since my basketball season was over my father asked when track started and what events I was looking to run. Like basketball, he would make it to most every track meet I would ever run. But my mind was still on basketball like everyone else.

"Koelbel said Chris Brust might play tonight," I put in.

"Ahh, if you guys get him back that could be a big boon going into the playoffs."

"Yeah, I guess the question is will he be one hundred percent."

We pulled off the main highway, which certainly felt like it was pitch black the whole way, and passed through a dimly lit area of town before pulling into the school parking lot at Comsewogue High School. We circled around a bit before parking to make sure we were near the entry to the gym. Neither of us had ever been here before.

Eventually, we saw a better-lit area with people entering and gambled that was the spot to park. We did so and headed inside. I didn't see any Babylon people immediately upon entering.

Comsewogue also had a newer gymnasium. It was large, clean, and had those glass backboards. When we walked over to what we presumed was the visitor side of the gym we saw the Farley family. Gary was sitting with his parents and with Virginia by his side. We went over and joined them. My father plunked down next to Mr. Farley, which left me flanking Virginia.

"Not great lighting on the drive," Mr. Farley said to my father.

"Yeah, it was so dark I thought we might drive off the edge of something," my father quipped back.

I noticed Virginia's friend was not with her and inquired. She said her family was doing something together that night and couldn't attend. None of the gang Gary usually traveled with were there either. I guess this game was not much of a draw. Even when Ernie arrived, he was alone with his parents. That was good. I didn't want to be the only unaccompanied guy there.

The JV game was already over and the varsity would be out in a few moments. As things grew more quiet, I finally worked up the nerve and chatted some with Virginia.

"Did you have any homework over the vacation?"

"A little, but I haven't done it yet."

"Me neither. Kalfus gave us a butt load of stuff, but I probably won't do it until Sunday. That jerk."

That got a laugh out of her and pumped me up a bit.

When the game eventually started Babylon got off to a quick start. We went up by nine after the first quarter and sixteen by halftime. Stanley Davis continued his torrid shooting, scoring ten in the first half. The game was highlighted by Chris Brust playing for the first time since his injury. He grabbed a couple of rebounds and put an offensive rebound back for a basket. He seemed to be moving well but playing tentatively, as if still afraid of reinjuring himself.

Not expecting Comsewogue to make a comeback, my friends and I walked around the school at halftime and a little beyond. We strolled down whatever halls were open and did not make it back until a minute before the final buzzer. The game ended in a not-unexpected blowout.

The win was significant in that Babylon had clinched at least a tie for the League V title and a place in the Suffolk County playoffs. Next up would be our final regular season game at home against Wyandanch. If we were to defeat them, we would win the title outright and get a first-round bye, which was much preferable.

Some who attended looked a little lethargic, almost wondering why they had ventured out for a game that would end so lopsided. As for my group, since we would be getting back late Ernie didn't think it worth extending the evening once we got home. So, we all dispersed until tomorrow.

The drive back home with my father should have been routine. I even contemplated napping. But the eeriness of the dark roads kept me awake. Then the Monaco started to sound odd, and something very scary happened. The protective doors that covered the headlights when the car was off went down and covered the lights.

"Oh crap," my father said.

Suddenly it felt as if we were locked in a dark closet, but moving at sixty miles an hour.

"Should we stop the car?" I asked, more than a little frightened.

Then the covers came up and we could see around us again. The road was straight, and we seemed to be the only ones on that stretch for the time being. So, we relaxed a bit.

"Thankfully that stop—"

Before I could finish my sentence, they came down again and once more we were driving blind. Actually, we could see a few feet ahead. My father slowed the car until we were barely moving. Then the headlamps went up again.

This happened two more times before they finally stayed up and remained on for the rest of the drive. Neither of us said a word for the rest of the journey out of superstitious fear. It became less scary when we got closer to Babylon where the roads were better lit, but the two of us were practically numb from the tension.

When we got home my father and I went inside where he immediately made himself a Manhattan. When my mother came out to greet us, we were seated at the kitchen table. When she saw my father's cocktail her first question was, "Did Babylon lose?" When my dad told her what had actually happened, she went pale and immediately grabbed and hugged me.

My parents took that car to the garage the next morning in the daylight. When the mechanic said he couldn't find anything wrong with it, they immediately set out looking for a new car. Come Monday Dad was driving a Ford Granada.

Back to School and the End of League V Play

The first Monday back after a vacation is among the least enjoyable days in a teenager's life. There was no more sleeping late, you had to pay attention, and there was that extra layer of discipline that seemed to be doled out with relish by certain teachers and administrators. The teachers themselves mostly weren't happy to be back, and they often let their bad moods roll downhill to us.

During math class that morning Mr. Kalfus started by walking around the room confirming that everyone present had done the hours of assignments he had given us over the break. One could sense his disappointment when he found that everyone had actually done their work. So, he picked a few unlucky volunteers to go to the blackboard and write out several of the calculations in detail. As soon as anyone faltered, he would berate the entire class by stating that none of us were bright enough to ever go to college.

Fortunately, after enduring that torture, I had art class and joined Bartsch at the front counter to discuss basketball and the team. The front had gotten more crowded with the varsity's continued success. Although few had my level of basketball interest the train was rolling and everybody was climbing on board.

"Did you think Chris Brust looked a little tentative on Friday?" I asked.

"Yeah, but that's to be expected. Big men are always worried about losing their legs, particularly after an injury."

"Will he play more tomorrow?"

"Yes, he'll probably get a little more time than last week. Koelbel wants to bring him along slowly. But not too slowly."

That made sense. Tomorrow's game shouldn't be a gimme. We expected Wyandanch to be tough again.

"Does Wyandanch have a shot at the playoffs?" I asked further.

"No, they already have five losses, and I doubt a fourth-place team would get a birth."

With that I went back to drawing and listened to other questions from the group. Bartsch enjoyed holding court as much as any teacher or coach.

I brought my lunch that day and when I went to sit at the eighth grade table, I noticed another tradition was breaking down. There were *girls* at our table. My world was blowing up.

Virginia was there seated next to Gary when I arrived and several of her friends had also taken up residence with us. I was only able to get a seat on the edge whereas most of my teammates who were already there had garnered seats toward the center in the mixed company. Any conversation I tried to input made me feel like I was yelling, so I remained quiet and in a foul mood.

When I left lunch, I had no idea what people were doing after school or when and where everyone would be sitting at the game tomorrow. The second item was more easily remedied as it would be an afternoon game with plenty of time after school to get there. Since Mr. Williams had ended extra practices after the vacation, my whole after-school day was open.

As soon as my last class had ended and I'd collected my stuff, I went by Virginia's locker to see if any activities were forming, but neither she nor any of her locker mates were present. I wandered around the hallways for a while after that but could not find any signs of life, so I dejectedly exited the building and trudged toward home. The temperature was still cold, but the sun was out, which made it feel a little less frigid.

As I was crossing Montauk, I made the decision to go into Waldman's to kill some time. Once inside I grabbed a copy of *Mad* magazine from the rack, took a seat, and asked Mr. Jaffie for an egg cream. I then put a dollar down on the counter.

While he was whipping up my drink, I opened the magazine to *Spy vs. Spy* for the latest laugh. I would read the whole magazine, but I always started there.

After serving up my egg cream, Mr. Jaffie looked at me and gave a sigh of disappointment.

"Is this going to be a pattern?" he asked. "Are you just going to come in now when you're depressed?"

"I'm not depressed, just . . . bored," I lied. "I have no practices until track season starts, so there's not a lot to do."

He studied my face and his expression led me to believe that he wasn't buying it.

We spoke for a while longer about things going on around town and I corrected a few of the scores he had recorded for the basketball season on his poster. He refilled my egg cream once as a thank-you. When I checked my watch, I saw it was five thirty and knew I had to get home. I said goodbye to Mr. Jaffie and headed out.

Normally my parents weren't too keen on us filling up on junk food before dinner, but I made up a story about how I had helped move some boxes at Waldman's and the soda was my compensation. They cut me a little slack. Dinner was again fish and vegetables that night to keep with my father's diet. He was beginning to struggle with the lean entrée choices and was not yet in the mood to continue the nightly current-events quizzes. This was the one side benefit from his recent health episode.

There were no more late nights now that the break had ended. We did stay up to watch one of our favorite television shows, *Happy Days*. I enjoyed the fifties era and high school theme of it. But my parents remarked that the haircuts and some other details were not quite accurate.

At ten, Pat and I turned in again, dreading our Top 40 alarm come morning. I didn't fall asleep as quickly as normal, partly due to the fact that I'd had no practice session to tire me out. My mind had also meandered back to the social breakdown after school and whether that would continue. In the end, I only got five hours slumber before morning came.

During the walk to school the next day I noticed that the temperature had started to break a bit. The mercury had risen to the mid-forties. This seemed to incite more collegiality with the other migrating students from our block. The extra livening up was also no doubt due to the excitement of where the basketball team might be headed. That was all anyone would talk about as we hashed out the thirty-minute stroll to BHS.

The morning PA announcements led with a statement encouraging everyone to show up for the game that afternoon to cheer on the Panthers to win and clinch their second straight League V title. We all knew that Wyandanch had given us a tough fight at their place a few weeks back and that they had also knocked off Amityville to clear the path for this chance to be the sole league champions. I'm sure Koelbel wasn't taking them lightly.

There was no discussion at lunch or in the halls as to whether anyone would be at the game. I found my crew was in our normal spot, ten rows up in the middle of the far home bleachers facing our bench come game time. I joined everyone about twenty minutes before the opening tip.

The players were not yet on the floor and our cheerleaders had just finished their pyramid. Next the Wyandanch cheerleaders came out and did an extremely entertaining routine that garnered both chuckles and plaudits from our crowd. They were a very pretty group of black girls who were probably among the most innovative cheering groups in the county.

Marching sideways from the far corner of the court, they tap-danced in unison while clapping their hands in sequence to a chant of "Watch out, watch out, here come the Warriors! Watch out, watch out, here come the Warriors!" Their procession went out to the midcourt and then made a backward ninety-degree turn toward the opposite corner. Their timing was perfect. At nearly the exact time the lead girl stepped on the pointed edge, the Wyandanch players came running out for their warm-ups to the applause from their fans.

However, being on our home court, their cheers were no match for ours. As soon as Glenn led the Panthers out, our fan noise totally drowned out the Wyandanch crowd. It was the first time since December that many of the fans had seen the whole team run the layup drill. Chris Brust looked unhampered in his running and the crowd seemed to gain energy from that.

Before the game started there was a ritual that the varsity team ran at the end of every home season. One at a time, each player was announced over the PA and called out to center court, bringing with them a carnation. They would give it to a correspondingly announced cheerleader in appreciation of their support during the year. Upon handing out the flower the two would share a brief kiss on the cheek before departing the court. It was a nice tradition despite the occasional goon yelling out, “Slip her the tongue!” from the crowd.

The cheerleaders would respond with their gratitude later on. They had each prepared a freshly cooked plate of cookies, brownies, or some kind of delight that would be given to the players after the game. We could see from our seats all of these tinfoil-covered dishes on the front-row bleachers where the cheerleaders resided during games.

After this, Babylon got off to another fast start, building up a twelve-point first-quarter lead. Wyandanch appeared very sluggish. Perhaps they knew they were out of county contention and were just mailing this one in. We were too far away to see much into their huddle but one could make out that their two bigger players were breathing very heavily during the break.

Nevertheless, the Warriors rebounded in the second quarter and cut into our lead by fast-breaking with a smaller lineup. When the buzzer sounded ending the first half, Babylon was only leading by seven.

“It’s not in the bag yet,” Gary said.

“Yeah, it looked like we were going to run them off the court at first,” I replied.

Many fans stayed seated during halftime to enjoy another entertaining routine by the Wyandanch cheerleaders. But when the second-half play began, our guys came out all business and crushed the remaining life out of the Warriors with a ten-to-nothing opening run to start the second half. As the lead widened, Koelbel was able to start substituting in. He brought each of his seniors off one at a time in their last-ever home game to some deserved applause from the fans.

First to come out was Gervais Barger, and then Stanley Davis, right before the end of the third quarter. Then Chuck Farley came out about midway through the fourth. Finally—even though he had only gotten to play a few minutes—the team’s bench-support leader, senior Mike Fischer, came out. He was so happy he gave Koelbel an impromptu hug. All were touched and a little emotional when the coach shook their hands affectionately as they departed the court.

Chris Brust got plenty of time in the second half and racked up ten points in a much stronger performance than at Comsewogue. Glenn led everybody with twenty points and sat out the entire fourth quarter as our lead ballooned to nineteen. He and Barry Davis did not participate in the ceremonies due to both of them being only juniors. In fact, every member of the team managed to get in the game and score as we cruised to an unexpectedly lopsided win. After the final buzzer went off, Mr. Cosci made his final announcement of the season.

"Congratulations to the 1974–75 League V champions, your Babylon Panthers."

Everyone in attendance, even the Wyandanch players and fans, applauded. The Babylon players then remained on the court after our opponents departed for the traditional cutting down of the nets for the second consecutive year.

There wasn't a ladder present, so Chris and Barry Davis stood under the basket and helped everyone up. Glenn substituted in when it was Barry's turn, but it took a few more people when Chris got to cut. Every team member would get to keep a piece of the net.

Everyone's mood was very jovial, both on and off the court. It had been a hard-fought campaign to win the league title. There were injuries, adversity, and downright despair at some points. But the team had come through every time they needed to and endured what was a tough league schedule.

I could see Koelbel's smile subside as he made his way to the locker room. He had gotten this far last year and had expected to go further. Babylon had been upset in the first round of the county playoffs and was forced to watch a team they had beaten in the regular season, Central Islip, go on to claim the crown.

Just before he got out of view, he looked down at the piece of net in his hand. I could tell that was not the rope he wanted. The second season—the real season—was about to begin.

The County Playoffs

Very few in the fanbase knew how the county playoffs worked, myself included. In those days, there were two major newspapers that covered the events of Long Island in which our high school sports would be included. *Newsday*, which is still around today, and the *Long Island Press*. We also had the local town paper, the *Babylon Beacon*.

None published a bracket detailing how play would progress win to win; they would only list the games that were occurring that day or the next. We knew that Babylon had received a bye due to winning the League Championship and we would not know our opponent until an earlier game in what was called the "outbracket" was played. As soon as we knew who we would be playing it would be announced on the morning PA system.

Due to this structure, our basketball team also had ten days off until its next game. This provided time to rest and get healthy, but also to grow a little rusty. I was sure Koelbel continued to work the team hard, but like everyone else I was unable to see anything as he kept the practices closed for the first week.

The smiles of exhilaration we had witnessed from the players following the league championship win and for a few days after slowly turned into stone-hard game faces. It was not advisable to try and speak to any of the players as the next game was steadily approaching. I would wave and smile when I saw any of the team but dared not launch into basketball talk.

On the next Monday morning, it was announced that our opponent in the first round of the playoffs would be Ward Melville. Ward Melville would come to be known as much as a place as it would be a school or team. They had the biggest gymnasium on Long Island at the time, and both county semifinals would be played there, with the winner advancing to play in the Nassau Coliseum.

During art class on Tuesday, I sat up front as usual in earshot of Mr. Bartsch but remained silent for most of the class. Many of my classmates were peppering him with questions regarding Ward Melville—how good were they, what was their record, and other blather. When the bell rang for the next class, I stepped up for a quick request.

"Could you convince Koelbel to let some of us sit in on the varsity practice?"

"I doubt it. But I'll ask. Come by the athletic office after school today and we'll see what he says."

"Great, thanks!"

Later at lunch that day I saw Gary, Ernie, and a few others to let them know what Bartsch had said. They were all eager to go but agreed to keep the group small to about five or six. If we showed up with a mob, Koelbel would surely kick us out.

The varsity practice had been moved up to three now that they were the only school team in need of a gym. The five of us skipped the after-school repartee with the girls, and all met at Koelbel's office. As we all filed in, he looked us up and down in his serious and yet comical glare.

"This is it," he stated. "The bleachers won't be out. You sit on the floor, no horsing around, and if you leave, you're gone for good. Understand?"

We all said yes and nodded in assent. Then we followed him down the middle aisle through the locker room as the players got ready. We took the stairs from there and emerged into the gym. Once at court level, he pointed to an area where we were to sit.

The five of us plopped down as silently instructed with our backs pressed up against the collapsed bleachers.

We were only there a few minutes before members of the team began trickling onto the court. When Glenn came out, he was dribbling a ball as usual and spied us sitting to the side. He detoured in front of us looking a little surprised.

"So, Coach K. let you guys in," he said.

"Yeah, but we can't talk or move," one of the others replied.

This gave him a chuckle as he dribbled on.

We all watched as the remaining players trickled out one and two at a time, much like they had three months earlier when the season had begun. But their appearance was somewhat changed. They looked hardened, like fighters who had taken what they thought were an opponent's best punches and were stronger for it.

The trepidation also showed, particularly among the players from last year's team who knew how quickly a dream season could end. Koelbel blew the whistle and they gathered at center court. I noticed that Koelbel had two JV players join the practice and was curious what they might be doing there.

We couldn't make out all of what Koelbel was saying but I definitely heard the words "full-court press." Obviously, that would be an item of focus today and moving forward, whether it was us pressing or breaking our opponents' press when they applied it. We would see shortly.

After the layup drills the teams broke into scrimmaging. Koelbel continued with the same starting five but regularly moved Chuck Farley, Chris Brust, and Weiner in and out of the first-string lineup. The JV players sat underneath one of the baskets waiting to be called for their services. After an hour of scrimmaging, Koelbel again brought the whole team out to center court.

At that point he added the two JV players to the six non-starters to assist in full-court defense. Obviously, this was the area he wanted to work on. The Babylon press break would usually have Glenn taking the ball out of bounds with Stanley at the foul line and Gervais positioned right behind him. Brian and Barry would be spread out wide to their left and right.

The first option to get the ball inbounds would be Stanley Davis setting a pick for Gervais Barger, who would then run diagonally toward the baseline to get a pass from Glenn. If he couldn't get open, Stanley would flash to the other side. Brian Vickers would be further out on the wing and would break long for a home-run pass if it was there. Meanwhile, Barry Davis would run to half-court and then turn back and go to the foul line for the final inbounding option. But it all had to be fast as the rules only allowed five seconds to inbound the ball.

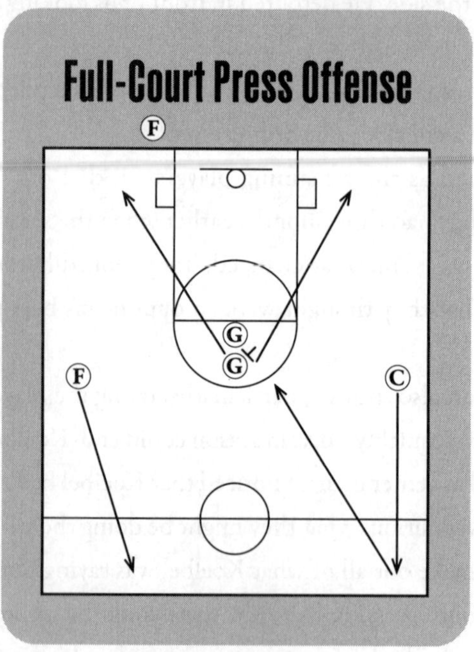

In order to make this more difficult, Mr. Bartsch, who was coaching the defense, was able to use all eight remaining players to do so. He had the giant Brust cover Glenn on the inbounds pass and deployed the others to cut off every conceivable lane. The reserve defense was effective as the first string failed to get the ball in after five tries.

They continued to run the play, again with Koelbel substituting the three key bench players. It worked more successfully after a while but not to Koelbel's satisfaction. To end the practice, he had the team run twenty interval sprints. It was the toughest practice I had seen to date and the players dragged to the various baskets to finish with their foul shots. Even Glenn would only go seven for ten that day.

Koelbel obviously believed the press break would be key to our success in the playoffs. While it needed more work, the rest of the offense looked in peak form. And most importantly the whole team was healthy.

After the break my friends and I gathered for a bit to discuss logistics to get to the game. Every one of our parents were said to be going so I thought nobody would need a ride. But then Ernie surprised me with a request.

"Do you mind if I ride with you and your dad Thursday?"

"Sure, your folks are going right?"

"Yeah, but they want to get there really early in case my brothers need anything."

"Will it be just you?"

"Two of us, if you don't mind," he said with a smile. "But she'll be at my house, so you won't have to stop in two places."

"Okay, we'll see you around six then."

It was still light out when I walked home. I took a different route by going down Carll Avenue, which would preclude the temptation to go into Waldman's and spend any more money. This took me past the public library where, two houses down, I saw a family friend, Mr. Conroy, exiting his car, most likely returning from work. He saw me right away.

"Hi, Tommy, how are you doing?"

"I'm great, Mr. Conroy. How are you?"

Don Conroy was a shorter man, nearer my own height, with a stout build, dark hair, and a very pleasant and jovial demeanor. Beneath his smile was a serious fellow who was very influential and seemed to know everything about life and getting things done in Babylon. Although not in any elected capacity at the time, if you wanted to buy a new house, were having trouble with your neighbors, or were trying to raise money for something, Don Conroy was the man to know.

As my family were big fans of the Godfather movies, in our house we would jokingly refer to him as The Don. My father would correctly predict that Mr. Conroy would someday be mayor of Babylon. He was a Republican, but one my father would easily cross party lines to give his vote.

"I assume you and your dad will be at the game on Thursday."

"Absolutely. You as well?"

"You bet."

The Conroys were almost a mirror image of our family. They had four children as well with two oldest being girls and the younger ones boys. Almost to a child each of our family members had a Conroy in their grade.

"How do you think we'll do?"

"I was just at the varsity practice, and we look great. Of course, anything can happen."

"True words indeed. Well, I'll see you there. Say hi to your folks."

With that, Don disappeared into his house, and I negotiated the rest of my journey home. It was just turning dark out when I walked past the new Ford Granada in the driveway. It was still clean and white, so it stood out a bit. I took a peek inside to assess the size for passengers to the game. The back seat was not quite as wide as the Monaco, so I probably wouldn't be able to ask more than three people. Ernie and his girlfriend made two, so I thought I had one more spot. However, at dinner that night Pat surprised me by announcing that he wanted to go to the game. So, the car was full.

When Thursday finally arrived, the school was electric again during the day. The players were walking tall, decked out in their dress attire. Every member I saw by this point had on some version of a leisure suit. It was clear that trend had definitely taken root in Babylon. The cheerleaders wore their uniforms during the day despite the cold temperature, and the banners and posters were everywhere.

As usual on a game day it seemed like classes took forever, and students were often caught in class not paying attention or talking too much during work time. Eventually the bell rang, and we all rushed home to finish our wait. My father had a meeting and did not get home until five thirty, which had me antsy right up until the time he walked through the door.

He had an urgency about him as well, knowing that we would want to get there early to secure parking and a good seat. He joined Pat and me in the kitchen for a quick sandwich to tide us over and we were out the door a little before six. As if he were performing a blessing before getting in the car, my father patted the lights on the Granada as he went by. These had no electronic coverings and would be visible at all times.

Despite buying it used, the Granada still had a new-car smell about it that I have always loved. We got to Ernie's house on time where he and his girlfriend waited by the door. Ernie locked the home door behind him as it appeared that he and his companion had been in the house alone.

Pat sat in the front while Ernie and his girl sat in the back with me, she being in the middle. Both new passengers said hi and thanked my father for the ride. The game was being played on a neutral court at Centereach High School, which was about thirty minutes away.

When we arrived, the parking lot was already three-quarters full, which meant a rather high fan-to-seat ratio inside. My calculations were correct as after we entered the gym there was little bleacher space remaining. Dr. Godfrey was about fifteen rows up on the near side and was waving to my father. I told him to go ahead and we would find our own friends wherever they were. Pat went with my father.

After a search, we found Gary, Virginia, and the other members of our crew in what appeared to be the main Babylon fan section. Thanks mostly to Ernie being who he was, people pushed aside and created three tight seats for us nestled down in the middle of it all. I looked around and saw that practically everyone I knew from school was here at the game.

The cheerleaders from each side were finishing up their opening routines and we all then waited for the teams to appear. Every game could be our last now, but Babylon was ready. At least I hoped so.

Too Many Fouls Make It Too Close

In organized basketball, a player can only accumulate a certain number of fouls during a game before being disqualified and can no longer play. A foul is generally some type of illegal personal contact with another player. In professional basketball a player will foul out after committing six such infractions, while in high school and college the limit is five.

Our team did look a little rusty in the first quarter against Ward Melville, particularly on defense. Stanley Davis drew the tough assignment again of guarding the other team's best player, who got off to a quick start. In trying to slow him down Stanley collected two early fouls, but Koelbel decided to keep him in the game.

Glenn and Barry Davis also picked up fouls in the opening period playing against some very physical Ward Melville big men. We were able to match them offensively, though, with Glenn and Stanley each scoring six points. Leaning on his now deeper lineup, Koelbel gave Stanley a breather and started with Chuck Farley in the second quarter.

Babylon went on a run to start the second as Glenn scored eight more points and Chuck hit a few open jump shots as the Panthers ran out to a ten-point lead.

Also, during the second quarter both Barry and Glenn picked up their second fouls and had to sit the half out on the bench. Chris Brust and Weiner came in and contributed some good play as Ward Melville was only able to whittle the lead down to eight before the break.

"The fouls are starting to add up," I said.

"Yeah, it's good we have the whole team healthy," Ernie replied.

The physical play started to take a toll on both teams with Glenn and Stanley picking up their third fouls, while Barry Davis collected his fourth and was one away from fouling out. Ward Melville was also in trouble as their sharpshooter, who was looking at a twenty-point night at his current pace, also had three fouls. But Glenn would also score eight points in the third as Babylon increased its lead to eleven.

Chris Brust started the fourth quarter for Barry Davis, but shortly into the period, Glenn picked up his fourth foul on a questionable offensive call. The Babylon fans erupted into boos but Koelbel was forced to sit Glenn for a few minutes. This gave Ward Melville an opportunity to play more aggressively, sensing Babylon's hesitancy to play hard defense. They subsequently went on a scoring run with Glenn out of the game and cut our lead to five halfway through the fourth quarter. Stanley had been carrying the offense during the quarter but then he picked up his fourth foul. At that point Koelbel made the decision to go for broke by putting all of his starters back in.

Barry Davis was forced to play less physical defense on the Ward Melville center, so they continued to pass it inside, which enabled them to cut Babylon's lead down to three points with a few minutes to go. I'm sure I wasn't alone in seeing visions of last year's first-round loss flash through my mind. Glenn had taken over the point guard duties and seemed to be playing a two-man game with Stanley, who had managed to draw a fourth foul on his defender, the Ward Melville sharpshooter.

Stanley kept driving and playing aggressively on both offense and defense. The effort paid off and with two minutes to go the Ward Melville shooter fouled out. Melville continued to play close for the remainder of the game but a three-point play by Glenn with ten seconds to go sealed a five-point win. It was a victory that was no doubt too close for comfort to many.

Our bench cleared to celebrate, but the euphoria was muted as most seemed to appreciate that a much better effort would be needed to go deeper into the tournament. The fans on both sides stood up looking almost as fatigued as the players. Koelbel shook hands with the opposing coach and retreated to the locker room shaking his head as he walked on.

"Well, a win is a win," Gary said.

Everybody nodded in agreement as we all started to make our way over to our respective cars. Ernie informed me that he would be heading home with his parents but asked if his girlfriend could drive home with us. This made me believe the earlier scenario might have been set up to get him some alone time with his girlfriend and that his parents might not have known about. Regardless, I told him that would be fine.

It was Thursday night and, seeing that we had school tomorrow, no extracurricular activities were planned. The ride home seemed shorter than the ride there as the weight of getting that first playoff victory was gone. We would probably know who we would be playing next by tomorrow morning. If not, it would be in the newspapers when I got home in the afternoon.

By the time we dropped Ernie's girlfriend off and made it home to Coppertree everyone in the house was asleep. We all followed suit as Pat and I headed upstairs to our room. Once there we changed and got into our respective twin beds, then he turned on the lamp next to his and set the alarm. We chatted a little bit before nodding off.

"Did you find anyone you knew at the game?"

"Yeah, I saw a few people at halftime but pretty much stayed with Dad and the elders to watch the game."

Pat had his group of friends but was not one to venture out. The fact that he wanted to go to a basketball game at all indicated to me that the whole school was caught up in the fever. I nodded off quickly after that. It seemed I was only asleep a few minutes before I was jarred awake by that stupid alarm playing Frankie Valli singing "My Eyes Adored You."

I guess I knew it could happen but hadn't counted on the surprise we all felt the next morning to hear that our Tuesday playoff game would be against none other than Amityville. After they fell out of contention in the League V race, many of us had somewhat put them in the rearview mirror. But here they were again turning up like a bad penny.

The mood in the hallways that day was excitement tempered by more than a little trepidation. Unlike the last time we played Amityville we would have our whole team healthy, which should give us the advantage. Although that didn't seem to matter when we played them. The rivalry ran deep, and we all knew that they were not about to lie down.

I dozed through my first few classes just waiting to get to art class and hear Mr. Bartsch's take and any latest information he might have on Amityville. I ran from my previous class to get there in time to obtain a good seat at his front art table. When I arrived, I saw that I was the first student of his class to get there, but he was in the midst of opining to a couple of starry-eyed senior girls who hung onto his every word. They had copped the best seats, but the one I grabbed was good enough.

I sat down a good minute before the bell rang.

"Muh-*kyoo*-en," he spat out. "Were you at the game last night?"

"Oh, absolutely. A little too close for comfort."

"No kidding. Now we're looking at Amityville again."

"Any idea how they played in their first two games in the playoffs?"

Since Amityville got in as a non-league champion, they had to play an extra outbracket game before the official first round.

"They crushed both of the teams they played. Won both games by about twenty points."

"So, they're back to what they were."

"Yeah, and maybe then some."

The table had filled up with other interested parties as class started. All of the chairs were taken and several people stood behind the seated to hear any details about the team. Even the two senior girls had ceased their flirting and were just listening in.

When school ended that day the five of us who had been permitted entry to the varsity practice hurried down to the East Gym to take our seats. When we arrived, Mr. Koelbel was closing the gym door despite it still being empty. He looked and saw all of our eager faces but was about to disappoint us.

"Sorry boys, no admittance today."

He must have seen the formation of the word "why" on my mouth as well as some of the others, but just held his hand up.

"I'm really sorry but you can't come today," he added. "Maybe I'll let you back in again on Monday."

That implied Saturday practice was off-limits as well. He was obviously not happy with last night's game. Resigned to our misfortune, the five of us walked dejectedly back down the hall to the gathering spot at Virginia's locker.

She was there with two of her friends talking as we all stepped up. The three of them actually laughed a bit at our forlorn expressions.

"What, did someone die?" she asked.

"No, we just can't sit in on practice," Gary answered for all of us.

"Tragedy," one of the other girls responded with a sarcastic laugh.

We all stood there for a while and talked about random things. Ernie as usual was trying to get a party together for the night. If I were going to be able to attend it would be late, as my father had alerted me earlier that we were all going out to dinner. And nobody opted out when the McKeown family did something together.

As I started to leave, Virginia tugged on my shirt sleeve to ask a question.

"Can we get a ride with you on Tuesday to the game?"

I assumed she would be going with the Farleys. I played it cool, or at least thought I had.

"Who's 'we' and how many?"

"Me, Gary, and my neighbor."

"Aren't the Farleys going?"

"Yes, but they are going very early and we'd rather go later."

I wondered to myself if they were trying to get some alone time as Ernie did on the last trip, but that notion was dispelled when she asked if they could be picked up at their separate houses. I was sure my father was anticipating me bringing some friends to the game, but the only question was whether Pat was coming. If so, we could likely only fit two.

"Let me check to see who's going from our family and I'll call or see you tomorrow."

She accepted that and said thanks as I headed home wondering what Pat's plan was.

Friday night was often pizza night at our house. Usually, we picked up a couple of pies and brought them home to eat. However, tonight my parents wanted to go out, so we booked a table at Manniello's, packed in the car, and headed into the village.

In order to accommodate the leaner nature of the Granada, Dorothy squeezed into the front between my parents while Pat, Peggy, and I sat in the back. That gave me the idea to perhaps recommend that configuration if Pat wanted to come to the game Tuesday. But I'd wait and see how that played out.

We parked behind the restaurant and used the rear entrance. The dining room was about three-quarters full when we entered, but the owner recognized my father with a smile and immediately went about constructing a table that would fit the six of us. My parents actually preferred a table of four next to a table of two so they could have their own conversation away from us. I would come to fully understand this preference when I eventually became a parent.

My father ordered a beer and my mother a glass of wine while we four had a pitcher of coke, un-spiked in this instance, of course. Mom, Dad, and Pat ordered pasta entrées while the girls and I split a large pizza. Pat no doubt figured he could steal a slice or two to complement his meal as my sisters ate like birds.

While we waited for our food, I asked Pat if he planned to go to the Amityville game. He responded he would have to think about it.

"Did you even enjoy the last one?" I asked. "You didn't seem to."

"How would you know? You were on the other side."

"Yes, with all of the other students that you didn't want to hang out with."

I sensed he didn't want to go but was perhaps angling for a trade. So, I waited for the offer.

"I'll stay home if next snowfall you do the whole driveway."

I quickly accepted as the weather had already started warming up and I seemed to always do most of the work in any case.

With the deal sealed the four of us moved the conversation to other things. Our food arrived and as I suspected Pat finished his meal and took not one but two slices from our pizza. It didn't affect me that much as the two girls barely finished one slice each. The rest of the night finished without incident, and I decided to stay in once we got home and not inquire what my school friends had cooked up.

Other than giving Virginia the green light on Saturday that her entire party could ride with us, I don't remember much else about that weekend. The focus was all on Tuesday when we would square up one more time with Amityville. If anyone had expectations for a boring game, they would be deeply disappointed.

The Run-Up

The five of us made sure to get to the Monday practice early so as not to get locked out. When we walked in Mr. Koelbel was on the court holding a basketball and bouncing it occasionally while talking to Mr. Bartsch. Koelbel had a stern look on his face, and when he saw us I was half expecting him to kick us out again. Rather, without saying a word he just pointed over to where we should sit, and we obliged.

When he saw the last player emerge from the locker room, Koelbel blew his whistle and gathered the team at midcourt for the usual start-of-practice talk. However, he spoke several minutes longer than usual. I only heard part of the speech, but it came down to, "They know us, and we know them. It's going to come down to who wants it more."

After going through the normal warm-up routines Koelbel had the team spend a lot of time on the half-court offense. He emphasized taking however long was necessary to get a good shot. He also ran a number of different configurations of players in varying positions on offense, melding Chuck Farley, Chris Brust, and Weiner in even more than usual. Perhaps the prior game's foul situation had the coach thinking he might need to go deeper into his bench and sooner. This would prove very prescient.

The additional JV players were present again and when the team practiced the press break, they wreaked lesser havoc. The offense was slowly adapting and getting the ball in more often. Koelbel again moved his three top bench players in and around with the starters to make sure they could run the play fluently.

By interval drills, the team looked pretty tired. After only ten runs the players broke to shoot their foul shots. I was not keeping track of anything on paper but paid close attention to Brian. He was still struggling and hit only five of ten as usual. His shot never seemed to have enough arc and when he missed, it died after hitting the front of the rim.

When the practice ended Koelbel yelled, "Be outside ready to go at four tomorrow!"

Then he and the players drifted up to the locker room.

My friends and I had been silent for nearly the entire three-hour practice. Ernie was the first to break the silence.

"What time does everyone plan on getting there tomorrow?"

"About an hour ahead of time," I replied for my group.

"I'll be there earlier and will try to save some seats."

The game would be played at a neutral location. Judging from the last game we were all certain that there would be a big crowd, and good seating would be at a premium.

At school the next day there was a lot of scrambling to find rides. I had to tell several people that my car had been filled up a week ago. The school didn't opt to provide a fan bus, so if you weren't heading over with an adult you weren't going. Eventually everyone I spoke to found a ride from someone or another, so Babylon would have its share of fans in attendance.

The school halls were decked out as befitting such an important game. It was all anyone could talk about in and out of class. Mr. Bartsch had so many questions yelled at him that day that he forbade anyone to speak for most of his class and turned the music way up.

I didn't see Koelbel all day and the players each had his "don't talk to me" face on. And we didn't dare.

My friends and I re-finalized our travel plans again during lunch. I gave the girls and Gary the times we would be there to pick them up. Jon Shiebler said his family planned to get there about the same time we did.

My father was home when I got there, so punctuality would not be a problem tonight. He assured me that there was enough gas in the car and that he knew the directions to where the game was being played. I was being such a pest that he finally banished me to my room until departure time.

Pat was at his desk doing homework when I walked in. He gave me a nod but was obviously deep in thought about something. I unpacked my bag and attempted to start a math assignment but just couldn't concentrate. I would just have to bear Kalfus's wrath tomorrow if he called on me.

I headed downstairs a little before five to keep my father on track. My mother was sitting in the living room reading a paperback, but my father was in his room. I joined her on the couch and checked the clock to see that we would need to leave in ten minutes.

"Is he going to be ready in time?" It was more a plea than a question.

"Give him a few more minutes and if he is not out by then I'll go get him," she responded with a smile.

My father emerged a few minutes later. He asked what we were going to do for dinner but my mother had made some sandwiches and wrapped them on two paper plates. She figured we could offer the whole gang some.

Dad grabbed a half and scarfed it down right away. I rewrapped the plate and stacked the two, one on top of the other. At that point we put our coats on and began our exit to the car. My mother gave us both a hug and wished us luck.

The sky was a dark gray as we got into the car, but the weather had been continually warming for the past few days. With the thermometer posting near fifty we no longer needed hats and gloves for short outings. When my father started the car, I checked the gas gauge. It rose to three quarters full. He gave me a sharp look as if I was questioning his honesty, so I looked away quickly.

Virginia and her friend were waiting at the door of her house when we arrived. They both hopped into the car with a smile and greeting of, "Hi, Tom. Hi, Mr. Muh-kyoo-en." Just about nobody ever got it right.

Gary was also waiting by his door when we arrived. Once we were in the driveway, he locked the house door behind and bounded down the stoop and into the car. He got in on the side where Virginia was and pushed her into the middle. Once everyone was secure my father backed out and we were on our way.

En route I passed the sandwiches around. The girls declined but Gary grabbed a few. Between the two of us and my father, we cleaned both plates.

The game was to be played at Half Hollow Hills High School, which was almost thirty minutes directly north of Babylon. If you looked at it on a map it was practically in the dead center of Long Island. Unlike the trip to Comsewogue a few weeks ago I recognized plenty of the cars along the way belonging to our Babylon friends and neighbors.

We drove up next to the Shieblers' station wagon which had a few paper signs posted to their windows reading Go Panthers and Sink the Tide. The second one didn't make much sense, but at least they were showing some spirit. As I looked around in a three-sixty fashion, I counted twelve cars of people we knew caravaning across two lanes. Many of these had signs of support as well.

I turned to my friends in the back seat with a smile and said, "It's going to be a crowded gym."

They all nodded, and I could see that the excitement level had gone up a notch. When the first car of our caravan pulled into the parking lot the driver gave a few honks on his horn, which set off a chain reaction that led to a series of honks from multiple cars announcing that Babylon fans had arrived. My father of course did not honk. It was not in his DNA.

We parked next to the Shieblers and Jon came running over to join us as we all exited the car. My father partnered up and walked over to the entrance with the Shiebler parents. The rest of the cars emptied, and we all clogged up the entrance for a few minutes as the attendant processed us through.

The gymnasium was one of the older ones still in use. It had wooden backboards and what seemed to be a smaller seating capacity than Babylon. We saw Ernie and his family on the opposite side of the gym when we walked in. He was pointing down to three rows of open-bleacher seating near him that was still available in the fast-filling gymnasium. Both parents and kids of our group hightailed it over as quickly as we could to claim them.

By the time we got seated I looked around and there did not seem to be any more availability. But the attendant kept letting people in who squeezed and cajoled their way into open segments of the bleacher in various places. We were up behind the Babylon bench. That whole side became the Babylon fan side while the other filled up just as densely with the Amityville faithful. As we all got pushed tighter and tighter together, someone wondered whether there was anyone back in the Village to keep the lights on.

As they had the last time, Amityville came out to warm up first. They were in their white uniforms, which meant they had the insignificant honor of being labeled the home team. Their fan base exploded with cheers that our side thought went on a little too long. In response our cheerleaders then began the chant, "This is Panther Country! This is Panther Country! . . ." We all joined in. The chant culminated again with our explosive cheer as Glenn led our Panthers out onto the floor.

No matter who we played, or how often we played an opponent, the Babylon opening warm-up ritual continued to have a hypnotic effect on all who watched it. Both sides quieted down for a few minutes as one by one our players bounce the ball off of that backboard. Even the Amityville players looked over in what appeared to be envy in that they did not have such a ritual in their routines.

Koelbel and Bartsch had walked out of the locker room trailing the team as usual. They split about ten feet before reaching the bench as Koelbel veered over toward the scorer's table to meet the Amityville coach for a pregame best-of-luck handshake. The two had what looked like apprehensive smiles on their faces as they spoke. No doubt they were both expecting another slugfest.

When the buzzer sounded the two teams returned to their benches. Koelbel spoke to his team as the starters took off their warm-up sweats. The starting five for both teams were the same as the last time we played. From where we sat, we could hear everything Koelbel said. He emphasized defense and waiting for the open shot, no matter how long it took.

Koelbel also indicated that if anyone felt tired to signal. He obviously planned on using every one of his top eight players this evening. When the team broke, Koelbel lightly grabbed Chuck Farley by the neck and directed him to the seat immediately on his left, indicating to me that Chuck would get lots of play and possibly very quickly.

The starters made their way to the center of the court and for the last time in several of their basketball careers gave their opponents a pregame handshake. Everything was on the line at this point. Each team had escaped with a two-point victory at home in the League season. The winner here would leave with a chance to be the first champion of all of Long Island, while the other would have their season ended.

The players all then moved to their respective starting positions. The teams' knowledge of the rules and of each other required little separation or movement by the officials. The lead referee surveyed the ten players one last time before moving between the two centers with the ball extended. The moment was riveting. Then after a short pause the official blew his whistle and tossed the ball up to start the game.

The Thrilla with the Villa

Sports historians often analyze the trio of fights between Muhammad Ali and Joe Frazier. They were all very close, with each winning one of the first two. Both knew the winner of the third would be remembered as the better and perhaps the greatest boxer of all time. Although the final may not have been the closest mathematically of the three—mainly because it didn't go the distance—it is remembered as the most heroic. The fight would be forever labeled the "Thrilla in Manila" because the two fighters slugged it out until both nearly dropped.

The third Babylon–Amityville game had the virtue of being both the closest and the most heroic. As the evening started and the Babylon fans crowded over to our side of the gym behind the team's bench, I had a small sense of confidence. After all, we had beaten them last time with a diminished squad. Now we had our whole roster available. Surely that would add to our margin of victory.

That small feeling of confidence dissipated after the starting lineups were introduced and I was reminded of how big and tough Amityville looked. Also, if there was an award for most fearsome game faces, I thought they would surely win. Our guys looked sure of themselves as well, but after the Koelbel-enforced private practices, I was sure they were not going in overconfident.

Amityville won the opening tip and scored the game's first basket. Babylon answered shortly after when Stanley Davis hit a short jump shot from the left side. The teams then traded baskets for the rest of the quarter with Babylon leading at the end of the first break by two points.

However, in the second quarter, Amityville somehow managed to stymie our offense by packing the inside and double-teaming Glenn at every opportunity. Stanley Davis single-handedly managed to keep Babylon in the game by continually finding small cracks in Amityville's defense and hitting mid-range jump shots.

Amityville continued to press their advantage, though, with Paul Smith getting a hot hand and scoring eight points in the quarter. When halftime arrived, Babylon trailed by six, with the Amityville fans and their sidelines whipped into a fury. They could smell revenge. As the teams went to the locker rooms for the break, our side was as quiet as it had been in months.

"What are they doing differently?" someone in our group asked.

"It's not them; we can't hit our shots," Ernie answered. "Thank God for Stanley."

My stomach was in too much of a knot to grab any food at halftime. I just sat there amongst everyone thinking, but not saying, *Is Amityville going to do it to us again?*

Well, it was not as if the team hadn't hit adversity before. Hopefully Koelbel would again come up with something at halftime to get us back on track. When both teams emerged for the second-half warm-ups, the coach was walking and talking with Glenn and Gervais Barger. He was possibly discussing some strategy toward the Amityville guards.

Babylon managed to steal the second-half tip as Amityville center Mark Jenkins tapped the ball backward toward Smith, but Gervais anticipated the path and intercepted the ball. Our first set play of the third quarter was run perfectly with Glenn getting an easy inside layup. Amityville answered with a quick bucket of their own from forward Tony Boyce, but on their next two possessions, they forced up missed shots.

I couldn't quite tell what we were doing differently, but the offense seemed to be back in gear. Glenn was getting open shots and getting to the foul line, and midway through the period, Chuck Farley had been inserted into the game and had nailed two open jump shots. Amityville didn't crumble by any means, but by the end of the third quarter, we had cut the lead back down to two points.

As the teams marched back out for the final quarter the announcer recapped the foul situation for both teams. Stanley Davis, Barry Davis, and Gervais Barger all had three fouls for Babylon. Meanwhile, Amityville center Mark Jenkins, forward Mike Sullivan, and guard Mike Voliton all had four for Amityville. This might end up being a war of attrition, I thought.

The flow of the game remained the same through most of the fourth quarter. Every time it seemed as if we were about to tie the game, Amityville would answer with a steal or rebound that would result in points. Smith and Voliton kept getting foul shots and sinking them with ease.

Then, with a minute and a half left, Stanley Davis hit a jump shot to cut the Amityville lead to two. But as Babylon was pressing on the inbound pass, Glenn stole the ball. He missed his shot, but Gervais Barger picked up the rebound and was fouled. Not only did Gervais connect on the two foul shots to tie the game, but Amityville center Mark Jenkins fouled out on the play. This was the first big exit of a player.

Amityville brought the ball up slowly on their next possession, seeming from my view to be holding the ball for the last shot. Then on an attempted post pass by Smith, Brian Vickers, who had been somewhat quiet so far, jumped in and stole the ball. Now it was Babylon who walked the ball slowly up the court playing for the last shot.

Glenn went one-on-one for the remainder of the period and seemed to break free for an open shot with only seconds remaining. We were all on our feet certain it would drop, but the ball rattled out as the buzzer sounded.

The game was heading to overtime.

Although we were all disappointed with Glenn's miss, in hindsight it seemed only right that these two teams would have to dig deeper before a winner emerged. In high school basketball during the seventies, overtime was only three minutes. The teams would now play as many extra three-minute sessions as it took to determine a winner.

Babylon should have had the upper hand going into overtime as in addition to Mark Jenkins, both Mike Sullivan and Mike Voliton had fouled out for

Amityville. Babylon had not lost anyone, but Stanley Davis, Barry Davis, and Gervais Barger had all picked up their fourth fouls. This meant they each had only one more foul to give before also being disqualified.

Amityville apparently didn't see themselves at a disadvantage as they took the initiative right away in the overtime by scoring the first basket and holding on to the lead for most of the extra session. Then, with less than two minutes to go, Gervais would foul out by hacking Babylon's archnemesis, Paul Smith. It had prevented an easy layup but sent Smith to the foul line needing to make only one shot to guarantee a tie, and two to send Babylon home for good.

If you have played enough basketball in your life there are certain sounds that you never forget. One is the beautiful *swish!* or *woosh!* of a ball passing smoothly through the net of the basket. The second is the deadly *thud* of a missed ball hitting lifelessly against the rim. The third and possibly most wrenching of all is the sound of a ball that rattles around for a few tenths of a second before either falling in or out. The sound is like a *bu-bu-bu-bunk*.

I could only see the back of Paul Smith's head from where I was sitting as he put up his seemingly perfect foul shot that I feared was arcing slowly toward a sure swish. But the ball ended up going a little too far and hit the back of the rim. From there it rattled back and forth twice within the rim for a few gripping moments. Then, like a kitten or puppy crawling out of a box, it snuck over the outside and fell to the floor. He'd missed. The crowds on both sides exhaled. The next shot gained more importance as a miss would give Babylon a chance to win. Again, I was unable to see his face, so it was hard to gauge how the first missed shot had affected Smith. However, as the official handed him the ball for his second shot, I did notice that his ritual was not the same as with the first, nor any of the several other foul shots he had taken that night. He rushed it by taking only one dribble, barely making a spin in his hands, before pushing off a quick shot. This one made the *thud* sound and the ball was pulled down by Brian Vickers, who immediately called time out.

"Holy crap, I'm going to have a heart attack," one of the adults near us shouted.

I grabbed Ernie around his shoulders from behind as everyone seemed to look for someone else to hug. We hadn't been paying much attention to the huddle, but the reality was we still needed to score in some fashion either to win or send the game into a second overtime. It was no mystery to anyone in the gym that Babylon wanted Glenn to take that shot.

There were twelve seconds left on the clock. The ball was moved up to half-court for the inbound where Glenn would throw the ball in and then hopefully collect it back from Chuck Farley, who was now the other guard as Stanley Davis had fouled out as well. The inbound went according to plan as Glenn connected to Chuck in the backcourt but no sooner had the pass been made than did two Amityville players converge on Glenn. Seeing no lane to get it back to Glenn, Chuck pushed forward toward the basket. When an Amityville player rushed toward him, Chuck hit an open Brian Vickers down on the block. As Brian went up for what seemed an easy layup, Amityville forward Tony Boyce came out of nowhere with a hard foul that knocked Brian to the ground and the ball with him.

It was Boyce's fourth foul, but I doubt he regretted the move in that moment. Brian had missed his last four foul shots and was likely not the person Koelbel or most of us wanted on the line. Between my past observations and what I'd seen all season, Brian was usually fifty percent from the line. Amityville probably liked their odds.

The Amityville coach called time-out to freeze Brian. We all listened in as Koelbel used a positive-reinforcement technique to stoke Brian's confidence. He discussed only what the team should do *after* Brian makes both foul shots. Glenn was next to his brother in the huddle with his arm around him.

As the teams broke back out onto the floor the other Babylon teammates all gave Brian a word of confidence and a pat on the rump. I thought of the irony that this shy young man with outlandish physical abilities now had all our hopes on his shoulders. In a minute he would be judged hero or scapegoat. The Amityville fans began to yell and jeer to distract him.

We could all see Brian's face at this end. His eyes looked down while waiting for the players of both teams to take their designated positions in the lane and behind him. The minutes of wait were long for us but must have seemed like forever to Brian.

When the referee backed up to hand the ball to Brian the noise from the Amityville side grew louder and louder. As Brian spread his large hands across the ball, I thought I saw a moment of doubt and was dismayed. When the first shot went up it looked low and showed no arc at all. The ball hit the front rim hard and almost crawled up and rolled over it. But instead, it fell backwards and hit the floor for a miss.

The Amityville side cheered but Glenn clenched his fist and walked over to affectionately grasp his brother's head and pull it close to his own. You didn't have to be down there to know Glenn was saying, "Come on. You can do this."

The second time the official gave Brian the ball he looked up higher than he had the first time, perhaps grasping what had gone wrong with the first shot. When he let go of the ball this time it sailed with a beautiful arc. Nobody could hear the *swish* sound as the Babylon side erupted just when the ball cleared the rim and dropped through the basket. We were all embracing each other and jumping up and down as Amityville quickly inbounded that ball and tried a desperate, full-length shot at the buzzer that carried wide and short of the basket. We were going to a second overtime.

Both teams at this point were deep into their benches. Barry Davis had fouled out for Babylon midway through the overtime and been replaced by Chris Brust. Amityville had not lost any additional players to the three that had left during regulation.

The second three-minute overtime didn't see much scoring. Amityville's remaining big man Tony Boyce scored on a short jumper to put them up by two. On the next play from our end Chris Brust converted a layup to tie the score. Then Amityville had a chance to retake the lead when a newly inserted bench player went to the foul line with a minute to go. However, he missed both shots.

Glenn grabbed the rebound and took the ball up court. He eyed the clock and was obviously looking to take the last shot again with too little time remaining for Amityville to respond. Smith was covering Glenn with the other guard cheating over whenever he got near the foul lane. When the clock read ten seconds to go Glenn made his move to the lane.

Glenn tried a pump fake but Smith stayed put right in his face. The other guard had broken toward Glenn to assist. This left Chuck Farley wide open for a jump shot. Glenn rifled the ball over and Chuck squared up to launch a shot as the buzzer sounded. The ball sailed through the net. The Babylon side erupted in cheers, but our joy was short-lived.

The head referee came running toward the scorer's table waving his arms and mouthing the words "No basket." Koelbel ran out immediately to confront the official as the Amityville coach and players were clapping and nodding their heads as if no other call could have been made. Koelbel's words and demonstrative antics of course had no impact on the referee's call. And since there was no instant replay, we were onto a third overtime.

As our coach headed back to the bench for yet another plan and pep talk to his team, I could hear the derisive words being shouted at the referee from our fans. "You're f----g blind!" "How much are they paying you?!" "What kind of idiot are you?!"

Ernie leaned backwards and whispered to me too low for anyone else to hear, "I didn't think he got it off in time either."

I agreed by just nodding my head, not being able to mouth those words myself.

We listened again as Koelbel was telling the team that upon winning the center tap this time we would hold the ball for the entire three-minute overtime. Then once again Glenn would try and get off the final shot or draw a foul. Chris Brust had three inches on Tony Boyce, who was now jumping center for Amityville, so our coach seemed certain that we would again win the tap.

When Chris Brust took up the center position at midcourt, he was flanked by the two Vickers brothers and the two Farley brothers. Weiner had been inserted when Stanley Davis fouled out. The five of them would try and play keep-away for one hundred and seventy seconds. The referee tossed the ball up and Chris did control the tap, pushing the ball back to Glenn.

Babylon continued running the 2-3 but in a stall mode with Glenn dribbling around and eating up the clock. Amityville surprisingly stayed back in their zone defense, which allowed Babylon to keep the ball in the hands of its best foul shooters, Glenn and Chuck Farley.

When the clock again got down to ten seconds Glenn managed to break past Smith and get to the lane; a reserve forward for Amityville arrived to cover him and Glenn made his signature move. He gave a head fake, wherein the Amityville player went sailing into the air enabling Glenn to lean in and make contact as he shot. The referee's whistle blew as the ball bounced off the rim. Our star player was heading to the line with two shots to win the game. The Babylon stands were rocking.

The Amityville coach had one time-out left but decided not to waste it trying to freeze Glenn. Apparently, he thought it would be better used after Glenn shot, as a time-out called then would advance the ball to half-court for the throw-in. Right now, however, all eyes were on our main man at the foul line.

Our fans were silent this time as the Amityville people yelled and jeered to try and distract Glenn as the referee gave him the ball. He did his ritual of bouncing the ball and looking up, then bouncing it again and locking in on the basket. Even with all the Amityville noise I could hear the *woosh!* as the ball sailed through the net. Then our side erupted at our one-point lead.

I hugged my dad, I hugged Ernie, the girls, everybody. But it wasn't over yet. The referee gave the ball back to Glenn and after the same deliberate steps he shot what looked like another perfect ball, but this one rattled out. Boyce grabbed the rebound and he immediately called time-out. Amityville would have one last chance.

We all listened in again to Koelbel's huddle as he emphasized not to foul. Amityville's best two remaining weapons were Smith and Boyce, who both had scored over twenty points. If Smith threw the ball in there would not be enough time to get it back to him for a shot. Chris would guard the inbound pass to limit visibility. Glenn would guard Boyce, but Brian would guard the next closest player and cheat over as much as he could to help.

The huddles broke and the players took the court once again. When everyone was in place Smith was indeed set to throw the ball in. He was in front of where we were sitting and near the midcourt line. When Chris Brust stepped in front of him, I could barely see the rest of the court and could only imagine Smith's view.

The referee blew his whistle and handed the ball to Smith. The official began counting to five with extended hand gesturing. On the third count Smith tried to throw over Chris, who batted the ball away. No time had run off the clock as the referee retrieved the ball to hand to Smith and again whistled and began counting.

This time Smith faked a high pass that got Chris to jump. Then he threw the ball side-armed on a beeline toward Boyce. The ball seemed to have eyes as it bypassed several outstretched arms, including Brian's, who didn't quite get over to help in time. Boyce grasped the ball uncomfortably close to the low block in good position for a short turnaround jumper. It wasn't an easy shot but definitely makeable.

I stared in horror with everyone and thought to myself, *Not again.*

What Next?

Memories play out in slow motion, which is often at odds with the speed at which they transpired in reality. As I remember Boyce receiving Smith's pass, in my mind it seemed an easy catch, turn, and shoot. However, there were only two seconds left on the clock, which actually meant less than two seconds as the electronic scoreboards of those days did not show tenths of a second.

Bearing that in mind, the Amityville star barely had enough time to touch and grasp the ball before pushing it toward the basket. And when he turned to shoot, Glenn's hand was right in his face.

The result?

The hurried shot barely hit the low corner of the backboard and fell away harmlessly without getting near the rim.

And time expired.

We all regained our breath as the Babylon bench had already stormed the court while several of the Amityville players had dropped to their knees with their heads in their hands in an apparent combination of despair and exhaustion. I watched as Koelbel leaned half over by the scorer's table to collect himself before walking toward his opponent for the final coaches' handshake of a game that neither team deserved to lose. After twelve quarters and three overtimes what separated Babylon from Amityville was a single point.

For several minutes everyone in the Babylon stands was hugging each other and jumping up and down. It once again felt like the bleachers were going to break. I turned to my father who just wiped his brow and said, "Jesus."

After celebrating amongst ourselves, many of the students in the stands rushed down to the railing separating the bleachers from the court in hopes of touching or getting a "five" with one of the players. The celebration on the court continued for a while, but eventually when the players came back to get their sweats and whatever was left around the bench, we all got a brief touch of somebody. Then the team ran off the court to the locker room entry on the other side of the gym. Eventually the noise and craziness began to calm down.

I watched across the way as the remaining Amityville fans filed out. They were orderly and respectful as I believe we had been when they took the football championship from us in the fall. It seemed like another lifetime ago. Finally, it was time to collect everyone and head for home.

"Man, has anyone stopped shaking?" I asked.

"That was just unbelievable," Virginia said.

I asked Gary if he was coming home with us. He said that he would remain with his family but the girls wanted to get home sooner and said they wanted to go with us. My father was fine with that. I caught him as he was still talking to Mr. Farley, Mr. Conroy, Dr. Godfrey, and others. All were still shaking their heads in disbelief.

Once we got in the car it took a while to get out of the parking lot as there was a myriad of people still mulling around talking. They stood in driving lanes meshed with all of the cars pulling out of their spots. When we did get onto the road the car got pretty quiet as both Virginia and her friend fell asleep in the back seat, while Dad and I continued to rehash moments in the game up front.

"I thought we were dead so many times," I said to him.

"Yeah, if we didn't have everybody back and healthy it probably would have gone the other way."

I liked how he now referred to the Babylon team as "we" or "us." West Islip and his city teams were now firmly behind in his rooting preferences. I would never have to ask if he wanted to go to a game again. He was as invested as I was in Babylon's success.

I had to wake both girls when we got back to their respective houses. Each mumbled what sounded like a thank you as my father dropped them off individually and waited for each to get into their houses and close the door behind them. Then we turned toward Coppertree.

Nobody was awake when we got home, but after I snuck quietly up to my room, I heard Pat's voice as soon as I walked in.

"Did we win?"

"By one point in triple overtime!"

"No kidding."

"Yeah, you missed the greatest high school basketball game in history."

"I thought you were gone longer than normal."

"I'll give you the rundown tomorrow, but right now I'm about to pass out."

Minutes after my head hit the pillow, I was asleep.

We barely made it to school on time the next day as all of the high-school-aged kids on our block clumped together while we made the morning walk up to BHS. All anyone could do was talk about and retell portions of the game in as much detail as they could remember. Then they would remark on how they thought we were done for or how an incredible play had saved the day. I relived every one of them as they were told.

I was literally just sitting down when the bell rang to start the school day. My homeroom was still loudly buzzing about the game, which induced the teacher to raise her voice several times to get everyone quiet and in their seat. She did manage to get us all settled down before the morning announcements began.

The announcements of course started with a brief but still thrilling recap of the game, which led to a cheer that emanated from every classroom in the building. That was followed by the news that we would be facing the defending county champion Central Islip on Saturday at Ward Melville. It would be my first time seeing what I had heard was the largest high school gymnasium on Long Island.

Mr. Kalfus tossed me out of his classroom that morning because I had not even attempted the homework that he had given out the prior day. He said he didn't care about basketball and wished me well as a future server at McDonald's. I knew he would let me back in tomorrow and only hoped the news did not reach my father. Dad was as much a disciplinarian as Kalfus and might ground me, but at this point he was not going to miss any more basketball games.

As I stood against the door in the hallway, I noticed the vice principal of the school berating another student who had been caught roaming the halls without a pass. During his tirade another student walked by and the vice principal sternly asked him to show his pass before letting him proceed. When he glanced over at me, I pointed behind at my classroom to indicate I was attached to that room, and he returned to his lecture of the first student.

At that moment I saw Glenn strolling down the hall in our direction. He was resplendent in a full-length overcoat covering his jeans and shirt with a bright pair of white Converse sneakers on his feet. As he got closer, I saw the vice principal look up and assumed he would ask for Glenn's pass. However, when he looked up and saw our star walk by, a smile broke across his face as he said, "Hi, Glenn, great game last night."

Unfazed, Glenn just kept walking. When he saw me, he reached out and patted my arm and gave me a wink. Babylon was pretty strict about not letting students roam the halls without a pass, but apparently Glenn had earned a little leeway this season.

I saw him again at lunch that day sitting at the senior table, despite being a junior. He was taking plaudits along with Gervais Barger and Stanley Davis. There wasn't a person, including those at our eighth grade table, who could speak about anything but the Amityville game that day. That would all change in the afternoon once Koelbel convened the day's practice.

Mr. Koelbel continued to let our little group attend the practices in silence every afternoon. Without asking permission we stealthily moved to the other side of the gym in hopes of hearing more from the coach's center-court huddles. The move paid off from the beginning as Koelbel's voice became much more audible to us.

The coach told the team it's now time to look forward. Central Islip (CI) were the defending champions. They had started the season slow but made it into the tournament through the outbracket. On the same night we had defeated Amityville they had knocked off the tournament's number one seed, Brentwood. CI would not be easy. They liked to fast-break and full-court press. And that was how we were going to beat them, Koelbel said.

The team spent half of the practice working on the press break, but continuing the play all the way through to the offensive set up. Koelbel emphasized that the inbound passer had five seconds to throw the ball in, and once the ball was inbounded the team had ten seconds to get it over half-court. That would be fifteen seconds on defense. Once over half-court, Koelbel stressed that the team needed to be patient. He wanted them to run the offense back and forth several times before shooting to tire them down. By the second half he anticipated CI would be out of gas.

My friends and I sat and watched as time and again the team ran the press offense. Eventually it got to the point where the offense was beating the seven-man defensive team on every inbound pass. I felt sympathy for the reserve players as again playing defense for hours on end was not the most fun part of the practice. But Koelbel knew that's how players felt and was counting on CI feeling the same way on Saturday.

I went right home after practice to make sure I had enough time to do both the previous and current days of homework, particularly math. Not doing assignments felt wrong to me, and I did want to make up for my incomplete items. So, I got to Kalfus's class early the next day and handed the previous assignment to him directly.

"What's this?" he asked while leaning down on his desk and peering over his glasses at me.

"Yesterday's assignment. It was disrespectful to not have it done."

"It's not for me, you know, it's for you. I assume you want to go to college."

"Yes, I just was at the triple-overtime game and was too tired when I got home."

"Why does that matter? You're never going to play basketball."

"I already do," I replied defensively. "Besides, there is school spirit even if I didn't."

He just shook his head as I walked away in frustration. I thought he would appreciate the game of basketball since it did incorporate a smattering of mathematics into its strategy. Apparently, I was wrong.

I wouldn't let my schoolwork slip again that year, but my basketball enthusiasm didn't waver either. Since the game was on Saturday in the afternoon, the school chartered another fan bus for any students who were without a means of getting there. As a result, I had no requests for rides until late Friday.

Pat had decided that he would attend the game, so I had two seats to spare. The Vickers, Farleys, Conroys, and Shieblers were all going. Virginia was going with the Farleys and the other girls were taking the fan bus. I was surprised when Joey Jaffie knocked on our door that evening and asked us for a ride. Apparently, he had come home from college for the weekend and the game. I was happy to reciprocate for all the other occasions where he'd helped me out in the same way. He asked for his younger brother and himself, so between the two of them our car was now full.

Mr. Koelbel was apparently happy with practices that week and had decided to give the team Friday off. If there was anything social going on that night I didn't hear about it, so I just stayed in for another dinner of pizza and watching television with my family. Nobody approached the house that night, so Max sat silently between my mother and me on the couch while I stroked his head.

The game tomorrow was scheduled for a two o'clock start. There was another semifinal game that would begin right after ours. I was hoping to convince my father to stay for that one but I doubted Pat would go for it. I understood that not everyone could sit through five hours of basketball. Maybe I could hitchhike home with another family.

I was also very anxious to see the giant Ward Melville gymnasium I'd kept hearing about. I was at last able to convince my father to leave at noon so we could get there a little early and walk around. He said he had been there for a conference once before but had not seen the inside of the gymnasium.

There was a lot to look forward to as the game approached. However, there would be one additional bonus from attending that I had not anticipated. One that would delight a basketball fan who would talk to anyone.

The Big Gym

We pulled into a half-filled Ward Melville parking lot a little before one o'clock and easily found a space in close proximity to the main entrance. Joey Jaffie sat in the front while I was flanked by Pat and Joey's younger brother in the back seat. Just as we were getting out of the car, we could hear in the near distance the growing sound of the Panther cheer.

I turned toward the entry driveway we had just used coming into the parking lot. There I looked just in time to see the yellow-and-black school fan bus pulling in with people hanging out of the windows yelling, "This is Panther Country! This is Panther Country!" Right on the tail of the bus was the caravan of Babylon faithful that had continued to grow in number with every win. The bus pulled up next to us while the dozen or so cars pulled in one by one into every space to its left in what felt like almost military precision.

Rather than hurry inside to secure seats, we waited to join with any newly arrived friends while my father also connected with some of the parents. It seemed all about community now as opposed to every man for himself. Once we were all grouped together, the big crowd bulled our way over to the entrance.

It was the first Saturday of March and the sun was out, but there was still a chill in the air with the temperature a little over fifty degrees. Once we settled into line and after waiting five minutes to be admitted, I did start to worry about getting a good seat. I looked around and realized that there must be at least seventy people in the queue just from Babylon. My fear, however, would be allayed once we got inside.

The Ward Melville gymnasium lived up to the hype and had to be twice the size of Babylon's East Gym. The court was of course the same size, but everything else was two to three times as large as what we were used to seeing. It had longer sets of bleachers that also went a few rows higher than ours. Blocks of people could walk behind the baskets and the back walls without stepping on the court as opposed to single-filing it as we had to in the East Gym. It also looked like there was about twenty feet from the railing of the bleachers to the benches, and then another five feet to the court. The place was huge by high school standards.

I had been to a few professional basketball games before and had seen more populated games. However, I couldn't have imagined a high school playing somewhere this incredible all of the time. It was probably a good stepping-stone to whomever moved on to play in the Nassau Coliseum.

We found satisfactory seats quickly enough. Our group sat behind the bench, but as the court was further away, we sat several rows closer up than normal to get a better view. The adults were in a clump right next to a larger group of students. I was wedged in between my father and Pat but behind Gary, Virginia, Ernie, and his latest girl. The distance and the acoustics were such that we would not be able to hear anything going on inside the huddle as we did in the Amityville game.

I looked at the clock and judged we still had twenty or so minutes before the teams came out for warm-ups, so I perused the continually growing crowds. The place would eventually fill up as both semifinal games would be played here today. Each would have their own dedicated fan base in tow.

As my gaze wandered around, I caught site of a familiar little man coming through the main entrance. He was surrounded by several people whispering in his ear while others rushed up to shake his hand. Eventually, I recognized him and tapped Ernie on the shoulder.

"Hey, that's Lou Carnesecca."

After looking over and squinting a little Ernie replied, "You're right."

Lou Carnesecca was the head coach of basketball at St. John's University. He had also been the head coach of the New York Nets of the American Basketball Association (ABA) just a few years prior. Word started circulating amongst the stands that college coaches were in attendance scouting the talent. Before the players would come out, I spotted Denny Crum, who was the head coach at Louisville University, and Lefty Driesell, the head coach at the University of Maryland. As a big fan of college basketball, I would attempt to hunt all of those coaches down after the game.

As we sat and waited out the minutes before the game I looked over and saw Gary had his arm around Virginia's waist. I was resigned to the fact she was lost to me. When I turned back, I saw that my brother was staring at me.

"What?" I said.

"Nothing. Just making sure you're okay."

"Okay? I'm at the county semifinal basketball game. I'm great."

I was too proud to admit any disappointments to my brother or anyone else close to my age. I would definitely not confess to someone who might act too sympathetic and embarrass me further.

The bleachers continued to fill up at a steady pace. The Central Islip faithful were out in full force. As it stood, this was their title, and we were going to have to take it away from them. I saw one big handwritten banner with their school's purple-and-gold lettering that read, REIGNING SUFFOLK COUNTY BASKETBALL CHAMPIONS.

Our cheerleaders came out first doing cartwheels and backflips and whipping us into cheers. Their routine culminated with their typical pyramid. The CI cheerleaders had their routine cut short as the teams queued up simultaneously, coming out of their respective locker rooms. This caused our stands to start stomping our feet, clapping our hands, and yelling out our chant. Our opposing fans responded with something similar, but it was too loud to make out what they were saying.

Then both teams took the floor for warm-ups and the fan bases erupted in applause. As usual, our opponents broke immediately into layups while Glenn lead the Panthers out in our mesmerizing backboard ritual. As usual it caused a few of our opponents' heads to turn in wonder.

Babylon would start the game at the basket that was nearest to where we were sitting and closest to their own bench. As the teams warmed up people continued filing into the gymnasium, and to my eventual astonishment the exceedingly large sets of bleachers there at Ward Melville began to reach capacity. As at the Amityville game in that much smaller gym, we had to squish in against each other. It was my luck that I was between two guys.

A little while after Babylon broke into normal layups, Glenn huddled at the foul line with Gervais Barger and Stanley Davis. He was both speaking with them and pointing toward the CI team. Obviously sketching out some possible game actions.

The players on both sides seemed to be oblivious to the college coaches in attendance. I watched the Central Islip players warm up. They weren't a big team but looked very athletic as they cruised in for layups adding some individual flare. Their reputation was to play fast and press hard for most of the game. It looked like they had the players to do it. The biggest question was whether or not we could wear them out. From viewing our practices, I knew that Koelbel was willing to go deep into his bench to do that.

Finally, the buzzer sounded, and the teams returned to their seats. The starting lineups for both teams were announced one by one as the players jogged to the closest foul circle to remain until all ten players' names were called. Babylon continued with the starting five of Glenn and Brian Vickers, Stanley Davis and Barry Davis, and Gervais Barger.

When the teams returned to their final huddles before the tap, the starters removed their sweats while listening intently to their coaches' final words. Koelbel bent into the huddle while speaking; I tried to guess what he was saying as he emphasized things with his hands. He wore the same maroon jacket as always. My father had learned that the coach didn't particularly care for the garment. He had originally worn it in case a brawl broke out during a game, as it was a coat he didn't care about ripping. Now it was different. Out of superstition he wasn't going to change anything amidst the current win streak.

As the starters made their way onto the floor, Koelbel again made sure Chuck Farley was seated right next to him, followed by Chris Brust, and "Weiner" Farley. The players all shook hands before the referee tossed the ball up. Central Islip won the tap and went first on offense.

Babylon immediately went into a pressure man-to-man half-court defense. After a few passes Central Islip was able to work the ball to one of their big men and score the first basket of the game. Then they immediately went into their full-court press. Glenn grabbed the ball to throw it inbounds.

In what may have been a surprise to our coach and team, Central Islip opted not to cover Glenn while he was trying to throw the ball inbounds. This allowed an extra defender to float between Gervais and Stanley to double-team whoever might be picked off. Glenn grimaced as he looked for an open man but did not get the ball inbounds before the referee called a five-second violation. This gave the ball back to CI under their own basket.

After a quick inbounds pass one of the Central Islip players hit a ten-foot jump shot and we were down four. They went into their press again, but Gervais was able to break free and receive the outbounds pass, which he shot back to the open Glenn to take up court. The open defender then went back to press Glenn, who methodically used as much time as possible to get the ball up.

Babylon worked the ball around a few times in the 2-3 offense before Stanley Davis sprung open to the left of the foul line and scored Babylon's first two points on a jump shot. However, Central Islip quickly inbounded the ball and rushed up court ahead of our defenders for another quick score. Then they went into their press again.

The referee's hand count was at four when Glenn threw the ball into Gervais, but after he caught the ball, the open defender surprised him and slapped it off Gervais's feet. It went out of bounds to Central Islip. At that point Koelbel had seen enough and called a time-out.

"Damn, their press is killing us," someone on our side stated, demonstrating a knack for the obvious.

"We need to slow things down," Ernie said in a quieter tone.

"You're right about that," my father responded as much to himself than to us.

I imagine that everyone agreed with the diagnosis. We all watched Koelbel as he demonstrably spoke with the team while using his two index fingers to point in opposite directions in order to illustrate some sort of play. The players nodded in assent before the referee whistled and they all headed back out onto the court.

Central Islip inbounded the ball, but another pass inside resulted in a shot being swatted away by our center, Barry Davis. This brought the Babylon crowd back to life as Gervais recovered the ball and pushed it up court before the Central Islip players could react. He was about to set up the offense but then caught Brian Vickers streaking along the opposite side and hit him with a bullet pass that the freshman laid in to cut the Central Islip lead to two.

The next time Central Islip scored and put on their press, we got to see Koelbel's adjustment. In what is a legal play, when Glenn was handed the ball by the official, Gervais broke to his right, dragging the two defenders with him. However, rather than stop inbounds, he continued beyond the endline. His defenders looked befuddled and did not follow him out. Glenn passed Gervais the ball at this point, then stepped inbounds with no defender on him to receive a pass back.

This got a reaction from both crowds. The Babylon side shook their heads, wondering what had just happened, while the CI faithful yelled, "Illegal!" Regardless, Glenn then pushed the ball up quickly. Lacking a defender, he dribbled the ball all the way to the basket for a layup that tied the score.

Babylon ran the play a few more times until Central Islip eventually adjusted and had a man guard Glenn on the inbound. We began to beat the press more easily, but they kept using it and trying to up-tempo the game. When the buzzer sounded for half time, the score was tied.

Fatigue and Crisis

Partly due to not wanting to lose my seat I didn't go hunting for the college coaches at halftime. Lefty Driesell was the only one of significant height and so I could see him from where I was sitting. He was under the far basket with a small group around him signing autographs. The other two might have been outside in the hallways but weren't visible. I figured they would be staying for the second game as well, so I would find them between games.

When the two teams emerged for the second half it was hard to tell during warm-ups if either side looked more worn than the other. Koelbel had used his three main substitutes amply in the first half. Chris Brust got a lot of time at center as Barry Davis had collected his third foul midway through the second quarter.

The game stayed tight through most of the third as Central Islip stuck with their full-court press, but Babylon gradually started beating it more easily. Glenn would pass the ball to Gervais Barger, who would most often give it right back and let our star grind down his defenders. Babylon burst out to a seven-point lead with a run at the end of the third quarter as Central Islip shots started falling short, evidence of tired legs.

Then we opened the fourth quarter with a nine-to-nothing run that put the game out of reach. With about three minutes to go somebody on our side of the bleachers started singing the song verse, "*Nah-nah nah nah, nah-nah nah nah, hey, hey, hey, goodbyyye!*" Before long we were all standing along with the cheerleaders and singing it to the chagrin of the CI faithful, who had started exiting the building.

With a minute to go Mr. Koelbel pulled the starters out one by one. They all got standing ovations to a man. I could see the college coaches writing in their notebooks when Glenn came off the floor to the biggest applause. The team had done it. They were on their way to the Nassau Coliseum to play for the championship. First for Suffolk County and then maybe for all of Long Island.

We all went down to the bottom of the bleachers but were too far away to get any connection with the players. Without checking with my father, I exited the bleachers to look for the college coaches. The first I found was Lefty Driesell. He gave me an autograph and said something that I could not even begin to make out due to his thick accent.

When I spoke to Lou Carnesecca, he was like an Italian version of Mr. Jaffie. He would talk to you and pat you on the cheek. I could picture him with a white apron, slicing deli meat and asking my mother about how her day was going.

I didn't get close to Denny Crum as he seemed to be outside smoking cigarettes all the time. But I had gotten two out of the three, which was good enough. So, I headed back to my seat to see that very few people had left. I had an argument with Pat, who wanted to leave right away while I wanted to stay to see the team come out and to watch the second game. My father brokered a truce that we would stay until halftime.

I asked around to see if anyone was staying for the whole second game but could not find anyone who had room in their car. The fan bus had already started loading up shortly after our game had ended, so I was stuck going the way I came.

My father had moved down to the bottom of the bleachers and was talking with Mr. Conroy and Dr. Godfrey while Pat stood quietly with the Jaffie brothers, who were going on about something. I was talking with Gary, Virginia, and some of the others, but Ernie had disappeared. He emerged a short while later to give us his always relied-upon social update.

"There is a party tonight around the corner from my house," he started. "It will get going around nine."

"That was fast," I said.

"Yeah, I think they were planning on only having it if we won."

I wondered whether it would be a parentless party but wasn't going to ask.

The second game got underway a half hour after the first had ended. We would be playing the winner, so many people had stayed to see at least part of the contest. The combatants were Sachem and Harborfields. Both teams looked very big and very white. It was hard to judge but from my vantage point it looked like each team had two or three players taller than our center, Barry Davis.

The score was close at the end of the first quarter, but the focus of our fans shifted when the Babylon players emerged from the locker room all showered and dressed in their fineries. They looked like a rock band in their suits. We stood to give them another round of applause as they moved into our seating area. Mr. Bartsch was with them, but Koelbel must still have been up in the locker room.

Brian made his way over to where we were while Glenn took up residence amidst a passel of upperclassmen girls. The rest spread out to their families or different friend sets. We all were patting Brian on the back and congratulating him. Brian had quietly emerged as the game's leading scorer with nineteen points. It seemed unbelievable that he was only a freshman. My grandest ambition in high school would be to make the varsity team in my junior year and play on the same team as him.

"Way to go, you were awesome," I said.

"Yeah, you guys really turned it on in the second half," someone else said.

"The strategy worked," Brian replied. "They were dead tired in the fourth quarter."

We continued peppering him with questions, oblivious to the game going on in front of us, which was nearly even at halftime.

When the buzzer sounded my brother sprang out of his seat like he was finally able to escape some torture-filled experience. I made one last round to see if I could find another ride but it was to no avail. So, I dejectedly followed my father and crew out for the drive home.

I wasn't that mad at Pat but still didn't speak to him on the way back. When we arrived, I immediately went up to my room and sulked. It would all get better, I figured, at the party later that night.

As I was heading out later on, I asked my parents to increase my curfew, but they wouldn't budge, and I had to be back home by eleven. The temperature was still on the chilly side but since there was no more snow or ice on the ground I rode my bicycle across town. The party was around the block from the Vickers house, so I went there first so I could walk over with Ernie. I locked my bike up in the Vickers's backyard and was let in the house by Brian.

Ernie was in his room getting duded up as usual, so I sat at the kitchen table and spoke with Brian some more.

"Who won the second game?" I asked.

"Harborfields, but it was close. Three points, I think."

At that moment Glenn walked in.

"Hey, Muh-kyoo-en, what's happening."

"Great game," I said.

"Thanks. Now we are on to the coliseum."

Glenn moved past me to grab a drink of water from the tap. After quenching his thirst, he headed toward the front door but stopped along the way to check himself in the hallway mirror. Then he yelled back that he would see us later.

No sooner had Glenn left than Ernie emerged, having put the final touches on his appearance. It was already after nine, so he was now anxious to get going. Brian had had enough for one day and said he was staying in, so we bid him farewell. We started our walk to the party.

It was only a ten-minute walk but Ernie and I still had some time to chat a little bit.

"Who of our crowd is going?" I asked.

"Pretty much everybody."

"Are you a bachelor tonight or are you meeting someone there?"

"Choice number one."

Three months tended to be his length of relationship. Ernie was a very pleasant and decent sort of guy, so I often wondered what language he used when he would break up with someone. It couldn't be that easy, but he did seem to get a lot of practice at it.

When we arrived at the party all was in full swing. The stereo was blaring the latest album from Earth, Wind & Fire. Some people were dancing but most were just hanging around smiling while talking and drinking. There was a keg of beer out in the backyard as well as a good amount of weed aroma. It was in many ways a typical Saturday night party in Babylon, but with a lot more to celebrate.

As we searched for our friends, we walked through a comfortable-looking living room which led into a kitchen. Then we went through a wooden door at the back of the kitchen and descended down a rickety staircase to a dank and poorly lit basement. And that's where we found our gang.

Somehow Ernie had managed to snag a beer during our search without my seeing him. Not everyone in the group had a drink, so I didn't stand out being empty-handed. Virginia was standing with Gary, so I moved over next to them to get his take on the late game.

"What did you think about Harborfields?" I asked.

"They're big. We're going to have to play Boo more, I think," Gary replied, referring to Chris Brust.

"Is the court the same size in the pros? I know the lane is wider."

"I don't know. That's a good question."

Virginia had been talking to the girl on her other side but turned back to tune in on our conversation.

"Hey," I said in my attempt to be casual.

"Oh, hi," she said in return. "How come you didn't stay for the second game? I figured if anyone would stay it would be you."

"Sibling issues," I replied. "I'll have to work on ride alternatives in advance if Pat wants to come to any future doubleheaders."

We talked a little more about school and other matters as Gary and some of the others went to get more beer. I guess he didn't consider me much of a threat by leaving me alone with her. Which, unfortunately, was the case.

The gang pretty much stayed in the basement for most of the evening in our carved-out little spot in the corner. As eleven approached I started to plan my exodus. I went upstairs to find a bathroom and located one down a hallway. I had left my coat on all night but had unzipped it while in the house, so I didn't need to search for it. Before I made my way toward the front door, I heard a crash and several loud gasps come from the living room.

When I made my way over to investigate, I saw a girl that I recognized as a junior passed out on the living room floor. She must have knocked over a tray while falling, as another girl was picking up some large shards of glass from the carpet. I didn't get close enough to see if she was still breathing. Several upper classmen were pushing people back to give her space. It looked like she wasn't moving.

I could hear someone in the kitchen calling 911. There was nothing I could do to help but it seemed indecent to leave with someone in trouble like this. So, I waited until the ambulance arrived but contributed nothing in the meantime.

Ernie and the others had come up from the basement to see what had happened. I told them what I knew, and they all just stared and muttered worriedly. It was certainly my first encounter of this kind and likely most of theirs as well.

Once I got over my shock, I did have the presence of mind to sneak into the kitchen and use the phone. I was relieved when Pat answered and not my father. I told him to just let our parents know I would be little late and miss curfew, but that everything was all right. He tried to ask some questions, but I quickly hung up.

The paramedics arrived, as did the police, and they all filed into the living room. The guy whose home it was explained that his parents were out but that he had a number where he could get in touch with them. I didn't hear much after that, but the girl was moved out of the house on a stretcher with what looked like an oxygen mask over her face. I waited to get verification that she was alive before sneaking out and rushing over to Ernie's to retrieve my bike so I could get home as soon as possible.

We had a big white methodist church on the edge of the village that had a large clock visible from anywhere nearby. As I pumped my bicycle across Montauk Highway and down Fire Island Avenue, I could see the time was ten to twelve. I had forgotten to bring gloves, so my bare hands were red from the cold as I steered my way home to hopefully lessen my own crisis, which I knew was upcoming.

When I got to the house, I put my bicycle in the garage and entered through Nana's apartment. Pat was still awake watching television, but she and my parents had seemingly gone to bed. Before I could ask Pat how Dad had taken the news, a loud and angry voice yelled from upstairs.

"Tom, get the hell up here!"

I had not averted anything.

Parties and Press

As I trudged up the stairs, I knew this would not be a pleasant conversation. I could explain that I had called to say that I would be late, but it would be tricky to provide details on what had happened without giving away that I was at a party filled with much older students.

"Do you know what time it is?" my father asked red-faced, looking like he would explode.

He was sitting at the kitchen table where most of our inquisitions took place.

"Yes, I always know what time it is. And I know that I am late."

"Well why didn't you call?"

"I did call," I said. "I gave the message to Pat."

My father called Pat upstairs, who verified that I had in fact called. He said that since Dad and Mom were asleep, he chose to put a note on the inside of the front door. I turned and looked down the first half flight of stairs and saw a piece of yellow legal paper taped to the door saying, "Tommy will be an hour late. No explanation."

This seemed to calm my father down a little.

"Your mother thought you were dead," my father exaggerated. "I don't want to ever see that look on her face again."

My father always chastised us about how our conduct worried my mother. She of course was always the reasonable one.

Just then my mother came into the kitchen looking as if she had just woken up. My father was still in a bit of a rage, so I didn't call him out on it. My mom had obviously been asleep and had not known or worried about the situation until now.

Finally, Dad got around to asking why I was late. I shaded the truth a little and said that I had gone to Ernie's house, and we went around the corner to what we thought was a small gathering. However, while we were hanging out in the basement things had gotten out of hand upstairs. I told them about the girl passing out and the ambulance.

"Is she all right?" my mother asked.

"The paramedic said she would be fine, but that's all I know."

"And you knew nothing about what was going on?" my father asked suspiciously.

"Nothing until I went upstairs to leave. Then I stayed until they took her away. I didn't know if we were allowed to leave or if they needed help. That's why I called."

My father looked skeptical, but my mother was fine with the explanation and told everyone to go to bed. And that's how the evening ended.

The next day I called Ernie to see if he knew anything about the girl. He said he heard that she had to get her stomach pumped after imbibing multiple types of alcohol, but that she was home now and doing fine.

"Did the police arrest anyone?" I asked him.

"No, but they stayed until the guy's parents got home. I left before then."

That was a relief. I checked the newspapers on Sunday and Monday and nothing about the incident was printed, so it turned out to be merely a family matter.

My father was not totally satisfied. We had a further conversation on Sunday where he stated that he wanted to know more details in the future about with whom and where I would be when I went out to these weekend night parties from now on. It wasn't a request, so I of course agreed.

On Monday I checked again with Ernie for any more details about the incident. He said he had seen her in school today, so he assumed she was fine. He said the word was that the parents had straightened everything out with the police when they got home. This was life in suburbia.

The rest of the week was like the countdown to the Super Bowl—not only in Babylon but all throughout Long Island. On Friday night the two county champions would be decided with Babylon playing Harborfields for the Suffolk Crown and Southside playing Malverne for Nassau bragging rights. If things shook out to a final game between us and Malverne, it might be slightly ironic. Mr. Koelbel was a graduate of Malverne High School.

Koelbel continued to let my friends and me attend the practices every day. He seemed to have lightened up a bit, as well. The practices continued to be run hard, but he emphasized time and again to the team how proud he was that they had gotten this far and to enjoy the experience in the coming weekend.

His battle plan had changed a little from the prior weeks. With Harborfields in the mix, he was now preparing for size rather than speed. Since our center Barry Davis would be smaller than three of the Harborfields players, six-foot-eight freshman Chris Brust started to get a lot more time with the first team. At times he would be in with Barry, and sometimes taking Barry's place.

Mr. Koelbel had always emphasized pump fakes to draw fouls. He would joke that big men were much less intimidating when they were sitting on the bench. Glenn was a master at this skill, but every player had it ingrained.

We learned that unlike the games played at individual high schools, the championship games at the Nassau Coliseum would require a paid ticket for everyone who attended. However, the ticket would allow admission to both championship games and to the nightcap game where Dr. J and the Nets would play the Denver Nuggets. I really hoped Pat would decide not to come because I knew he would not want to stay for the pro game.

As practice was ending on Wednesday, Mr. Koelbel called me over to talk. I looked at my friends who just shrugged their shoulders not knowing what it was about. So, I darted over to see what the coach needed.

"Muh-*kyoo*-en," he started. "I need your home address."

"Are you sending me a gift or something?"

He laughed. "No, I have to pick up something from your dad."

This was exciting, I thought. I ripped out a page of notebook paper and wrote it down for him. I also gave him a general description verbally of where we lived. He seemed to know the area.

"Tell your dad I'll be by about eight."

I just nodded as he took off up to the locker room. He gave no indication as to what he would be collecting so I had nothing else to tell my friends. After lingering a little while longer with the gang we all broke for home.

When I got to Coppertree it was still about an hour before dinner, so I tracked down my father. He was in his office, which was a side room at the bottom of the stairs going up to the third floor of our house where the kids' bedrooms were. My parents slept on the second floor.

My dad seemed to have cooled down since our confrontation on Saturday night, but I was always on guard to "not poke the bear." That was an expression my siblings and I used that meant if Dad's in a good mood, don't ask for too much. Despite the closeness of our relationship, I usually was the one who went over the line and set the bear growling.

"Hi, Dad."

"How are you doing, bud?"

"Mr. Koelbel told me that he is coming over to the house tonight."

"Yeah, he was hoping to see a copy of our union contract. They might be about to go into negotiations themselves."

"I could have brought it to school."

"Better he just sees it and takes notes. I don't know if I can legally give him a copy."

"Well, he said he would be here at eight. Do you need to go get beer?"

I said that as a joke, but it made my father get up and go check the refrigerator. After he made sure of our supply I went up to my room and told Pat about Koelbel's impending visit. I was sure he would drop in to banter a little with the coach.

We had spaghetti for dinner that night and everyone was present except Nana, who ate downstairs as usual. This was due mostly to the fact that she ate earlier than we did. I guess my father had union politics on his mind because his quiz that night was about the AFT (American Federation of Teachers). The question was: Who was the organization's head? And it was answered by all of us at the same time. Albert Shanker. He was a talented man, from what I knew, but had a horrible last name.

I was doing my homework at the kitchen table when I saw headlights shine through our bay window indicating that a car was pulling up to the front of the house. Max immediately started barking as I looked out to see who it was. Mr. Koelbel had a unique car, a "Volkswagen Thing." Of course it was German, looked like a jeep, and my recollection is that part of its marketability was that it could easily be taken apart and the pieces rearranged.

I sat in the living room and held onto Max while my father let Mr. Koelbel in the house. The dog would not attack strangers but would bark aggressively until heeled by my father's command. My father took the dog from me and walked him up to Koelbel. He had the coach give Max a dog biscuit and from that point on they were friends. Max, however, did stay in the room with his eyes on Koelbel the whole time.

My father asked me to leave them alone for about thirty minutes, so I took my homework up to my room. Pat was at work over at his desk and I took up the parallel position at mine. After about twenty minutes, Pat closed a large textbook in such an emphatic fashion that I guessed he was finished for the night.

"Is he downstairs?"

"Yeah, he and Dad are talking union stuff. He told me to give them a half hour, so you can probably head down."

Pat put his books away and descended the staircase. I had another couple of pages from my history book to read so I didn't join them for a short while longer. When I made my way back downstairs the contract talk was done.

My father and Mr. Koelbel were sitting at the edge of the dining room table that bridged into the living room. Each had a Schaefer Beer in front of them. My father said he drank Shaefer because it was the only major beer brewed in New York, but it didn't hurt that it wasn't very expensive.

Mr. Koelbel was in the middle of telling the story of why Babylon was playing in League V against much larger schools.

"The ones that are close to our student size are all way out east," he said. "We used to travel out there during the week and not get back until ten at night. The parents complained so much that we got put into League V where the schools are a lot bigger but closer by."

"Yeah, Peg and I have taken the family out there for some trips," my father replied. "It's still pretty rural."

"Picture it ten years ago; it was all farmers."

Calling someone a "farmer" was a form of insult where I grew up, like "hick." It all emanated from Manhattan. The people in the city called the people on Long Island farmers, Nassau County called people in Suffolk farmers, and even western Suffolk called those in eastern Suffolk County farmers. That would all change when the Hamptons became ritzy in the eighties.

"How do you think you'll do against Harborfields?" I asked.

"It should be a tight game," Koelbel replied. "It took them until overtime to beat Smithtown West, so I'd say we're pretty even."

"They looked big," my father said.

"Yeah, we're going to need to play everyone and hopefully get them into foul trouble."

"By the way," I interjected, "are there any differences in the court sizes between high school and the pro?"

"They're the same width of fifty feet," Koelbel answered. "But the professional court is ten feet longer at ninety-four feet. But I doubt that will make much of a difference."

Pat remained mostly quiet as we spoke about basketball. However, the fact that he was here at all led me to believe he would likely come to the game. I might need a plan B for a ride home.

As the evening started to grow late, Koelbel looked at his watch and deemed it time to go. He drained his remaining beer before rising. Max jumped up at the movement. Apparently Koelbel had tamed him as he was able to pat the dog on the head and calm him down.

"Thanks for the help on this, Pat," he said shaking my father's hand.

My brother and I also stood up and shook the coach's hand as he made his way to the door. My father wished him luck on Friday and added that we would all be there. With that, Mr. Koelbel took his leave. We watched as his weird "Thing" car pulled out of the driveway and turned the corner.

The whole farmer rhetoric would start to pick up steam as we approached championship weekend. The first Long Island Champion would definitely come from Nassau, according to all of the papers, but Babylon wasn't focused on that yet. Winning the school's first county championship was our immediate priority, and that chance was now only two days away.

Friday Night Showdown

It had been a long week, but Friday had finally arrived. The hallways of BHS were as electric as they had been all season, but I noticed the player's vibes were a little different. For the entire second half of the season, they had all been stone-faced on gameday, but today they seemed much looser. They looked like they were having fun.

Mr. Koelbel had run the practices in his usual hard-pressing and disciplined manner, but toward the end of the week he was also emphasizing for the team to enjoy the moment. It seemed that message had taken root. Whenever I saw one of the players in passing that day they were smiling and living large.

The tradition of wearing suits to games had risen to a new level. Many of the players looked like they were dressed for the prom by sporting velvet jackets, ruffled shirts, and bow ties. I heard Glenn mention to some classmates that he planned to be "styling" at the coliseum. In any event, it had a contagious effect.

The newspapers that day differed somewhat in their coverage. *The Long Island Press* dedicated a full page to previewing the games. It had a write-up on each team with some pictures of their coaches and top players. Also, for the first time I saw a printed bracket of the remaining showdowns. Not that we needed one at this point.

Newsday, on the other hand, dedicated only a short paragraph to the contest reading, "Nassau, Suffolk Finals Today." Then it provided the times for the games. The Nassau title game would be at 3 p.m., with the Suffolk final following at 5 p.m. As the Nassau Coliseum was thirty minutes away with no traffic, this likely meant that we would see none of the prior game to preview a potential opponent. However, Mr. Bartsch would be leaving school early to serve as a scout for the team.

Most of the teachers were as caught up in the excitement that day as the students. All except for one, of course. Mr. Kalfus gave my class a "ball breaking" calculus test that morning. He claimed the best time to test is when the pupils are distracted. Kalfus was a brilliant man, but I often wondered if we went to war which side he would fight on.

Mr. Bartsch was still around for art class that morning. He had pinned the page from the *Long Island Press* to his bulletin board. That was actually where I saw it first, since the paper was not delivered to our house until the afternoon. Some of us went over to read the synopsis, but most of the students just hung around at the front table asking questions and discussing the upcoming contest.

At lunch everyone was busy securing rides. The school did take the uncharacteristic step of securing a fan bus despite it being a night game. Still, most would rather get a ride in a car. I was in the unusual mode of trying to get a ride home from the game from someone who would also be staying to see the Nets, who would be playing after the high school games were complete. I was still assuming Pat would petition my father to leave after Babylon had played.

"You can come home with us if you need," Gary had said. "George is home from school, so we'll be taking a second car."

George was the oldest Farley who'd been Babylon's center the year before.

"Thanks, I'll let you know afterwards."

I had gotten over him and Virginia and was focused on the team winning at this point.

I didn't see Ernie until after lunch, but when I did, I wasn't sure how I had missed him all day. He was dressed up all sharp in a suit as if he were playing. I ran over to get the details.

"What are you all dressed up for?"

"Ah, you never need a reason to look good."

That was indeed his motto.

"Well, I'm glad my father can't see you. He'd probably make me wear a suit too."

That got a laugh. We coordinated plans to meet up at the game and went our separate ways for the rest of the day.

When the bell rang to end the school day, I ran all the way home in hopes my father would be there so we could get an early start and possibly see the end of the Nassau championship. I was happy to see that he was home, but we ended up having to wait on Pat, who had stayed late at school for some reason. Of all the days, I thought.

Pat finally arrived home a little before four and the three of us hastily departed with only a single hurried "goodbye" to the rest of the family. It was rush hour traffic, but we were heading in the reverse direction, so we cruised along at normal speed while looking over at the bumper-to-bumper mess of people commuting home from working in Manhattan. I didn't know why they didn't take the train.

When we pulled into the coliseum parking lot it looked to be about a third full, so it was no challenge finding a space. If this many cars had been at a single high school, even Ward Melville, they would never have fit. But this was a professional arena.

The weather was seasonable, and the skies were still light. We started to see people we knew as we got closer to the entrance. I located the big yellow fan bus and cursed to myself that they had beaten us there and maybe saw some of the Nassau game.

When we bought our tickets, we were told that we could sit anywhere we could find for the high school games, but if we stayed for the Nets game, we would have to relocate to the uppermost level to a special designated area to sit. The attendant also reminded us that we would need to present our tickets again, so she cautioned us not to lose them.

I had been to two professional basketball games before in my life. Both had been held here at the Nassau Coliseum. But the awe I felt at that age whenever I entered a professional sports arena was almost breathtaking. It wasn't just the size or advanced electronics, but the history. The players who I had only seen on television played here. That feeling would diminish somewhat as I got older but never totally dissipate.

After we came through the small tunnel to the lower section of the arena, I took it all in. Although the coliseum had seating behind the baskets, very few people were there. This was the type of venue where the glass backboards would actually serve their original purpose of allowing the fan to better see the court. The fans from both sides were numerous but would have plenty of seating on their respective sides.

The first game had already concluded when we walked into the arena, however the score was still up on the big electronic cube that hung over the court. Southside had defeated Malverne 89–74. Only a few Babylon people had arrived to see any of that game, and it was mostly over by that point. I did hear that Southside had a star named Chuckie Smith who had scored thirty-five points and that this was the team's third county championship in five years. They would be a tough opponent if we got to them.

We saw the Shiebler family first and made our way over toward them figuring the rest of the gang would show up at some point. Mr. Shiebler had used his family's coats as corner markers in an attempt to block off about forty seats. I guess we'd see if that was a good reservation system.

Shortly after, the Vickerses and Farleys arrived to join us in that "reserved" area. I had imagined they might have been somewhere near the locker rooms providing some last-minute support to their playing family members. I confirmed the fact with Ernie.

"Did you see your brothers in the locker room?"

"No, we weren't allowed in but talked to them outside."

"How'd they seem?"

"Loose, like it was a pickup game."

Gary gave the same report with Virginia sitting at his side. She gave me a smile, which I returned.

Pat was sitting over with Jon Shiebler's older brother. The two didn't really hang out together but seemed to be speaking cordially enough. The Conroy family and a portion of the large Godfrey clan had arrived as well. The two dads had parked themselves behind my father, and they all and Mr. Shiebler seemed to be hashing out a sideline game plan for the Panthers.

By the time two teams came out for warm-ups, the bulk of the Babylon fans I expected to be at the game had arrived. Despite Harborfields being almost double our size in student population, it appeared that we were matching them almost person for person from a fan base ratio. When both sides cheered for their teams, it didn't seem quite as loud in the larger professional venue. But I'm sure our guys heard it.

When the buzzer sent the two teams back to their benches, a very professional voice came across the public address system. It echoed through all corners of the arena.

"Welcome to the Nassau Coliseum and tonight's Suffolk County High School Championship game, pitting the Tornadoes of Harborfields against the Panthers of Babylon."

The speaker then introduced the starters for each side, including the details of their height and school year. Some of our fans were taken aback a bit when they heard how tall the Harborfields front line was. Someone muttered, "We're going to be shooting over some large dudes."

Koelbel was sticking with the same starting five. Glenn was the last player to be introduced. Then the coaches were announced, and Mr. Koelbel began walking over to his opponent for the pregame handshake. He was sticking with his lucky maroon jacket. It was funny to me now that I knew the story behind it.

I noticed that our three main substitutes, Chuck Farley, Chris Brust, and Steven Farley (Weiner) all had taken their sweats off despite being on the bench. Koelbel was obviously planning to play eight players and use them early on.

"Do you think Weiner will get some time tonight?" I asked Gary.

"Depends on the foul situation. Chris will likely see a good deal of time with the size of their frontcourt."

Despite being our starting center, Barry Davis was the fourth-tallest amongst the ten starters. Chris Brust, on the other hand, matched Harborfields tallest player in height. However, he was only a freshman and had missed much of the season.

While the teams huddled getting their final instructions, both sets of cheerleaders had a chance to come out and do their shows. The arena size made it tough to hear them, but we all recognized the familiar routine of our girls. Cartwheels, claps, and the culminating human pyramid at the end. The Harborfields routine wasn't much different other than the fact that their pyramid was not built. They merely ended with four girls doing splits with two behind them crouched and one in the back standing with her hands straight up. All had pom-poms, though.

Barry Davis had won most of his center taps to date, but this one would be a challenge in that he was giving away two to three inches. One of things we had spied while watching the varsity practices during the week was that Koelbel had put in a trick play to steal the tap. Barry had executed it against Chris several times during scrimmages. I was curious if he would pull it out on the opening tap or wait until later in the game.

As the players made their way out onto the court, I shared the little nugget I had received about the pro courts being ten feet longer. It got a few nods but no verbal reactions. Perhaps they all thought I was showing off.

After the players concluded their handshaking with each other and were properly separated and positioned by the two referees, the head official bounced the ball once and made his way between the two centers. He put the whistle in his mouth and extended the ball between the two crouching pivot men.

The coliseum went silent for the few seconds as the official held the ball motionless. Then simultaneously he tossed the ball up and blew his whistle. It was game on.

The Best of Suffolk

Mr. Koelbel was not going to leave any tricks in the bag. He instituted his center-tap play from the very beginning as Barry Davis swatted the ball backwards before it hit its zenith. This launched the Harborfields coach out of his chair to protest, but the officials apparently had not seen any infraction. As a result, the ball ended up in Gervais Barger's hands and Babylon had the first possession.

Consistent with their play all season, the Panthers moved the ball patiently back to back and side to side within the 2-3 offense looking for the best shot. After almost two full minutes Glenn broke free on the block and Stanley Davis hit him with a pass that led to the first two points of the game. The Babylon players then retreated back on defense but played pressure man-to-man up top, meeting the Harborfields guards at midcourt. Our forwards and center packed into the lanes so as to assist each other in guarding our opponents' larger inside players.

The teams traded baskets for most of the first period. On Babylon's last possession of the quarter Glenn used his pump-fake move to draw a foul on Harborfields's leading scorer. The ball trickled into the basket as Glenn was knocked backwards and down. He would make the accompanying free throw, and a few moments later the buzzer sounded with Babylon holding a three-point lead as the teams retreated to their benches. The foul was also the second on the Harborfields player, who was forced to sit out of the game for a while.

With Harborfields down one of their big men, Babylon broke free in the second quarter. Stanley Davis hit a few long jump shots that were pretty darn close to the ABA three-point line, while Glenn poured it on and scored thirteen points in the quarter. Our interior defense was frustrating their big men who could not get the ball to go in the basket while their guards could not convert any open outside shots. Harborfields would muster only seven points in the second period as Babylon raced to a nineteen-point lead at the half.

The only negative moment for us was when Barry Davis collected his third foul and was forced to sit out the last two minutes of the second. Regardless, when the buzzer went off to signal halftime, we were all feeling pretty good. The teams rushed off the court with the Babylon players patting each other on the back as if the game were over. Even Mr. Koelbel was sporting a small mid-game smile.

"Wow, everything is working to perfection," I said to no one in particular.

"Yeah, but there are two halves in a game," one negative parent spouted in response from behind me.

I ignored the remark and didn't turn around.

As I was not as worried about losing my seat in the spacious arena during the break, I joined Ernie and left to treat myself to a hot dog and a Coke. He bought the same, but we both ate them near the concession stands. Bringing food back to our seats would invite all our male friends to ask for some and neither of us was in a mind to share.

He and I chatted a bit about the game but mostly ate our food in peace. We then made our way back into the arena just as the buzzer sounded to end halftime. Having completed their warm-ups, the players were making their way back out to midcourt as Ernie and I pushed past and upended people to get to our seats. It looked like Koelbel was going to stay with Barry Davis at center despite his foul situation.

Once again Koelbel's trick play stole the tap from Harborfields, which further enraged their coach, who stomped up and down by his bench. However, our players came out a little sluggish to start the half. We missed our first three shots and Harborfields was able to close the lead to thirteen. Then Barry Davis got his fourth foul and had to go back to the bench. This brought in freshman Chris Brust at the pivot.

Harborfields immediately went after Brust on offense and managed to cut the Babylon lead to nine by the end of the third quarter. Suddenly we were not so confident as before.

"I told you not to get arrogant," the naysayer behind me put in.

Again, I didn't acknowledge the remark but just kept my eyes on the court.

Koelbel put Barry back to start the fourth quarter but would platoon him with Brust for the remainder of the game. We regained our composure as the period began and started hitting more shots. Brian Vickers and Stanley Davis each had four points by sinking a couple of baskets to steady the offense. A key play came with five minutes to go, when the lead was cut down to seven points. Glenn went up and missed a bank shot where we all thought he had gotten fouled. The ball then rolled around the rim and out. Then it seemed to touch several outstretched hands over the next few seconds, almost in slow motion, before it landed in the grasp of Chris Brust, who easily laid the ball into the basket to increase the lead to nine again. That play seemed to take the remaining steam out of Harborfields.

Babylon then went into the stall version of the offense for the final minutes of the game, with Glenn at point passing around to Stanley and Gervais daring Harborfields to foul us. Whenever they did, our players converted the free throws. The lead remained at nine as the clock ticked under a minute. The noise started to rise from the Babylon crowd as we realized the county crown was about to be ours.

With seven seconds left in the game Koelbel called time-out in order to take his starters out to the roaring applause of the faithful and to the hugs of their hardworking and grateful substitutes. Harborfields would score one more bucket to close the final score to 62–55, but that was it. The celebration for Babylon was on.

The players began grabbing each other on the floor while we in the stands were jumping up and down and hugging as well. During those minutes a group of men began setting up a table at half-court. They positioned a microphone by running a long cord underneath the scorer's table to what I assumed was a power supply. Then several other men came out carrying three trophies, which were placed upon the table.

A different man than the one who announced the game eventually stepped up to the microphone and began speaking.

“Hello, everyone. Wasn’t that a great game?”

The applause in response to his remark was of course much louder from the Babylon side of the court.

“We would first like to present the runner-up trophy to a fantastic Harborfields team.”

We all clapped perfunctorily as the Harborfields coach made his way to the table along with his player captains to accept the smallest of the three trophies. The coach embraced the trophy while his players stood next to him with their heads down and their hands on their hips. It must be difficult to get that close, I thought.

When the speaker returned to the microphone, he then announced what we’d all been waiting to hear.

“Now, let’s congratulate the 1975 Suffolk County basketball champions, the Babylon Panthers.”

As we all broke into cheers, Mr. Koelbel and his three captains, Glenn, Stanley Davis, and Gervais Barger made the march out to accept the biggest trophy on the table. The players strode slowly but confidently across the hardwood as if they had expected to be there. Then the three each held a piece of the triple-decker award and then hoisted it up for all of us to see.

After posing for a few pictures, Gervais assumed control of the entire trophy. Then the speaker came on to present the final award, which I assumed was the MVP trophy. Stanley must have guessed the same thing as all of us because he grabbed Glenn by the arm and turned him around to face the speaker. Then he gave him a little push.

“We have one final presentation tonight” the same speaker began. “It is the award for the Suffolk County Playoff’s Most Valuable Player.”

We all watched in anticipation despite knowing who the winner would be. Regardless, the speaker drew revealing the name out for a few more seconds of build up before announcing it.

“The most valuable player for 1975 is Glenn Vickers of the Babylon Panthers.”

Loud applause again broke out as Glenn strode forth by himself this time and took the trophy with a gracious smile. He posed for a few pictures with members of the committee while positioning the trophy appropriately between them. Then Glenn walked back to the bench while lifting the award over his head as our fans gave one final outburst of emotion-filled applause.

At that point the teams and presenters left the court while the attendants started shepherding all of us high school fans out of the high-priced seats for the Nets game and directing us up into the rafters where those who would be staying for the pro game would need to sit. As my dad and I were exiting through the small tunnels, Pat came running up to inform us that he had secured a ride home with the Jaffies. That meant if my father wanted to stay for the Nets game he could. He then patted Pat on the back and said to take the ride, as he would prefer to stay.

Once we were out in the concession halls again that the rimmed the arena, Ernie came rushing toward me.

"Hey, do you want to come down to where the team will be exiting the locker room?"

"You bet I do," I said before checking with my father.

As I looked at him my father waved me away and made his way over to Mr. Conroy and some of the other adults.

Ernie then led a gang of us down and along the hallways to the lowest level of the coliseum. It wasn't a restricted area but was one that seemed less trafficked. There was a concession stand nearby where I grabbed another Coke and then joined the others by a big double doorway with glass windows that had the word RESTRICTED printed above it in red letters on a silver backing.

We all waited for about thirty minutes before one of the gang peered through the glass and yelled, "Here they come!"

A few seconds later the doors swung open and the team strolled through. They were all in their dress clothes. Some still had wet hair from showering. They were all smiles as they came past us slapping hands and looking like winners.

I had my Coke in my right hand and was slapping five with my left as Brian came up to me and asked for some of my drink. I of course handed it to him. Then after he drank nearly half of it, Gervais asked if he could have one as well. At that point I just waved my hand and said, "It's all yours."

Mr. Bartsch came out, but not Koelbel. I found out later that he was doing an interview with a *Newsday* reporter. He had a new life ahead of him now. Bartsch had always been quite at home hanging out with the students. He always seemed like one big kid himself.

We all stayed in that little concession area well into the Nets game. It felt like an exclusive private reception room as the players hung around and talked to us and each other. Eventually it all broke up and the players joined the masses, but we'd had our special time with them. Before he walked out Glenn came over to where the younger group was standing and put his hand on Ernie and my backs.

"Well, guys," he said. "How about that?"

"We knew you had it all the way," I said.

"Then you were the only ones."

Glenn laughed and exited with the rest.

I got separated from the gang on my way up to our section for the Nets game. I had to ask several people where to go as the description on the ticket wasn't overly clear. Finally, I made it up to the top of the arena and over to the remaining Babylon faithful. It looked like fifty or so people had remained for the pro game. I checked the score on the big electronic cube, and it was tied at half time.

My father was busy speaking with the same group as before. I got his attention so he knew I was back but then went to join my friends. Most of the gang was still there and sitting together.

We all watched the game with one eye while continually talking with each other about our school's championship. Dr. J did make a few colossal dunks that pried our full attention away for a minute or two here and there. However, the night was still all about the Babylon Panther victory.

The Nets ended up losing that night and after the late-night drive home my father and I were ready to sleep. Tomorrow we would get our heads right and start thinking about the matchup for the first-ever Long Island crown. Having not seen any of the Southside game, I was sure we could beat anyone. I would find out the next day that most of the press and coaches on Long Island did not share that opinion.

The Underdog

The word *underdog* has its origins in the late 1800s and referred to a dog in a dogfight who had lost. That definition, however, implied a done deal. As the phrase has been adopted in the modern sports era, it took on a present-tense meaning designating the person or team that is expected to lose, but sometimes doesn't.

As many of us read the newspapers Saturday we became very well acquainted with that word. After going through the accounts of the Babylon victory over Harborfields and the Southside victory over Malverne, I read through several descriptions of Southside as being a heavy favorite that should easily dispense with Babylon. The source of much of this downplaying of our chances was, surprisingly, other basketball coaches in Suffolk County.

My father was going to lunch with Mr. Koelbel and several other dads in the village as a celebration and report-gathering of how the coach himself felt about our chances. They were of course going to the Villager and it would be in part a liquid lunch. When he returned, Dad gave me the type of recap that both surprised and brought me down a little.

"It seems many of Roy's colleagues don't like our chances," he said. "This being Suffolk's first shot at Nassau County, many of them wanted one of the historical powers like Brentwood to carry the banner. Not Cinderella Babylon."

"Did someone actually say that?" I asked.

"Well, Roy said he's heard things like 'The only way for Babylon to keep the score close would be to miss the bus tomorrow.'"

Knowing Mr. Koelbel, though, he would probably use those comments to his advantage. I started noting in the articles where the coach was actually quoted as referring to Southside as "awesome" and a real "super team." He continually peddled the notion that his team would mostly just enjoy the ride, and what happened would happen. He told *Newsday* that he wouldn't even hold a practice on Saturday, stating that he preferred to give his team a rest.

There was one positive surprise that came from the lunch, though. The high school championship game would be played at 8 p.m. at night but would be preceded by another Nets home game. Mr. Koelbel had been given a hundred tickets to dispense to team family members and others for that game. My father had collected three of them for Pat, him, and me. I wasn't sure Pat would be as excited as I was, but he'd have to sacrifice if he wanted to see the Babylon game.

None of my school crowd was planning on being out late that Saturday night but several of us got together midafternoon at Manniello's for a between-meal slice of pizza. The school had planned another fan bus for Sunday but that would only make it there in time for the high school game. Everyone at our gathering would be attending the pro game, so they were heading with family. Virginia, of course, was going with the Farleys.

"We're going to get there an hour before the Nets game," Ernie said.

"Why is that?" I asked.

"The players want to soak it in a little more."

Glenn and many of the players had been upping their wardrobe as we got deeper into the playoffs. I'm sure he'd look sharp. The [illegible] didn't sound to me like a team who was expecting to lose that night. That was welcome news.

During pizza Gary told us that he had seen Southside play one time over the summer. He attested to the fact that they played an up-tempo game and that they were similar to Central Islip. However, he added the caveat that they were just bigger and better at it.

When I came home later that day my mother was in the kitchen cleaning up and beginning to put dinner together. I asked if I could help with anything, and she requested that I set the table. Again, it would only be the six of us as Nana Mary would've eaten dinner downstairs already.

While I was putting out the plates I was suddenly hit by a sense of guilt.

"I'm sorry, Mom," I started. "I never think to ask if you wanted to go to the games."

She smiled in her always reassuring way and said, "I don't want to go until you're playing."

Her words were as good as her hugs and always made me feel much better. I set the rest of the table and asked if she needed me to do anything else. She responded in the negative but alerted me that dinner would be ready in an hour. That said, I went up toward my room.

I saw my sisters across the short hallway playing a board game. Not caring to join in or visit, I retired to my room to find Pat wasn't there. Thus, I grabbed my Nerf ball and hoop, set it up on the back of the door, and began shooting miniature foul shots.

Time passed by quickly during my indoor hoop session, and before I knew it my mother was calling us down to a dinner of chicken, rice, and broccoli. I was still a little full from eating pizza but didn't say anything. We all were responsible for our own drinks, and I would likely have milk.

Pat had been down in Nana's watching television. His expression was what I had expected when Dad told him we had Nets tickets and that he would need to attend both games if he wanted to see Babylon play for the title. After a grimace he said he still wanted to go.

We had no current-events quiz that night as my father was as consumed with the championship game tomorrow as I was. Even my sisters were asking questions about the teams and players. I knew one of Gary's sisters was a classmate of Peggy's so there must be some banter going back and forth in the lower grades as well.

As an offering to Pat my father did concede to not arrive at the Nets game early in order to watch practice. We targeted getting there as close to tip time as possible. That didn't seem to make Pat any happier. So be it, I thought.

After dinner broke, we all adjourned in our separate directions before convening down at Nana Mary's to see what was on television that night as we had our tea and dessert. At seventy-nine she was always up for the task and had been boiling water and pulling out cakes from the refrigerator. (Have I mentioned that we really were very spoiled?)

The movie of the week was one that Pat and I had seen a few years earlier called *Westworld*, about a robot-themed vacation destination where the robots become evil. My brother and I were happy to watch it again because we had enjoyed it so much the first time. I wondered if it might be too scary for my sisters but said nothing.

My father had a favorite armchair that was always his when he was around. My mother usually sat on the couch with one of my sisters cuddled up at each side, while my brother and I plopped down on the floor. We had thick carpeting, so sitting there was not uncomfortable when augmented by a few pillows. After Nana got everybody served, she settled into her rocker with her own cup of tea shortly after the movie had started.

I could tell that my parents enjoyed the movie, but it did rattle my sisters, which, in turn, prompted my father to scold Pat and me for not informing them how scary it was. We responded that we were their ages when we saw it originally and thought there would be no harm. That prompted a scowl from him but no apologies or retractions. He didn't like not getting the last word.

The movie ended at eleven and we all went up to bed from there. Pat and I stayed awake a little longer in our room with him reading a comic book and me shooting some more Nerfoop. Finally, we dozed off some time after midnight.

My father took Nana to church at St. Joe's early the next morning but let the rest of us sleep in. The Nets game would start at 3 p.m., so we had to get on the road at two in order to arrive at the coliseum on time. Despite the excitement of seeing a professional game my mind was focused on the Long Island Championship game later on. I still could not believe how poorly all the press and other coaches thought Babylon would perform in the game.

"Why do they think Southside is so much better?" I asked my father.

"It's a city thing," he responded. "They're closer to Manhattan and people think they compete at a higher level. I was checking their schedule, and it does seem that Southside has played a few high-profile, non-league games around the state this season and did pretty well."

In my mind I wasn't taking a defeatist attitude, but I still thought it was great that we had won the county championship. However, if we got a drilling in this game that might be the lasting impression in everyone's minds. I had faith Koelbel and Glenn would figure something out.

The parking lot at the coliseum was near capacity when we arrived. Dr. J always filled up the house. As it was a pro game, we had assigned seating and no control over being close to our friends. By chance, as we walked in, Mr. Koelbel was strolling by. He saw us and came over.

"Hey, Pat, boys."

"Hi, Roy," my father said. "I guess you didn't take everyone's advice and just stay home."

Mr. Koelbel laughed. The coach seemed very loose. Pat and I stood by for a few minutes and listened in while he and my father chatted, but then we went ahead of our father to see if any of our friends had arrived yet and where they were sitting.

The tickets Mr. Koelbel had procured seemed to be spread out as a I saw a few people here and there, but no particularly large clump of Babylon attendees were visible anywhere. I wasn't able to spot Ernie or Gary about. Perhaps they were down visiting with their siblings in one of the closed-off areas near the locker room.

Pat and I followed where our ticket stubs directed us and eventually found our seats. They were located in a pretty good area. We were in the section behind one of the baskets about twenty rows back and to the left. We had a great view of the Nets bench and were on the side where the home team was warming up. The players looked to be twice the size they appeared on television.

There were only a few minutes left in warm-ups, but the two of us got to see Dr. J sail in for a couple of unguarded but awesome dunks. Even Pat was a little awed despite not being much of a sports fan. My father joined us just as the buzzer sounded to call the teams back to the bench for the starting-lineup announcements and other pregame activities.

Dad caught us up on the latest from Mr. Koelbel. The coach was laughing at how badly everybody thought the Panthers were going to do. He said the team was using it as a motivating factor but that his players were all in a good head space and that he was expecting a good game from his squad. We would see.

The Nets were playing the Utah Stars and a young phenom, Moses Malone, who had gone professional right out of high school. The home team got off to a slow start but caught up midway through the second period. It was nip-and-tuck from there on, but the Nets pulled away at the end for an eleven-point win. Dr. J did make one incredible dunk on our side of the court that was definitely the highlight of the game. Two Utah players had been in position to block the shot, but the Doc went in with such force that I thought the opponent's arms might break off.

After the pro game was over, we had to go back outside and enter again in general-admission fashion as all the seats became first come, first served again. When we reentered, I saw Mr. Shiebler again blocking forty or fifty prime seats by putting his family coats around the perimeter. Nobody challenged him and thus we all had prime seating again. I went over and sat by Jon and his brother. Slowly the rest of the familiar Babylon faces began to appear and our section started to fill up.

The Farleys and Vickerses were the last to arrive, having apparently spent time with their family members before the game. Then at about a quarter to eight the two teams emerged simultaneously from different entries onto the court for warm-ups. Again, we looked so much cooler because of our opening routine.

Southside high school were the Cyclones. Their team colors were red and blue, but because they were designated as the home team, they wore white uniforms with the red-and-blue trim. Their uniforms looked a little like those the Nets had just worn. The similarity projected a superior aura to me. Babylon was outfitted in our away black uniforms with orange trim and numbering. The stark contrast in colors assured that there would be no confusing the two teams from appearance.

At the top of the hour, the buzzer sounded and the two teams returned to their benches. The same announcer that had called the Friday-night county championship came over the speaker again to welcome everyone to the first-ever Long Island championship game. Both sides erupted in partisan applause. The announcer proceeded to introduce the starting lineups and coaches as usual. Babylon started the same lineup. When Southside was introduced, we all took note of one person from their starting lineup, Chuckie Smith. He was the current darling of the high school sports press and the man we were supposed to fear.

Smith looked to be about as tall as Glenn. He had a decent-sized afro and sported a big smile. His walk had a bounce to it that made him seem more athletic than those around him. One could tell by the way his teammates acted around him that they knew he was their meal ticket.

The Southside coach had a very young-looking face to me. He was of decent height but shorter than most of his players. The confident look on his face seemed to be one of a man who was ready to preside over a dynasty. Was he thinking we would be a challenge or just a bump in the road?

The Babylon fans were on the same side as we had been on Friday night with Southside's faithful straight across on the other—although there did seem to be one person somewhere nearby who either didn't like Babylon or at least didn't care much for our chances of winning. After the introductions he made a snide remark that was overheard by several of us.

"Babylon is going to wish they stayed home tonight," the man said.

"That's what Harborfields said," someone shot back.

"Southside ain't Harborfields," was his cocky retort.

We all took another look toward the court, but nobody responded again. Maybe it would be better to wait and watch, I thought, as many others likely did as well.

The two teams' starting players went to midcourt for their final opening tip of the season. For some it was the end of a career. Barry went inside to the small circle to jump and everyone on Babylon assembled around accordingly. One team was about to get an education, but which one?

Two Counties Collide

Southside won the opening tip and immediately went to work by scoring a quick basket when a streaking Chuckie Smith caught a half-court pass from a teammate, resulting in an easy layup. Then the Cyclones set up their full-court press. It took almost the whole five seconds, but Glenn got the ball inbounded to Gervais, who raced the ball up court and passed the ball to Brian Vickers, who hurried a short jump shot that fell dead off the rim.

The rebound was picked off by one of Southside's big men who threw an outlet pass to Chuckie Smith. Smith pushed the ball up court and found another teammate under the basket for yet another easy lay-in, and Southside was up four to nothing. Babylon did not score their first basket until three minutes had gone by when Glenn hit a jump shot from the middle of the lane.

Midway through the first quarter a Southside player intercepted a pass from Gervais to Stanley, which led to another fast-break layup. That resulted in a 14–7 Southside lead. At that point, Mr. Koelbel yelled for a time-out. Thus far, the Cyclones were indeed looking like a "super team."

During the time-out the uninvited voice from nearby spoke up again.

"I told you Southside was good."

This time nobody looked back or said anything. So far, the voice had been correct, but we weren't done yet.

When the teams came back out onto the court Glenn received the ball to throw in with Southside still in their full-court press. Babylon ran its inbounds play, but this time did not race the ball up court. Gervais patiently dribbled across half-court and slowed things down. This was pure Koelbel; he was going to make Southside play some defense.

Gervais and Stanley Davis directed the offense back and forth several times from out top before Glenn flashed up forward to receive a ball at the foul line. Chuckie Smith was guarding him. Glenn made his patented move of driving to the lane and then with a pump fake got Smith into the air to draw a foul while also sinking the basket. After Glenn hit the accompanying foul shot the lead was cut to four. Then Babylon went into its full-court press.

Chuckie got the inbound pass with Gervais right in his face. The Southside guard had some difficulty dribbling side to side up the court and barely beat the ten-second count. He passed the ball to the other guard and Southside went about setting up its offense. The slowdown of play didn't suit them and one of their forwards missed a short jump shot. Barry Davis grabbed the rebound. He passed the ball to Stanley Davis, who again slowly moved the ball up court.

Once again Babylon worked their half-court offense patiently and slowed the pace of the game. The result was nearly the same as the last play with Glenn receiving a pass from Stanley and scoring a midrange jump shot over Chuckie Smith. The Southside star was now having to work hard on defense as well as offense.

Babylon made its way back into the game and closed within one point with thirty seconds to go in the first quarter. Then, recently inserted Chuck Farley hit a twenty-foot jump shot that gave the Panthers their first lead of the game. Our side of the coliseum erupted in applause. Stanley Davis would add another jump shot before the quarter ended to increase the lead to three.

As the Panthers retreated to their bench, I could see Mike Fischer spring up and lead the reserves in applause while clapping those playing on the back as they came over. The Panthers were pumped. We had taken Southside's initial punch and returned it with interest.

There was no sound from the nearby voice of doubt, so someone in our crowd decided to provide some feedback.

"We told you. Southside may be good, but Babylon is better."

"Not bad, not bad," the voice responded. "But one quarter does not make a game."

He was right, but we had captured the momentum, and it was game on.

Babylon came out with the original starting five to begin the second quarter. The pace continued as Koelbel had obviously directed. We ground their run-and-gun offense to a slow crawl. Glenn continued to score and draw fouls while Southside grew more and more frustrated. Chuckie Smith could not shake Gervais, and the Cyclones continued rushing shots and throwing the ball away.

Koelbel used his bench to keep fresh legs in the game as Chuck Farley, Chris Brust, and Weiner all got significant minutes in the second quarter. Glenn scored eight points in the quarter but Brian, Stanley Davis, and Barry Davis all contributed four. When the half ended, Babylon had built its lead to seven. Southside was suddenly looking extremely mortal.

I caught up with my father at halftime to see if he would buy me a hot dog and a Coke. He was talking to Mr. Conroy when I approached.

"Unbelievable," Mr. Conroy said. "Glenn is taking it to another level."

"Yeah, they sure have Southside frustrated," my father answered.

He didn't break away from the conversation but just handed me two dollars without looking—enough for me to make my purchase. I bought my goods and located Ernie and Gary over at a stand-up table, where we ate for a few minutes and discussed the game. I had seen Virginia with Gary earlier but she must have waited back inside at the seats.

We got lost in our conversation rehashing what had happened so far before the buzzer jarred us back to life. I hurriedly forced the rest of my hot dog down and rushed back with the gang carrying the rest of my Coke. When we got back to our seats the teams had already made their way out for the second-half tip. Again, we had our regular starting five out there to start the third quarter.

I turned to look off to the side to see if the Southside enthusiast was still nearby. He was there but chose to be silent. No doubt he was waiting to see a second-half burst from the Cyclones before piping up again.

If the Southside faithful were looking for a restart in their favor during the third quarter, they would be sorely disappointed. With a combination of patient offense and stifling defense, Babylon continued to crush the life out of the Cyclones. In a scenario they had likely not experienced, Southside continued rushing shots and committing turnovers while enduring the precision play of a Babylon team that continually scored and drew fouls. We were led, of course, by the stellar play of Glenn Vickers, who had nearly thirty points by the end of the third, with most of it coming from free throws.

Chuckie Smith did not score during the entire third period as Gervais followed him wherever he went. By the fourth quarter, Southside looked beat as their guards were walking the ball up court. To add insult to injury, Chuckie Smith fouled out with just over two minutes to go. With the game well in hand, Mr. Koelbel started taking his senior stars out one at a time as he did at the end of the regular season.

Gervais again came first and everyone on our side cheered. He did not score in the game but his relentless defense on Chuckie Smith was essential to the win. Gervais had also doled out eleven assists and brought the ball up court most of the night. He gave and received a big hug from Mr. Koelbel.

Next came Stanley Davis. Stanley's opportune scoring and ability to transition between forward and guard all season made sure the Panthers could endure the mid-season injury plague. He was the team's second-leading scorer and had always hit that timely jump shot when it was most needed. Stanley exited the game with eight points and to a loud eruption from our fans.

Chuck Farley had likely not had the season he had hoped for, but being able to accept his slightly diminished role following his injury added greatly to the team's second half of the season run. The Babylon faithful knew this and gave him a round applause worthy of his contribution.

Barry Davis and Brian Vickers came out later at the same time. Both had scored double figures in this championship game. But more importantly to Babylon, they would both be back to play next year. In fact, Brian's high school career had only just begun.

Finally, with a minute left, Koelbel brought out the man of the hour—and from our standpoint the man of the year—Glenn Vickers. That night, on the biggest stage in the history of Long Island basketball, he was the brightest star in our universe. His final tally was thirty-three points on nine field goals and fifteen for nineteen from the foul line. Mr. Koelbel and Mr. Bartsch greeted Glenn as he exited the floor. Also, in a show of great sportsmanship the Southside fans joined those of Babylon in applauding Glenn.

After Glenn's cheers wound down the voice behind us made his final remarks, mostly to himself, I think, but we all heard him.

"Wow, I don't know what the heck happened to Southside."

The response was yelled back in almost unison from several different people: "Babylon is what happened to Southside!"

With that rebuke, the man picked up his coat, left his seat, and surely exited the building. We would not miss him. The game still had twenty seconds left, and Mr. Koelbel was able to play everyone on the team. It was something they would all be able to talk about the rest of their lives.

As those final seconds ticked down, the team stars watched from the sidelines as their dedicated substitutes got their moments of glory. Gervais stood between Glenn and Stanley sporting his giant smile with his arms around both of their shoulders. Barry was smiling and clapping while intermittently pointing to different team members on the court in support. Brian just smiled quietly, as was his nature, and left the celebrating to the others. When the final buzzer went off, they all joined their teammates on the court in a giant celebratory group hug.

Mr. Koelbel walked over to shake hands with his adversary, who, even from my vantage point, looked to be in shock. In the stands we continued applauding, but to us the game had ended twenty minutes ago. Everybody would now stay to see the presentation of the first-ever Long Island Basketball Championship trophy. Also, the Babylon team would get to cut down their last nets of the season.

Koelbel went to the center this time with the entire team to accept the championship trophy. After getting their runner-up award, the Southside team quickly left the floor. It was now just Panther Black out on the court with Koelbel and his lucky maroon jacket in the middle hoisting the giant trophy up for all to see. This brought another thunderous applause.

The fans continued to watch as the nets were cut down but less attentively as we started to talk more amongst ourselves. Virginia came over and gave me a big hug almost out of the blue.

"What's that for?" I laughed. "I didn't play."

"Just a thanks for all of the rides this year," she replied.

"No problem, we had room."

"I know, but I've always known."

I knew what she was saying, and for one of the few moments in my life, I didn't ruin a moment by speaking. I just smiled and nodded my head in acknowledgment. She then walked back to her seat and eventual ride home with the Farleys. It was a nice moment.

After the final strand was cut and the team began exiting the floor, we all headed toward the exits. The Southside fans were long gone, and due to the size of the parking lot at the coliseum, we had no traffic problems getting out or once on the highway. Pat opted for the back seat to spread out while I took the front where I could recap the game with my father.

"What do you think?" he asked once the coliseum was out of sight.

"I think we have a great chance of getting back here next year," I replied. "Glenn is only a junior and we have all those underclassmen. We'll miss Stanley and Gervais, of course."

"I agree. You also won't be the Cinderella you were this year."

"Right, everyone will have Babylon circled on their schedule."

We drove along a little further in relative science. Then I picked up the conversation again.

"You know, if I can continue to up my game over the next few years, I might make the varsity when Brian and Chris are seniors. Then maybe I'll get to play in the coliseum."

"It's good to have dreams," my father said.

"Not dreams, Dad: goals."

My father didn't like to be corrected, but he just smiled at my response. That might have been what he meant anyway.

That's how the 1974–75 Babylon basketball season concluded. One of the smallest school districts on Long Island had become its first ever champion. A great coach, a great team, and a once-in-a-generation player made the dream a reality. They overcame injuries, a brutal schedule, and a doubting press, and they will always be remembered as the first.

As for me, I'll always remember the time when all of Long Island was Panther Country.

The 1974–75 Long Island Basketball Champions, the Babylon Panthers

Coach Koelbel and team captains (*from left*)
Stanley Davis, Gervais Barger, and Glenn Vickers

Epilogue

There were no state championships in New York back in the seventies. As mentioned earlier, this was the first time any team on Long Island had ever played beyond the county finals. There were state rankings that were usually dominated by New York City teams, but my recollection was that we cracked the top echelon after the 1974–75 season.

For the program, winning the Long Island Championship that year would indeed come at a price as Babylon would enter the next season as the team to beat in everyone's eyes. In addition to all of the vanquished and disappointed public-school teams that we went through from '74 to '75, many of the top private schools on Long Island would reach out to play Babylon as well. I heard from Mr. Koelbel that they did not like a Long Island champion being crowned in a tournament that did not include them. So, 1975–76 would be another interesting year, but in a different manner. However, that's the stuff of sequels.

Mr. Koelbel would remain Babylon's head coach for the 1975–76 season but would leave that post the following year to become the BHS athletic director. He would remain as AD for another decade or so before retiring. Koelbel was omnipresent at Babylon during those years, walking the halls and teaching gym, employing his wit and humor every chance he got.

I was able to find and reach out to the coach to corroborate some of the facts in the book. He is ninety years old now and living in Florida. Our conversations contained some of the same ribbing and banter as when I was in Junior High. It's been great fun.

In a way, many of us in Babylon came to invest some of our dreams in the future of Glenn Vickers. In addition to his bringing glory to Babylon, much of the populace became consumed with where he would go to college, and whether we see him in televised games. During his senior year in high school, Glenn became one of the top college basketball recruits in the country. We all hoped maybe he would someday play in the pros.

Glenn had his pick of schools but ended up selecting a regional New York college that had hired a charismatic young coach who had pursued Glenn relentlessly. The school was Iona College and their new coach was Jim Valvano. Acquiring Glenn allowed Valvano to build a nationally ranked program at Iona. That was due to the fact that many other Long Island stars would head there wanting to play with Glenn in the succeeding years. Although it wasn't UCLA or one of the Atlantic Coast conference teams, Glenn flourished at Iona and ranks today in the school's all-time top ten for scoring, assists, and free throws. A benefit for all of his Babylon fans was that it was not that far away. Many of us could travel to see him play other New York teams like St. Johns and Seton Hall. I saw him play several times in Madison Square Garden.

I caught up with Glenn for lunch back in Babylon while I was in my editing phase of this book. We had a great catch-up session and he was able to fill in some details that definitely added to my story. Glenn is working on a book of his own that will take a more investigatory look at life in the seventies and eighties, which I look forward to reading.

I remained close friends with Ernie for the rest of my high school life. He stayed with basketball through his senior year, although not quite as tied to it as his brothers. Ernie was also a serious student, and we spent as much time together in class as we did outside of it. However, he would always remain that glowing center of the activity when it came to social gatherings for our class. Wherever he was, that's where the action was.

Unfortunately, Ernie came to an untimely demise in his mid-twenties. Only months after graduating from medical school, he had some sort of seizure and died before ever entering into practice. He and I had grown apart over the years due to settling in different parts of the country. However, every time I did see him it was like we had just been together, and he always made a priority of pronouncing my last name correctly. He was that type of guy.

I'll never forget how I found out about his death. I had moved to Dallas, Texas, sometime in the late eighties and was on the phone speaking with my mother. She was looking through the mail as we spoke and came across the latest edition of the *Babylon Beacon*. Jokingly, she said she would catch me up on the current village gossip. Instead, her voice dropped and after a few moments of silence she told me she was looking at a picture of Ernie above his obituary. I didn't have enough time to travel up for the service, but my brother Pat went in my stead. It was a very sad day.

One of the very pleasant by-products of writing this book is that I got to meet Paul Smith for the first time through his son Tristan. As it turns out they both live about an hour away from where I have resided since 1986 in Dallas. Following basketball season, Paul would team again with backcourt mate Mike Voliton to win the county championship in the 880-yard relay in track. He also may have gotten some payback in basketball as well, with Tristan leading Amityville to two state titles during his high school tenure at Amityville and being named the Suffolk County player of the year in 2001.

My relationship with my father remained strong throughout my youth. He always remained dedicated to his family and tried to attend any game or event in which I participated. I often enjoyed strategizing and discussing my academic and athletic pursuits with him.

I felt a little guilty that I got more of my father's time than my siblings, but I did pursue it more. I would always drag him to sporting events or games that I wanted to see, knowing that he would enjoy them as well. Whether we were cruising in the Granada or cringing in the Monaco, my father and I spent countless hours on the roads of Long Island looking for whatever venue hosted the event we were attending that day. It may seem odd, but it was the time in the car when it was just him and me that I enjoyed the most.

Unfortunately, Dad's time with all of us would be limited. He suffered another heart seizure when I was home from college for Thanksgiving weekend in 1980. Mr. Conroy got an ambulance to our house in record time. But an hour after we arrived at the hospital, Dr. Godfrey came out with a tear in his eye and his arms spread out wide. He couldn't seem to speak, but his lips read, "He's gone."

My father did live to see me achieve my goal of playing varsity basketball at Babylon for two seasons. I left no particular mark other than being part of the last dynasty team in 1977–78 during my junior year. Gary, Ernie, and I joined a team captained by Brian Vickers, who had become the mainstay of the program after Glenn graduated. Brian would lead more with his actions rather than his words, as he would always remain a quiet guy. If anyone ever asked me why Brian didn't speak much, my reply was always, "Because he doesn't have to." Unfortunately, Brian passed away a few years ago as well. I don't know the cause.

It was not long after college that I relocated south and eventually settled just outside of Dallas. However, my mother remained in Babylon, as did two of my siblings, so I often return for extended visits throughout the year. It's remarkable to me how little Babylon has changed in fifty years. I mean that in the most complimentary way.

The village area is only a walk away from most homes where one can find all sorts of shops and eateries. It's still a place where everybody knows their neighbors, and anyone can drive down to the water and enjoy a cup of coffee while staring out at the sea. It turns out comedian Rodney Dangerfield was from Babylon. He remarked in one of his routines that the place was so small that one day, he plugged in his electric razor and the train stopped.

The high school is in the same place and doesn't look much different from the outside. The playing fields have been resurfaced many times but are in the same locations. The school did install a marquee out front that brandished whatever champion sports teams might emerge any given year. I've often pictured it with the words 1974–75 LONG ISLAND BASKETBALL CHAMPIONS across it.

Babylon has always been a great place to live in the summer with the sun and the beaches nearby. During those five golden years in the middle of the seventies, it was also a great place to live in the winter. Every year, our basketball program would put forth a county contender that would rally the populace to crowd the gymnasium on Friday nights. Several coaches would succeed Koelbel over the years. Most had ability, but none had his unique character.

I've lived in Texas for almost forty years now, but I still call Babylon home. Probably because that was where my mother lived. Sadly, she died only weeks before I finished this book. Mom had actually been reading chapter by chapter as I progressed through the initial draft. I knew she wouldn't be critical because she believed all her kids were wonderful. That's the woman she was.

I can't help but be nostalgic whenever I'm in Babylon. My entire family gets together multiple times when my wife, kids, and I would come north to visit. At least one of the meals we always enjoy together on every visit is a pizza from the Village, where we reminisce about Friday nights and growing up in Babylon. Manniello's is long gone but several others have replaced it with equally delicious pies.

During those trips I'll often drive through the main Village area, down to the docks, cross over Coppertree Lane, and pass by the high school to mentally relive the memories. I've told my own family often what it was like growing up in Babylon and what occurred there. After years of of repetition, they eventually said, "Why don't you write a book?"

What a great idea!

Acknowledgments

I would like to begin by thanking my loving wife, Ann, for believing in me and providing the support needed to write this book. The joy and light that are our children Kelly Ann and Brian remind me every day that looking at the positive things that have happened on one's journey makes future chapters much more enjoyable.

I would also like to thank my parents for providing the stable and loving home for me and my three siblings that I believe made us all the people we are today.

Finally, I would like to thank my publisher and friend Milli Brown, who I've known for years but was there ready when I decided it was time for me to become an author.

Glossary of Basketball Terms

alley-oop: a play in which a player leaps to catch a pass above the basket and then dunks the ball

assist: an action whereby a player passes the ball to a teammate in a way that results in a made basket

bank shot: a shot that rebounds off the backboard and into the basket

bench player: a substitute player who sits on the bench and is ready to replace a starter if needed

boxing out: a defensive technique that involves positioning yourself between an opponent and the basket to gain an advantage on a rebound

center: the position of usually the tallest player on the team who most often plays near the basket

center tap: a jump ball between the centers of the opposing teams, held in the circle at the center of the court, as at the beginning of a period or half

corner pass: a pass to a player in the strongside corner

double pump shot: a technique that consists of making two shooting moves while in the air with the first intended as a fake and the second being the actual shot

fast break: an offensive strategy where a team tries to move the ball up the court and score as quickly as possible

first-string: the strongest players on the team who are usually the first to play in a game

forced shot: a shot that a player is forced to take when they are not in control of their body or balance

forwards: positions that play near the basket while rebounding and defending taller players

foul: an illegal action that gives one team an unfair advantage over the other

foul shot: an unopposed shot taken from behind the free-throw line after a foul is called against an opposing player; synonymous with *free throw*

full-court press: a defensive style in which the defense applies pressure to the offensive team the entire length of the court

guards: positions responsible for running the offense and setting the pace, usually assigned to the best dribblers and passers on the team and who are also often the smaller players

half-court press: a defensive strategy in basketball where the defensive team only pressures the offensive team once they enter the half of the court where they'll shoot

head-fake: a type of feint in which someone moves their head to fake an intended change in direction and thereby deceive opponents

hot hand: a term used to designate a player who is on a streak of making many shots in a row

inbounding: when a player passes the ball into play from out of bounds

jump shot (jumper): a basketball technique where a player jumps straight up and releases the ball toward the basket

layup: a shot where a player leaps from below the basket and uses one hand to bounce the ball off the backboard and into the basket

no-look pass: when a player throws the ball to a teammate without looking directly at that same teammate

pick (screen): a legal block set by an offensive player to free up a teammate to receive a pass or take a shot

the post: the area of the court between the free-throw line and the baseline, where players can position themselves to score

rebound: when a player retrieves a live ball immediately following a shot

rubber match: a final game to be played after each team has won an equal number of the prior games, usually referring to two out of three

run-and-gun offense: a high-scoring basketball play style that involves quick movement, passing, and field goal attempts

steal: when a defensive player legally takes the ball away from an offensive player, causing a turnover and a change of possession

strong side: the side of the court where the ball is currently located

turnover: when a team loses possession of the ball to the opposing team before a player attempts a shot

weak side: the side of the court where the ball is not currently located

zone defense: a basketball defensive strategy where each player is assigned to guard a specific area of the court as opposed to guarding an individual player

1975 Basketball Championship

New York State Section XI

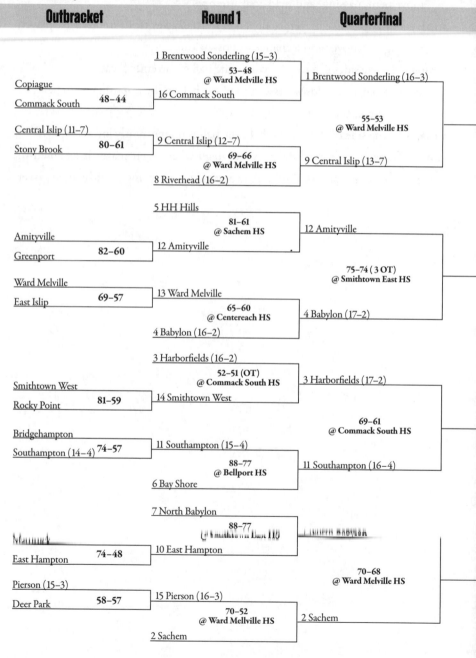

Suffolk County

Outbracket

Copiague vs. Commack South	48–44
Central Islip (11–7) vs. Stony Brook	80–61
Amityville vs. Greenport	82–60
Ward Melville vs. East Islip	69–57
Smithtown West vs. Rocky Point	81–59
Bridgehampton vs. Southampton (14–4)	74–57
Mattituck vs. East Hampton	74–48
Pierson (15–3) vs. Deer Park	58–57

Round 1

1 Brentwood Sonderling (15–3) vs. 16 Commack South	53–48	@ Ward Melville HS
9 Central Islip (12–7) vs. 8 Riverhead (16–2)	69–66	@ Ward Melville HS
5 HH Hills vs. 12 Amityville	81–61	@ Sachem HS
13 Ward Melville vs. 4 Babylon (16–2)	65–60	@ Centereach HS
3 Harborfields (16–2) vs. 14 Smithtown West	52–51 (OT)	@ Commack South HS
11 Southampton (15–4) vs. 6 Bay Shore	88–77	@ Bellport HS
7 North Babylon vs. 10 East Hampton	88–77	@ Smithtown East HS
15 Pierson (16–3) vs. 2 Sachem	70–52	@ Ward Mellville HS

Quarterfinal

1 Brentwood Sonderling (16–3) vs. 9 Central Islip (13–7)	55–53	@ Ward Melville HS
12 Amityville vs. 4 Babylon (17–2)	75–74 (3 OT)	@ Smithtown East HS
3 Harborfields (17–2) vs. 11 Southampton (16–4)	69–61	@ Commack South HS
7 North Babylon vs. 2 Sachem	70–68	@ Ward Melville HS

Nassau County

Semifinal

Final

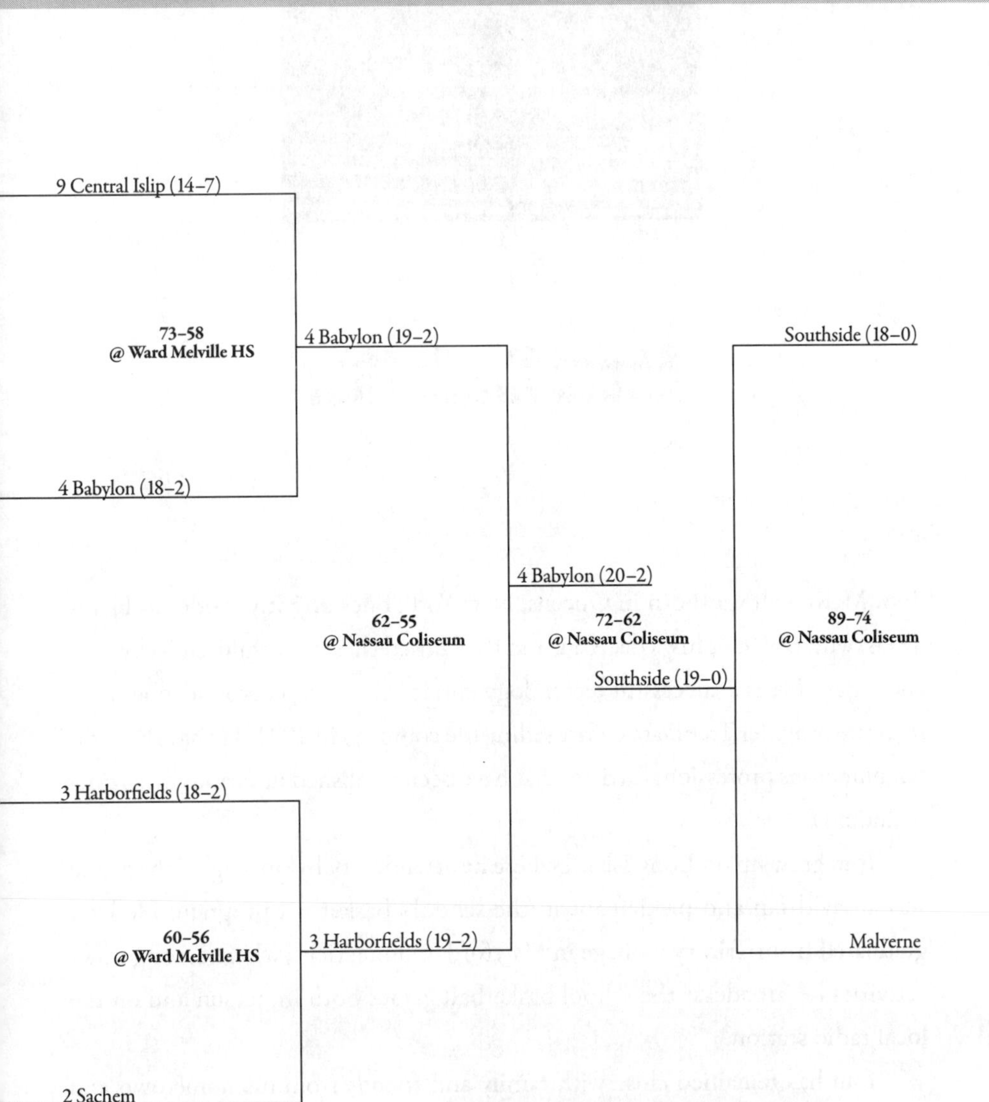

Champion: **Babylon**

MVP: **Glenn Vickers**

About the Author

Tom McKeown was born in Queens, New York, but currently resides in Plano, Texas, where he met his wife, Ann, and they raised their two children Kelly Ann and Brian. He is a successful technology entrepreneur who cofounded and ran software provider TrenData before selling the company in 2021. He has also written numerous professional articles that have been published in various magazines including Forbes.

Tom grew up on Long Island where he attended Babylon High School and was an avid fan and participant in the school's basketball program. He later graduated from Trinity College in Hartford, Connecticut, where among other activities he broadcast the school basketball games both in person and on the local radio station.

Tom has remained close with family and friends from his hometown and visits several times a year. He remembers fondly the mid-1970s when his high school basketball team was a regional power and the envy of many surrounding schools.